THE SICARII IN JOSEPHUS'S *JUDEAN WAR*

RHETORICAL ANALYSIS AND HISTORICAL OBSERVATIONS

Society of Biblical Literature

Early Judaism and Its Literature

Judith H. Newman,
Series Editor

Number 27

THE SICARII IN JOSEPHUS'S *JUDEAN WAR*

RHETORICAL ANALYSIS AND
HISTORICAL OBSERVATIONS

THE SICARII IN JOSEPHUS'S *JUDEAN WAR*

RHETORICAL ANALYSIS AND
HISTORICAL OBSERVATIONS

Mark Andrew Brighton

Society of Biblical Literature
Atlanta

THE SICARII IN JOSEPHUS'S *JUDEAN WAR*
RHETORICAL ANALYSIS AND
HISTORICAL OBSERVATIONS

Library of Congress Cataloging-in-Publication Data

Brighton, Mark.
   The Sicarii in Josephus's Judean war : rhetorical analysis and historical observations / by Mark Andrew Brighton.
      p. cm. — (Early Judaism and its literature ; no. 27)
   Includes bibliographical references and index.
   ISBN 978-1-58983-406-4 (paper binding : alk. paper)
   1. Zealots (Jewish party)—History. 2. Jews—History—168 B.C.-135 A.D.
3. Jews—History—Rebellion, 66-73. 4. Jews—Politics and government—To 70 A.D.
I. Title.
DS122.7.B75 2009
933'.05—dc22

2009001549

16 15 14 13 12 11 10 09   5 4 3 2 1
Printed in the United States of America on acid-free, recycled paper conforming to ANSI /NISO Z39.48–1992 (R1997) and ISO 9706:1994 standards for paper permanence.

For Michelle

"She is clothed with strength and dignity;
she can laugh at the days to come."

CONTENTS

Acknowledgments

This book is a revision of my dissertation, submitted in the Classics Department of the University of California at Irvine. A work of this nature never sees the light of day without the assistance of many people. So it is my pleasure to acknowledge them here.

I would first like to express my deepest thanks to Prof. Steve Mason at York University, who in addition to his many teaching responsibilities, scholarly pursuits, editorial responsibilities, and publications took me on as an advisee. He never failed both to challenge and encourage me as he introduced me to Josephus. Also, during the preparation of the revised manuscript his comments proved invaluable. This book would have never been possible without his genuine interest and unfailing assistance. Steve is one who possesses true *humanitas*.

Thanks are due also to the many professors who inspired and supported me at the University of California, Irvine. Deserving special mention are the members of my dissertation committee, Prof. Dana Sutton and Prof. Andrew Zissos. I am indebted to your encouragement and interest in my work. I am indebted to Concordia University, which granted me time to get started on revising the manuscript for publication, and to the publishing editors, whose suggestions for clarification and corrections of infelicities not only improved the manuscript but also saved me from future embarrassment. In particular I wish to thank the anonymous reviewer, whose pointed comments were invaluable.

Finally, but not least, I wish to thank my family. Michelle, Lauren, and Nick, you fill my life with joy and purpose. I would never have been able to devote myself to the many hours of this project without your unfailing love and understanding.

ABBREVIATIONS

AJP	*American Journal of Philology*
ANRW	*Aufstieg und Niedergang der römischen Welt: Geschichte und Kultur Roms im Spiegel der neueren Forschung.* Edited by H. Temporini and W. Hasse. New York and Berlin: Walter de Gruyter, 1972–
Ant.	Josephus, *Antiquities*
Apion	Josephus, *Contra Apion*
CQ	*Classical Quarterly*
GRBS	*Greek, Roman, and Byzantine Studies*
HTR	*Harvard Theological Review*
JBL	*Journal of Biblical Literature*
JJS	*Journal of Jewish Studies*
JQR	*Jewish Quarterly Review*
JR	*Journal of Religion*
JRS	*Journal of Roman Studies*
JSNT	*Journal for the Study of the New Testament*
JSJ	*Journal for the Study of Judaism*
JSPSup	Journal for the Study of the Pseudepigrapha Supplement Series
JSQ	*Jewish Studies Quarterly*
NT	*Novum Testamentum*
TAPA	*Transactions of the American Philological Association*
TDNT	*Theological Dictionary of the New Testament.* Edited by G. Kittel and G. Friedrich. Translated by G. W. Bromiley. 10 vols. Grand Rapids: Eerdmans, 1964–76.
TLZ	*Theologische Literaturzeitung*
War	Josephus, *The Judean War*
ZNW	*Zeitschrift für die Neutestamentliche Wissenschaft und die Kunde der älteren Kirche*
ZPE	*Zeitschrift für Papyrologie und Epigraphik*

PREFACE

I suppose this study began many years ago when I first hiked up the snake path to the top of Masada to see the ruins of Herod's fortress, the visible remains of the Roman camps, and the slope on the western side where the siege engines were brought to bear. Like so many others before me, I too was swept away in my imagination at the drama of that last battle in the Judean war. Who were these last defenders? How did they manage to hold out for so long? Why did they kill themselves rather than surrender? And so in the course of my graduate studies I eventually resolved to learn more not only about Masada but also about Josephus, for it is impossible to know about one without the other.

In the course of my investigation I discovered that no comprehensive study of the Sicarii, the last defenders at Masada in Josephus's *Judean War* (often and erroneously called "Zealots"), had yet been done. Those who had paid attention to the Sicarii had done so selectively, focusing only on a few isolated passages, and largely in a secondary manner, aiming at some purpose other than the identity and the activities of the Sicarii themselves. Scholars are also divided in their assessment of the historical existence, nature, and activities of the Sicarii, in part because of their disagreement concerning the rhetorical elements in Josephus's presentation. This study, therefore, is my attempt to address these areas and provide a holistic study of the Sicarii in *The Judean War*, focusing in the first place on all those passages where the Sicarii are explicitly mentioned or where their presence and activity must be inferred from the context. Each of these passages is analyzed for its rhetorical elements, and then literary and historical conclusions are presented. This study shows that within the narrative of the *Judean War*, "Sicarii" is a label that was originally applied to a group of bandits who embarked on high profile assassinations in the early stages of the war. Josephus adopted this label to develop and bring to a resolution several major themes in *War*. This examination leads to the conclusion that from a historical perspective, "Sicarii" was a somewhat fluid term used to describe Jews of the Judean revolt who were associated with acts of violence against their own people for religious/political ends.

Finally, I must include a word about the presentation of Josephus's text below. In order to make this study more accessible, I have included my own translations for all the relevant Greek material in *War*. But I also want to allow the specialist ready access to Josephus's own words and so I have included the Greek in every case. One particular mentor of mine in years gone by would often insist that every translation was an interpretation, and this will become immediately apparent for those who consult the Greek when reading my renditions, particularly in the translation of certain concepts that Josephus regularly employs in the Sicarii narratives such as "necessity" (ἀνάγκη), "sedition" (στάσις), or "daring" (τόλμα). This is, of course, the nature of the task of translating ancient concepts into modern idiom, but I want to draw attention to one issue in particular. Masada is known as the place were the last Jewish rebels against Rome committed "suicide." This term, however, is unfortunate for several reasons. One is that of the 960 who died there, strictly speaking only one committed suicide. The rest submitted themselves to death voluntarily. More important, however, Timothy Hill points out that "suicide" is a term that brings agency to mind whereas the Romans, Josephus's primary audience, were more concerned about honor when discussing such deaths.[1] Since honor appears also to be Josephus's concern when describing the deaths at Masada, we shall, therefore, avoid the term "suicide" throughout this study unless referring to or quoting another author's usage.

---

1. See Timothy Hill, *Ambitiosa Mors: Suicide and Self in Roman Thought and Literature*, ed. Dirk Obbink and Andrew Dyck (Studies in Classics; New York and London: Routledge, 2004), 1–29.

CHAPTER ONE

SCHOLARLY STUDIES CONCERNING
THE SICARII IN *THE JUDEAN WAR*

Why study the Sicarii in Josephus's *Judean War*? There are many reasons. As far as we know, Josephus is the first Greek author to use the term, aside from a single occurrence in Luke-Acts (Acts 21:38), and so questions naturally arise. Whom is Josephus describing? How and why does he employ such a striking term? These questions are complicated by the fact that the Sicarii are the protagonists in the episode at Masada, which is not only one of the more dramatic narratives in *War* but also is subject to sharply divided scholarly assessments of how Josephus characterizes those who preferred death rather than surrender to the Romans. The speeches put in the mouth of Eleazar b. Yair, the Sicarii leader, and the circumstances of the voluntary deaths have brought some to comment on the nobility of these last rebels,[1] others on their madness and fanaticism.[2] Complicating matters still further are some competing rhetorical elements at play in *War* that have gone unnoticed because Josephus has routinely been mined exclusively for the information he might give on other matters, such as archaeology, the New Testament environment, or the Flavian emperors. The result is that scholars have, in Steve Mason's words, tended to "fragment his writings into little bits of data" and largely ignored such basic matters as the various structural, thematic, and rhetorical elements of Josephus's works.[3] There is still the need to place the Sicarii firmly and in a comprehensive manner within the structure and rhetoric

---

1. As L. H. Feldman, "Masada: A Critique of Recent Scholarship," in *Christianity, Judaism, and Other Greco-Roman Cults: Studies for Morton Smith*, ed. J. Neusner (Leiden: Brill, 1975), 237. Also Tessa Rajak, *Josephus, the Historian and His Society*, 2nd ed. (London: Gerald Duckworth, 2002), 220. With the exception of a new introduction, this edition remains substantially unchanged from the first, published by Fortress Press in 1983.

2. See David J. Ladouceur, "Josephus and Masada," in *Josephus, Judaism, and Christianity*, ed. Louis H. Feldman and Gohei Hata (Detroit: Wayne State University Press, 1987), 101. More recently, Honora Howell Chapman, "Spectacle and Theater in Josephus's *Bellum Judaicum*" (Ph.D. diss., Stanford University, 1998), 6.

3. Steve Mason, *Josephus and the New Testament*, 2nd ed. (Peabody: Hendrickson, 2003), 31. Mason provides a summary of how Josephus has been misused and ignored as an author in this book's first chapter, entitled "The Use and Abuse of Josephus."

of *War*. Indeed, we shall see that it is precisely the failure to do so that has led in part to sharply divided assessments about Masada and the historical identity of the Sicarii.

Before we turn to these matters, however, our study properly begins with a survey of scholarship about the Sicarii in the *Judean War*. The scholars to be considered in this chapter are divided according to whether their analyses tend more toward a historical or a literary assessment of the Sicarii, and they are arranged chronologically. This survey will demonstrate how the historical identity of the Sicarii is complicated by the rhetorical elements of *War*.

The Historical Perspective

A survey of scholars who offer a historical assessment about the identity and activities of the Sicarii may properly begin with Emil Schürer, who in his magisterial work, *A History of the Jewish People in the Time of Jesus Christ*, articulated the long-standard view that the Sicarii were an armed and fanatical offshoot of the Zealots. There he states that the Zealots originated under the leadership of Judas the Galilean and the Pharisee Saddok, who in 6 c.e. organized opposition to the imposition of Roman authority and taxation in Judea under Quirinius. Josephus presents both these characters in *Ant.* 18.1f., but early in *War's* narrative he focuses on Judas alone.

> [117] Now when Archelaus's region was defined as a province, a procurator of the equestrian rank among the Romans, Coponius, was sent out, having from Caesar authority of capital punishment. [118] At this time a certain Galilean man, Judas by name, urged his countrymen to revolt, reproaching them if they would put up with paying taxes to Romans and would endure mortal masters next to God. Now this person was a teacher of his own sect, which was not at all like the others. (2.117–18)

> [117] τῆς δὲ Ἀρχελάου χώρας εἰς ἐπαρχίαν περιγραφείσης ἐπίτροπος τῆς ἱππικῆς παρὰ Ῥωμαίοις τάξεως Κωπώνιος πέμπεται μέχρι τοῦ κτείνειν λαβὼν παρὰ Καίσαρος ἐξουσίαν [118] ἐπὶ τούτου τις ἀνὴρ Γαλιλαῖος Ἰούδας ὄνομα εἰς ἀπόστασιν ἐνῆγε τοὺς ἐπιχωρίους κακίζων εἰ φόρον τε Ῥωμαίοις τελεῖν ὑπομενοῦσιν καὶ μετὰ τὸν θεὸν οἴσουσι θνητοὺς δεσπότας ἦν δ' οὗτος σοφιστὴς ἰδίας αἱρέσεως οὐδὲν τοῖς ἄλλοις προσεοικώς·

At this point Josephus goes on to describe what he considers to be the three legitimate Jewish sects; the Essenes, the Pharisees, and the Sadducees.

It must be noted that Josephus nowhere refers to Zealots in this passage or in the context. Nevertheless, Schürer makes the connection through the activities of Judas's descendants, Menahem and Eleazar. Menahem, his son, apparently became an early leader among the "Zealots" at Jerusalem, for after Menahem gained control of the rebels there, Josephus states that he "had gone up (to the temple) in pompous fashion to worship, decked out in royal attire and accompanied by armed Zealots (2.444)."[4] Josephus states that some Jews then rebelled against his leadership and killed him there. At this point Eleazar, another descendant of Judas, withdrew to Masada and there became the leader of the Sicarii (2.447 and 7.254). Thus, Schürer maintains that those who employed the sword against the Romans in the effort to hasten the rebellion against Rome were known as Zealots, and it was they who nursed the "fires of revolution which sixty years later burst forth into flames."[5]

As to the Sicarii, they did not arise until the governorship of Felix as a "fanatical faction of the patriots."[6] Here Schürer makes reference to *War* 2.254–55, where Josephus states:

> [254] Now when the country was cleared, a different type of bandit sprang up in Jerusalem, the so-called Sicarii, murdering people in the middle of the city in broad daylight. [255] Especially during the festivals they would mix with the crowd, hiding small daggers in their garments, and stab their opponents. Then when they fell dead, their murderers became part of those who cried out in indignation. Thus, by means of this air of plausibility they remained completely undiscovered.

> [254] καθαρθείσης δὲ τῆς χώρας ἕτερον εἶδος λῃστῶν ἐν Ἱεροσολύμοις ἐπεφύετο οἱ καλούμενοι σικάριοι μεθ' ἡμέραν καὶ ἐν μέσῃ τῇ πόλει φονεύοντες ἀνθρώπους [255] μάλιστα [δὲ] ἐν ταῖς ἑορταῖς μισγόμενοι τῷ πλήθει καὶ ταῖς ἐσθῆσιν ὑποκρύπτοντες μικρὰ ξιφίδια τούτοις ἔνυττον τοὺς διαφόρους ἔπειτα πεσόντων μέρος ἐγίνοντο τῶν ἐπαγανακτούντων οἱ πεφονευκότες διὸ καὶ παντάπασιν ὑπὸ ἀξιοπιστίας ἦσαν ἀνεύρετοι.

Their fanaticism and use of daggers to murder their political opponents, especially during the Jewish festivals, earned the Sicarii their name and made them distinct from the Zealots.[7] In this manner Schürer set the stage for scholarly debate about the origins, identity, and activities of the Sicarii. In particular, scholars have spent much time investigating their relationship with the Zealots.

---

4. σοβαρὸς γὰρ ἀναβεβήκει προσκυνήσων ἐσθῆτί τε βασιλικῇ κεκοσμημένος καὶ τοὺς ζηλωτὰς ἐνόπλους ἐφελκόμενος. We will see below that there is good reason to translate ζηλωτάς not as "Zealots" but as "fanatics."

5. Emil Schürer, *A History of the Jewish People in the Time of Jesus Christ*, 3 vols. (Edinburgh: T & T Clark, 1890), I.ii.80–81.

6. Ibid., I.ii.178. By "patriots" Schürer presumably means the Zealots, though he does not make explicit the term here. At I.ii.80 he makes the connection between "patriotic resolutes" and Zealots.

7. Ibid., I.ii.178. Schürer draws attention to the "lex Cornelia de Sicariis," passed under Sulla, and notes that "Sicarius" was generally to be understood as a murderer (I.ii.179). He says little about Masada aside from the essentials of Josephus's report and the "horror" expressed by the Romans at the suicides (I.ii.189).

Martin Hengel, in the enlarged and translated edition of *Die Zeloten* (1961, 1976), offered a now-classic presentation of the origins, growth, characteristics, and activities of the Zealots from 6 C.E. to 70 C.E. Unlike Schürer, Hengel maintains that the Sicarii were a violent section of a general insurrectional movement, called by Josephus "bandits" (ληϲταί), and were not an independent party among the Zealots. He states that the connection between the Sicarii at Masada and Judas of Galilee at *War* 7.254, where Josephus says the Sicarii leader was a descendant of Judas, is made on the basis of common ideology and ancestry and should not be understood to mean that the Sicarii already existed in 6 C.E. It was not until certain bandits later adopted a new method of fighting in Jerusalem that the Romans began to apply the label "Sicarii."[8] Their use of the term should not be understood as datum for the existence of a group historically known as such.

Hengel suggests that Josephus adopted this Roman label perhaps with the "aim of defining various groups more precisely" and not to indicate a separate rebel faction.[9] For the Sicarii shared with all the other rebel groups named by Josephus (excepting the Idumeans) a common, fundamentally religious and eschatological ideology that resulted in common activities and goals.[10] For Hengel, then, "Sicarii" amounts to little more than a rhetorical label.

Shortly after Hengel first published *The Zealots* in German, Solomon Zeitlin wrote a brief response, and contrary to both Schürer and Hengel, he maintained that the Sicarii and Zealots were two distinct and "mutually hostile" groups.[11] He expressed these ideas more fully in a subsequent article on Masada, written after Yigael Yadin's excavations there and partly in response to Yadin's publication on his findings. There he says that the Zealots and the Sicarii had different leaders, agendas, and activities. The Zealots had Eleazar, son of Simon, as their leader, were characterized not by any philosophy but primarily by their continual intent to pursue war with Rome, and stayed all the while in Jerusalem until it fell, at which point they disappeared. The Sicarii, on the other hand, were followers of the "Fourth Philosophy," founded by Judas of Galilee in 6 C.E. This philosophy was characterized in particular by the slogan that the Jews ought to have "no master but God." After Judas was killed, his son Menahem became the leader of the movement. When the latter was killed in Jerusalem, another relative, Eleazar son of Yair, led the group to Masada, where they took no further part in the war against Rome but rather endeavored to spread their teaching elsewhere, as in Egypt.[12]

---

8. Martin Hengel, *The Zealots*, trans. David Smith, 2nd ed. (Edinburgh: T & T Clark, 1989), 46f., 396–97.

9. Ibid., 48, 400.

10. Ibid., 139, 382f.

11. Solomon Zeitlin, "Zealots and Sicarii," *JBL* 81 (1962): 395. See also Zeitlin, "The Sicarii and Masada," *JQR* 57 (1967): 263.

12. Solomon Zeitlin, "Masada and the Sicarii, the Occupants of Masada," *JQR* 55 (1965): 316f.

Discussion about the historical identity of the Sicarii took a turn with the publication of Yadin's semi-popular account of the archaeological dig at Masada, not only because he did not preserve the distinction, so carefully maintained by Zeitlin, between the Sicarii and Zealots, but also because Yadin viewed the "Zealots" who committed "suicide" there to be a symbol of national courage. He speaks of "our great national figures, heroes who chose death over a life of physical and moral serfdom."[13] So, scholarly discussion about the Sicarii focused for a time less on their relations with the Zealots and more on the nature of their activities, particularly at Masada. Indeed, Yadin's conclusions elicited a series of responses by Trude Weiss-Rosmarin, who also made no distinction between the Sicarii and the Zealots but was otherwise sharply critical of Yadin's conclusions. In a 1966 article she states that the heroes of the period were not the "Zealots" of Masada but Rabbi Yohannan ben Zakkai and his followers, who chose life for the preservation of Israel. *"The Spirit of Masada was not Jewish!* It was the spirit of the conquering-and-dying hero of Greek and Roman literature, the glorification of death which remains the most popular motif of the literature today." Alternatively, life occupies the "highest rung" of Jewish values and is never hopeless.[14]

In a following article dealing with the same topic, Weiss-Rosmarin goes much further and states that Josephus's story about Masada was largely unhistorical. Josephus invented it to ease his troubled conscience about the thirty-nine deaths at Jotapata, for which he was responsible.[15] She states that the archaeological evidence is equivocal, and Josephus's own story is riddled with contradictions. Her reasons: (1) Josephus could not have recorded the speeches verbatim; (2) the breach in the wall could have been defended for a time; (3) fighters of valor would not commit suicide; (4) the suicides and murder were not commanded by Jewish law, contrary to the words Josephus places in the mouth of Eleazar; (5) it cannot be determined whether the skeletal remains found in a cave there are likely to be those who defended Masada; (6) only some rooms in the casemate wall were burned, probably as a defensive smoke-screen, and not the entire fortress as a final act of defiance, as Josephus reports; (7) lots are not cast with ostraca, as Josephus indicates in the Masada story, but with stones; and (8) the Romans would have viewed the suicides as acts of cowardice.[16] Her conclusions,

---

13. Yigael Yadin, *Masada: Herod's Fortress and the Zealot's Last Stand* (New York: Random House, 1966), 3. Yadin's book deals primarily with the archaeological finds at Masada, but it is difficult at times to assess his data, as, for example, the presence of lots, evidence of fire and destruction, the presence of a synagogue, etc., inasmuch as it is presented with such obvious bias.

14. Trude Weiss-Rosmarin, "Masada and Yavneh," *Jewish Spectator* 31 (1966): 4–7. Emphasis hers.

15. See *War* 3.336–91. We will return to this matter below.

16. Weiss-Rosmarin, "Masada, Josephus and Yadin," *Jewish Spectator* 32 (1967): 5, 32–33, 44–45, 78–79. All these arguments have been answered in detail by Feldman, "Masada: A Critique of Recent Scholarship," 218–48.

which presage scholarly treatments of the literary balance between the deaths at Masada and those at Jotapata (further below), are worth quoting:

> The Josephus-Yadin image of the death of the last defenders of Masada is not one of heroes but of COWARDS who chose suicide in preference to doing battle and dying in self-defense. This negative image is the projection of Josephus' tortured conscience trying to find surcease from his self-reproaches which never let him forget that he did not shrink from sacrificing thirty-nine lives so that he could save himself by betrayal and treason. By means of *the fiction* of suicide of the 960 last defenders of Masada Josephus *convinced himself* that instead of wronging and deceiving his companions in the pit at Jotapata he, in fact, bestowed upon them the crown of immortal heroism—the heroism he *fabricated* for Eleazar Ben Ya'ir and his fellow Sicarii.[17]

Thus, Josephus ennobled the suicides at Masada so that his behavior at Jotapata would appear less reprehensible. The upshot is that whatever Josephus tells also about the Sicarii at Masada cannot be trusted.

Yadin's book also prompted Zeitlin to reenter the arena with a much more critical response. He wrote that the Sicarii were not heroes but fanatical enemies of the Jewish state, whose philosophy led them to commit acts of war against their own countrymen and who simply "delivered" Masada into Roman hands.[18] Neither were the Sicarii devout Jews, because suicide has no place in "the views of the (Jewish) sages." About Eleazar's speeches, he agrees with Weiss-Rosmarin to the degree that they were Josephus's invention and designed to stand in opposition to the speech that Josephus himself gave at Jotapata.[19] Moreover, he says that devout Jews do not kill in the temple precincts. Neither do they kidnap and plunder their own countrymen, as Josephus presents the Sicarii doing.[20]

Wrestling with many of these same issues, Sidney Hoenig agrees with much of Weiss-Rosmarin's argument and concludes that the Sicarii cannot be understood as heroes. But he departs from Weiss-Rosmarin by admitting that Josephus could not have fabricated the story in all its details because Josephus undoubtedly obtained knowledge of what transpired at Masada from official Roman records and in any case would not have dared to lie about the actual events of the war in Roman imperial circles.[21] So the suicides at least must have occurred. Hoenig adds that although Josephus hated these rebels and as a Jew was repulsed by suicide, he nevertheless embellished the story in such a manner so that the deaths would

---

17. Weiss-Rosmarin, "Masada, Josephus and Yadin," 32. Emphasis hers.
18. Solomon Zeitlin, "The Sicarii and Masada," 259–62.
19. Ibid., 258.
20. Ibid., 265–66.
21. Sidney B. Hoenig, "The Sicarii in Masada—Glory or Infamy?" *Tradition* 11 (1970): 11, 16.

have been admired by the Romans. Following Weiss-Rosmarin, Hoenig believes Josephus did this as "vicarious personal compensation for Jotapata."[22]

Several years later Shimon Appelbaum made a fresh approach to the identity of the Sicarii and Zealots by a review of the information given and the terminology employed by Josephus. He proposes that the Zealots and the Sicarii arose in the background of Galilean banditry, the roots of which went back to local reaction against Herod, a foreign rival to the last of the Hasmoneans.[23] He observes that "bandit" (λῃστής) is the most common term Josephus employs in describing the rebels, a term that, along with its Latin counterpart (latrones), referred in Roman parlance to all criminals using armed violence as distinct from the armed forces of states.[24] In this way Josephus employed an indiscriminate Roman term and used it to "denigrate the Zealots and conceal their religious and social motives."[25]

About the Sicarii, Appelbaum states that two things made them distinctive; their emphasis that God is the only ruler and their fight against the Jews who submitted to the Roman census. Appelbaum adds that *sicarii* is a term informed by the *Lex Cornelia de sicariis et veneficiis* (83 B.C.E. *Institutes* 4.18.5) and was used by the Romans, along with λῃσταί, to describe insurgents in general. Josephus then applied the term exclusively to the rebels at Masada.[26]

Writing primarily for scholars in New Testament studies, Otto Betz brings together several strands already mentioned above. Similar to Appelbaum, Betz maintains that Josephus adopts the standpoint of Roman law when he calls the "hated freedom-fighters of the first Jewish revolt 'robbers' and 'assassins.'" In addition to the *lex Cornelia*, Betz cites Quintilian (*Inst. Orat.* 10.1.12) for a broad (murderer) and narrow (assassin) definition of Sicarii.[27] These were the "guerrillas" in the Zealot movement who were distinguished not by their ideology, which they shared with other rebel groups, but by the "courageous nature of their effort, which held life cheap, whether their own or that of others."[28] Motivated not by greed, fanaticism, or lust for power, which causes are attributable to the "polemically distorted" account of Josephus, but by righteous zeal for the Torah and the insistence that God alone is Lord, they opposed all authorities, including

---

22. Ibid., 16.

23. S. Appelbaum, "The Zealots: The Case for Revaluation," *JRS* 61(1971): 159.

24. See also Otto Betz, "σικάριος," in *TDNT* 7:278 n. 3, where he cites Pomponius, "Enemies are those who declare war against us, or against whom we declare war. The rest are "bandits" or "robbers." (Hostes hi sunt, qui nobis aut quibus nos publice bellum decrevimus; ceteri 'latrones' aut 'praedones' sunt.)

25. Appelbaum, "The Zealots," 163.

26. Ibid., 159, 160, 163.

27. Betz, "σικάριος," 278 n. 1. "We also loosely name 'sicarii' all who have committed murder with a sword" (Per abusionem sicarios etiam omnes vocamus, qui caedem telo quocumque commiserint).

28. Ibid., 279.

Jewish priests involved in a "politics of compromise," and embarked upon theft, destruction, and the burning of archives as means to overthrow "unrighteous mammon" and establish "the eternal jubilee of freedom and equality."[29]

Morton Smith, in a pungently worded critical review of scholarship on the origins and terminology of Zealots and Sicarii, insists that the two were distinct from each other and that the Sicarii predate the Zealots. He endorses H. St. John Thackeray's translation of *War* 2.444, where τοὺς ζηλωτάς who accompanied Menahem are represented as "fanatics" and not "Zealots," and thus he rejects this narrative as evidence for the unity of these two groups.[30] He adds that the listing of rebel groups at *War* 7.253–74, where the Sicarii and Zealots find separate billing, also makes this distinction clear. The Sicarii stem from the sect of Judas, whatever name it had, but they did not distinguish themselves by their murders until the mid-fifties, when Roman administration began to "disintegrate."[31] But Smith maintains that the labels "zealot" and *sicarii* were not static. Admiration for Phinehas, the archetypical figure who embodied "zeal" for the Lord, was widespread in Judea from Maccabean times, and many could thus be known as Zealots. Similarly, not every "assassin" was a member of the Sicarii.[32]

R. A. Horsley took a fresh approach to the question of the origins and identity of the Jewish rebel groups mentioned in *War* by employing modern theories of social banditry. Following Eric Hobsbawm, Horsley states that social banditry arises "in traditional agrarian societies where peasants are exploited by governments and landowners, particularly in situations where peasants are economically vulnerable and governments are administratively inefficient." Such banditry increases in times of economic crises, during which times such people are popularly perceived as "champions of justice for the common people."[33] Horsley states that the socio-economic conditions of Judea in the first century exhibited precisely these conditions. Herod's administration and many building projects resulted in a severe economic burden, a decrease in small land ownership, the rise of tenants, and an oversupply of workers.[34] Horsley adduces further evidence for these conditions in the governorship of Albinus (*War* 2.272–73), whose taxation

---

29. Ibid., 280.

30. Morton Smith, "Zealots and Sicarii, Their Origins and Relation," *HTR* 64 (1971): 7–8.

31. Ibid., 18. A similar point is made by M. Stern, who also connects the origins of the Sicarii to the sect of Judas but suggests that what was "new" about the Sicarii at 2.254–57 was their emergence at this time in "massive numbers" and with a new technique of violence. See M. Stern, "Sicarii and Zealots" in *Society and Religion in the Second Temple Period*, ed. Michael Avi-Yonah and Zvi Baras (Jerusalem: Massada Publishing, 1977), 263–301.

32. Ibid., 3, 18. See Numbers 25:6–13, where the priest Phinehas took up the spear in his zeal and was commended for his example.

33. Richard A. Horsley and John S. Hanson, *Bandits, Prophets, and Messiahs* (San Francisco: Harper & Row, 1985), 48–49. See also Richard A. Horsley, "Josephus and the Bandits," *JSJ* 10 (1979): 49.

34. Horsley and Hanson, *Bandits, Prophets, and Messiahs*, 50, 58–59.

polarized the rich from the poor. Thus, when Albinus freed many brigands who had been imprisoned by Festus, these joined the revolt.[35] In sum, contra Hengel, Horsley understands "bandit" (λῃσταί) not as a generalized pejorative and merely rhetorical label, but as a term to denote actual social brigands.

Moreover, he states they are not to be confused with the Sicarii. The activities of these latter are more appropriately those of "terrorists," insurgents who fight against foreign domination when normal means of legitimate coercion are closed and who often direct their violence at fellow nationals who collaborate with the enemy.[36] The Sicarii exhibited just these qualities by their murder of Jonathan, the "symbol of sacerdotal aristocracy's collaboration with the alien Roman rulers and its exploitation of the people."[37] Though Horsley acknowledges that they shared certain ideological characteristics with Zealots and other rebel groups, their aggressive tactics were distinctive and unprecedented. Peaceful recourse, no longer deemed a viable option, gave way to attacks directed not against the Romans but exclusively against fellow Jews.[38]

Thus, sociologically, the bandits and Sicarii were distinct and should not be viewed, contra Hengel and others, as branches of one Zealot party.[39] This, Horsley says, is to be maintained despite the episode about the royal ambitions of the Sicarii with Menahem in *War* 2.409f., where Josephus calls the Sicarii "bandits." This was done merely for pejorative reasons. The entry of Menahem into Jerusalem was, according to Horsley, an attempt by the Sicarii to enthrone this character as the Jewish Messiah, the long-standing culmination of their opposition to Rome.[40] Subsequent to his murder, the Sicarii simply withdrew from Jerusalem, perhaps disillusioned that the Jews would reject this divine plan of liberation.[41]

In his book *The Ruling Class of Judaea*, Martin Goodman writes an account of the breakdown of the ruling class and how it contributed to the Jewish revolt against Rome. The "ruling class" with whom Rome attempted to establish cooperative relations commanded no respect either from the Jewish people or from Rome. This ruling class was therefore unable to deal effectively with the social, economic, political, and religious crises of the decades leading to the revolt. In this context, the Sicarii, according to Goodman, are best understood as little more than hired assassins. For one thing, at their first appearance in *War* (2.254–55) Goodman finds it "striking" that Josephus neglected to connect the Sicarii with the Fourth Philosophy, both of which he "heartily disliked."[42] Josephus calls

---

35. Horsley, "Bandits," 58.
36. Horsley, "The Sicarii: Ancient Jewish 'Terrorist,'" *JR* 59 (1979): 438–39.
37. Ibid., 440. Cf. *War* 2:254–57.
38. Horsley and Hanson, *Bandits, Prophets, and Messiahs*, 201–2.
39. Ibid., 241 n. 1. The authors call this a "synthetic misunderstanding."
40. Ibid., 119.
41. Horsley, "The Sicarii," 456–57.
42. Martin Goodman, *The Ruling Class of Judaea* (Cambridge: Cambridge University Press, 1987), 94–95, 214.

attention only to their *modus operandi* and not to any ideology. Similarly, Goodman finds it unlikely that they were "principled anti-Roman terrorists" for then it would indeed be difficult to explain why Felix, when prefect of Judea (52–59 C.E.), would hire such anti-Roman terrorists to assassinate the high priest Jonathan, as Josephus records in *Ant.* 20.162–63. The principled anti-Roman rhetoric in Eleazar's suicide speech at Masada (*War* 7.323f.), therefore, has as its "sole function" to serve as a literary balance to Josephus's own anti-suicide speech at Jotapata (*War* 3.362f.) and thus it yields no historical data for Sicarii rhetoric. Similarly, the suicides themselves are better explained as acts of fear than as devotion to liberty.[43]

In summarizing the scholarly debate about the origins, identity, and activities of the Sicarii, it would be appropriate here also to draw attention to the articles of Baila R. Shargel and Yael Zerubavel, for they both raise issues not only about the popular understanding of the deaths at Masada, but also about the motivation behind Yadin's archaeological excavations and his historical assessment of the Sicarii. Shargel writes that in popular Jewish consciousness, Masada became a myth that dramatized how the new Jewish state (1948) was a continuation of the second Jewish commonwealth.[44] Such an understanding also informed certain activities of Yadin's excavation. She writes:

> For Yadin, the message of Masada was simply and clearly the transcendent value of independence and the myth of the Zealot suicide was intended to integrate the entire population of Israel around the resolution never again to return to a state of what he called "physical and moral serfdom." He assured an Israeli population that was already committed to the slogan, "Masada shall not fall again," that freedom and independence were irreversible.[45]

The article is an exploration of how this myth receded into the background not because of a more careful reading of Josephus or an examination of the archaeological remains, but because of those changing political circumstances that made Masada more a symbol of Jewish "stiff-necked refusal to compromise" and thus what Israel "did *not* want to become."[46] Zerubavel similarly traces the rise and evolution of the Masada myth. She likens the work of Yadin to other times where "archaeology was mobilized to promote nationalist ideology" founded upon a "highly selective representation of the historical record."[47] Thus, the popular narrative elaborates where Josephus is silent and glosses over other elements to

---

43. Ibid., 214.

44. Baila R. Shargel, "The Evolution of the Masada Myth," *Judaism* 28 (1979): 361.

45. Ibid., 367.

46. Ibid., 367. Shargel here quotes a May 7, 1973 *Newsweek* article.

47. Yael Zerubavel, "The Death of Memory and the Memory of Death: Masada and the Holocaust as Historical Metaphors," *Representations* 45 (1994): 75–76, 84.

focus on the "defenders'" courage. The narrative similarly avoids the term "suicide" and speaks of "patriotic death."[48]

In concluding the summary of historical scholarship on the Sicarii, we return to Horsley, who in his book *Galilee: History, Politics, People*, offered a reinterpretation of Galilean history to the end of the Second Temple period. Horsley broke from what he called the dominant "paradigm" by which scholars had traditionally understood and presented Galilee as a place of sharp distinctions between Jewish and Hellenistic and Jewish and Christian cultural elements.[49] He presents a rather more complex social, religious, and political interpretation by bringing modern political-social theories and archaeological evidence to bear on the data from Josephus. Here he expands on his earlier ideas and denies any evidence for a longstanding, organized "nationalistic" or "resistance" movement between 4 B.C.E. and 66–70 C.E. as is "imagined" in the Zealot movement because the Zealots did not even emerge until the winter of 67–68 C.E. and then only in Jerusalem. As to the Sicarii, Horsley insists that their activity should be viewed also in the larger context of spreading anarchy in Jerusalem. He writes:

> Jerusalem had been slipping into increasing anarchy for several years. Banditry had become virtually epidemic in the countryside in the aftermath of drought, famine, and the resultant indebtedness and hunger. The principal high-priestly families, with their hired gangs of thugs, not only were feuding among themselves, but had become predatory, seizing by force from the threshing floors the tithes intended for the ordinary priests (Ant. 20.180, 206–7). Completely frustrated at the high priests' continuing collaboration with the Romans, a group of sages/teachers called Sicarii or "Daggermen" turned to assassinating key high-priestly figures. (B.J. 2.254–57)[50]

And so the Sicarii are little more than localized social phenomena.

THE LITERARY PERSPECTIVE

The foregoing summary makes clear that part of the problem in deriving a solid historical assessment of the rise, characteristics, and activities of the Sicarii stems from the disparate understandings of the rhetorical elements of Josephus's presentation. We have, for example, at several points seen how scholars have simply dismissed certain literary claims about the Sicarii as nothing more than rhetorical display. Thus Goodman rejects Eleazar's speech at Masada as a source of the

---

48. Ibid., 76–77. For a historical and sociological analysis of the rise of the Masada myth, which he calls a "fabricated moralistic claim," see Nachman Ben-Yehuda, *The Masada Myth: Collective Mythmaking in Israel* (Madison: University of Wisconsin Press, 1995); and idem, *Sacrificing Truth: Archaeology and the Myth of Masada* (Amherst: Humanity Books, 2002).

49. Richard A. Horsley, *Galilee: History, Politics, People* (Valley Forge, PA: Trinity Press International, 1995), 3–5.

50. Ibid., 74.

Sicarii ideology. Hengel states that the various names of the rebel groups provide evidence only of Josephus keeping them distinct in his narrative and not of their actual existence. Zeitlin, on the other hand, not only insists on a historically distinct group of Sicarii; he traces their origin to Judas of Galilee. Horsley dismisses this connection.

This disparity serves as an introduction to the following summary of what scholars have stated about the literary and rhetorical elements of Josephus's presentation of the Sicarii, and we begin with the work of O. Michel and O. Bauernfeind. They offer a brief literary analysis of Eleazar's speeches at Masada, paying attention to the integration of Judaic and Hellenistic elements. They propose in particular that the second speech, a "deuterosis" of the first, ends with the emphasis that "we are born to die." They connect this thought with Ecclesiastes 9:4f., where Qoheleth taught that life, not death, was man's misfortune. In this manner, Josephus has Eleazar emerge as a "preacher of death" (*Todesprediger*) for the Jewish people.[51] By contrast, Josephus, who "saw himself as a kind of rhetorical and historically significant opponent to the defenders at Masada," presents the alternative in his own speech before the walls of Jerusalem—submit to the Romans and live. "For Josephus wants to save the Jewish diaspora through his own fate and the composition of *War*."[52]

The authors also comment on the manner by which Josephus describes the suicides. "The death is no martyrdom in the true sense but the act of men who must bow under ἀνάγκη (necessity) as the recognized will of God."[53] Since it is directed toward God, Josephus describes the deaths via words that also have Jewish cultic overtones and speak of "liturgical order," such as "sacrifice" (σφαγή), or the fact that ten men were chosen to kill the rest, a number that in light of Ruth 4:2 reminds the reader of a valid representation of the Jewish people. Thus, the killings become a "congregation event."[54]

Sidney Hoenig might properly fit in the historical presentation above because he echoes some of Weiss-Rosmarin's arguments. But unlike her, he insists that due to the circumstances of the writing process, Josephus could not have fabricated the suicides. "Not only did he have access to Roman archives and Jewish information, but the Roman officers of the war were still alive and his writings on Masada were circulated in the imperial circles."[55] Only the manner of the suicides and the speeches were fabrications designed "to impress his readers with sympathy and drama."[56]

As asserted above, the events of Masada are subject to widely diverse inter-

---

51. O. Bauernfeind and O. Michel, "Die Beiden Eleazarreden in Jos. Bell. 7,323–336; 7,34–388," *ZNW* 58 (1967): 268.
52. Ibid., 268, 269.
53. Ibid., 269.
54. Ibid., 272.
55. Hoenig, "Sicarii in Masada," 16.
56. Ibid., 12. But Hoenig does not explain why Josephus would choose to arouse sympa-

pretations. Valentin Nikiprowetzky, for example, asks, "How can this Sicarii leader, that is to say, if one follows Josephus, this vulgar criminal be at the same time a hero capable of showing in the face of death a calm, a disinterest, a height of feelings worthy of a Socrates or of a Marcus Arelius?" He points out that the suicides are positively portrayed, that suicide had acquired from Maccabean times a positive value and in the eyes of the insurgents was a type of religious sacrifice, preventing not only the defilements of the Romans but also leading one to the divine. Taken all together, the fact that Josephus has the Sicarii repent of their ideals at the point of such a death is psychologically and logically incoherent.[57]

The answer to this problem, according to Nikiprowetzky, is not to be found in the identification of disparate sources that Josephus may have employed but rather in the "ideological demands" placed upon Josephus.[58] Of these Nikiprowetzky identifies three "apologetic themes" that run throughout *War*, by which the disparate elements of Masada might be harmonized. These are, first, "a war of oracles," by which Josephus exposes the false hopes of the rebels. These false hopes are addressed at *War* 6.289–315 in particular, where Josephus exposes the popular interpretations of various celestial phenomena and bizarre events at Jerusalem in the midst of the revolt.[59] Second is "an imperial mystique," according to which Josephus puts in the mouth of Eleazar that all things have passed to the Romans, thus answering the needs of imperial propaganda. But this statement is qualified, for at the same time as Josephus has Eleazar admit that God has assigned the Jewish race to destruction, Josephus sees in the Roman victory God's chastisement, following in the tradition of the Maccabean martyrs, and not total abandonment.[60] Third is the Messianism of Josephus. Nikiprowetzky, on the basis of such passages as *Ant.* 14.125 and 10.206–10, understands that Josephus has not abandoned the messianic hopes of the Jewish nation. This attitude, apparent in *Antiquities*, is brought to Masada via the suggestive manner by which he describes the deaths—the emotion, the "sublime" character, the "rhetorical glitter," the speeches, all these positive elements applied to those he had just called criminals—as well as by the admiration the Romans expressed for the act. Such coloring is attributable to this hope "barely expressed, but unquestionably present."[61]

Helgo Lindner isolated the speeches of Agrippa, Josephus before the walls

---

thy in the minds of the Romans for those whom he acknowledges Josephus hated as causes of the war.

57. Valentin Nikiprowetzky, "La Mort d'Eléazar Fils de Jaïre et les Courants Apologétiques dans le De Bello Judaico de Flavius Josèphe," in *Hommages á André Dupont-Sommer* (Paris: Librairie d'Amerique et d'Orient Adrien-Maisonneuve, 1971), 468, 470, 471.

58. Ibid., 490.

59. Ibid., 473f. But Nikiprowetzky here addresses more the attitudes of the Zealots than those of the Sicarii at Masada.

60. Ibid., 482–83.

61. Ibid., 489–90.

of Jerusalem, and Eleazar at Masada as the passages where Josephus would show most clearly the themes of *War*, and the speeches thus provided the method of his study.[62] The "theological / salvation-history lesson" (*theologisch-heilsgeschichtliche Belehrung*) that Josephus thus conveys through the themes of these speeches is, among other things, that Roman power is incontestable and that rebellion is untimely and suicidal, for God has placed all things under the Romans. Though not explicitly about the Sicarii, his comments about the rhetorical elements of Eleazar's speech are important in this regard, for Lindner maintains that Josephus has "foisted upon" Eleazar his own historical interpretation. That is, the reprehensible nature of the entire Zealot (*sic*) movement, exemplified in Eleazar, is in fact the conviction of Josephus.[63] Like Michel and Bauernfeind, Lindner believed that Josephus presents Eleazar as a "preacher of death," who serves as an example of the "way of death" for the Jewish people.[64] But while the former authors based this conclusion on connections to Jewish Wisdom literature, Lindner arrives at this conclusion strictly via a comparison of the three speeches. Striving for freedom, according to Agrippa, is untimely (2.355). Eleazar also came to recognize this fact (7.327). The rebels' slogan of freedom thus becomes a slogan for death because history offers no more choice. The speech of Josephus before Jerusalem, emphasizing submission to Rome, demonstrates the alternative—surrender to the Romans and live.[65] Thus, Eleazar serves as a negative example for the Jewish people who continue to rebel against Rome.

We have seen how Nikiprowetzky harmonized the seemingly disparate manner by which Josephus grants noble qualities to the Sicarii at Masada via discernable themes running throughout *War*. In two stimulating articles David Ladouceur took a slightly different approach.[66] Beginning with an analysis of Eleazar's speeches and following Menaham Luz, he notes first that the form and content are derived from Greek models, the *Phaedo* standing out in particular. In such a manner, Ladouceur states that Josephus transformed Eleazar into a "philosopher figure," which is a distortion of the "actual absorptions of the Sicarii."[67] Ladouceur therefore insists that the episode must be read in its Greco-Roman political environment, whereby Eleazar "echoes the opponents of the Flavian regime." As evidence, Ladouceur adduces Vespasian's hatred for Hel-

---

62. Helgo Lindner, *Die Geschichtsauffassung des Flavius Josephus im Bellum Judaicum* (Leiden: Brill, 1972), 19.

63. Ibid., 39.

64. Ibid., 39–40.

65. Ibid., 39.

66. David J. Ladouceur, "Masada: A Consideration of the Literary Evidence," *GRBS* 21 (1980); and idem, "Josephus and Masada," in *Josephus, Judaism, and Christianity*. The 1987 article is a repetition and expansion of the 1980 article.

67. Ladouceur, "Josephus and Masada," 97–99. For Menahem Luz's arguments, see "Eleazar's Second Speech on Masada and Its Literary Precedents," *Rheinisches Museum für Philologie* 126 (1983): 25–43.

vidius Priscus, who "forever praised democracy and denounced monarchy" (Dio 65.12.2), and the Cynic philosophers, who were "actuated" by Stoic principles as part of the political opposition (Dio 66.13.1).[68] By putting such words in Eleazar's mouth, "distinctions are blurred as a Jewish fanatic takes on the outlines of a home-grown opponent of Vespasian's rule."[69]

Ladouceur also insists on the clear literary connection with Josephus's speech against suicide at Jotapata, the obvious *antilogos*. "In this context it is therefore not implausible to sense political overtones in Josephus' speech as well. . . . In a sense his own speech (at Jotapata) becomes not only a moral rejection of suicide but also an assertion of political allegiance to Vespasian and Titus."[70] In sum, the episode at Masada must ultimately be interpreted as irony in light of the Stoic opposition to the Flavians and viewed in contrast to Josephus's own speech at Jotapata. Josephus in *War* draws his readers' attention to a proper response to the Flavian regime.

Shaye Cohen focused his attention on the credibility of Josephus's account of the events at Masada in light of the archaeological discoveries at the site. The approach was to examine other cases of mass suicide in antiquity and compare Josephus's narrative both with these episodes and the archaeological record.[71] From the literary parallels, he concludes that suicide was an action of last resort, was often embellished, and was generally praised by ancient authors.[72] Cohen identifies embellishment in Josephus's account also. The Romans, for example, would not have stopped attacking after the walls were breached.[73]

For "apologetic" reasons, Cohen proposes, Josephus gives two speeches to Eleazar. This, in the first place, allows the latter to admit his wrong. But Josephus also has Eleazar utter the "blasphemous" notion that God had rejected his people. Josephus does this so that he might demonstrate to his readers how "the theology of the Sicarii leads to the renunciation of one of the core doctrines of Judaism, the eternal election of Israel."[74] In this way Eleazar serves as a symbol of the "fate of all who would follow in their footsteps and resist Rome."[75] But Cohen also maintains that by patterning the structure of the suicides after collective suicides in the Greco-Roman tradition, where it was an object of amazement and

---

68. Ibid., 99–100.

69. Ibid., 101.

70. Ladouceur, "Masada," 257.

71. Shaye Cohen, "Masada: Literary Tradition, Archaeological Remains, and the Credibility of Josephus," *JJS* 33 (1982): 385–405. Cohen selects sixteen episodes from Herodotus, Xenophon, Polybius, Livy, Appian, Plutarch, Pausanias, Justinus, and Orosius.

72. Ibid., 392.

73. Ibid., 396.

74. Ibid., 396, 404.

75. Ibid., 396, 404. Cohen echoes Lindner here and states, "The way of the Sicarii is the way of death." He, too, identifies Eleazar's second speech as the *antilogos* to Josephus's at Jotapata. The speech thus serves a "purely literary" purpose (397).

admiration, Josephus unintentionally ennobled the act.[76] For Cohen, then, the disparate elements of the narrative arise from Josephus's inexperience with this literary tradition.

The interplay of Josephus' literary technique with reliable historical information about the Sicarii has been touched on at several points in comments by Tessa Rajak. She observes, for example, that the Sicarii at Masada echo the sentiments of Judas, the founder of a "Fourth Philosophy," but this philosophy, placed next to the other three treated by Josephus, "all looks suspiciously like Josephus' own schematization, made for the benefit of his Greek readers."[77] And so caution is in order when suggesting any direct connection between the Sicarii and an organized philosophy stemming from Judas in 6 c.e.

Rajak, however, speaks more directly about Josephus's portrayal of the Sicarii in the Masada narrative. She insists that the two speeches of Eleazar were designed by Josephus to evoke reader respect, and this because of Josephus's competing loyalties as a Jew writing in Rome under Flavian patronage. She writes:

> The pull of the Flavians is not made to supersede earlier loyalties, and adulation of the emperors is rarely close to the heart of his work. Though we cannot altogether eliminate that disturbing figure, Josephus the flatterer of the conquering emperors, this Josephus must be put in his place.[78]

Thus, while *War* might well have ended with the triumph in Rome, Josephus devotes space to Masada, which serves as a "counterweight," and momentarily holds up for the reader's admiration those he loves to hate. Though this may be inconsistent, the reconciliation of competing allegiances brings with it its own inconsistencies.[79]

Menahem Luz, focusing more narrowly, published an article on the literary precedents in Greek literature to Eleazar's second speech and makes the following observations. Eleazar's reference to the immortality of the soul (7.341–48) corresponds to Socrates' reply to Cebes in the *Phaedo* (78–80c), a well-known Platonic commonplace as evidenced by its parallels in the consolation literature, such as Seneca (*Ep.* 58.23–34, 77.4f.). Eleazar's comments about the repose of sleep (7.349–50) Luz similarly traces to Plato via the *consolationes* as a better match than Cicero (*De. Div.* 1.64), proposed by Morel. The example of the Indians (7.351–57), he proposes, is derived from Clearchus, though he notes Morel's proposal of Strabo (15.57.10–11). Finally, Eleazar's comment that the horrors of war offer proof that life is not worth living (7.358–88) he takes to be a Platonic commonplace also derived from the *Phaedo* (62c).[80] Several conclusions follow:

---

76. Ibid., 404.
77. Rajak, *Josephus*, 89.
78. Ibid., 221.
79. Ibid., 221.
80. Menahem Luz, "Eleazar's Second Speech on Masada and Its Literary Precedents,"

(1) the parallels between the second speech and the consolation pieces are too many to be coincidental; (2) the speech of Eleazar thus fits well with general discussions on death contemporary with Josephus; and (3) a Greek reader, recognizing these concepts, would not have been disturbed by them coming from the mouth of a Jewish Zealot, for "such an ancient reader would have recognized a fictitious, set-speech when he saw one."[81]

In 1998 Honora Chapman submitted her doctoral dissertation on Josephus's use of theatrical elements as a narrative device in *War*. Although she did not focus on the Sicarii directly, one of the primary sections she produced as evidence for her thesis concerned Masada, and so her comments are pertinent here. For Chapman, the Sicarii at Masada illustrate the improper response to Roman power, which results in death. She brings together some of the ideas listed above as, for example, that Eleazar's speech illustrates the wrong choice, whereas Josephus's at Jotapata illustrates the correct choice, or, following Ladouceur, that Eleazar is made to sound like the political opposition.[82]

Where she expands on these ideas with respect to the Masada narrative is in her attempt to unify the elements of *War* 7 under the theme of Roman power. Thus, not only is Masada the "centerpiece example of the greater Roman power encountering the weaker Jewish opponent," but this same theme carries over into the Alexandrian narrative, where the activities of the Sicarii are presented as an infecting madness and where their defiance of Roman power entails death "even for the very young."[83]

Finally both Jan Willem Van Henten and Rajak have proposed a fresh look at the Sicarii at Masada through the motifs of Jewish "martyr" texts and the idea of a noble death, and so these two scholars may be mentioned together. Expanding on his earlier published work, *The Maccabean Martyrs*, and with 2 and 4 Maccabees as his primary texts, Van Henten proposes the following stock elements of a Jewish "martyr" text: (1) the issuance of an enactment, the transgression of which brings death; (2) enforcement of the enactment brings the Jews' loyalty into conflict; (3) when forced to choose, the Jews choose to die rather than obey; (4) the

---

Rheinisches Museum für Philologie 126 (1983): 25f. For W. Morel see "Eine Rede bei Josephus," *Rheinisches Museum für Philologie* 75 (1926): 106–114.

81. Ibid., 43

82. Chapman, "Spectacle and Theater," 165–67, 179f. See now also her article "Spectacle in Josephus' *Jewish War*," in *Flavius Josephus and Flavian Rome* ed. Jonathan Edmondson, Steve Mason, and James Rives (New York: Oxford University Press, 2005), although here she does not treat the Masada narrative.

83. Chapman, "Spectacle and Theater," 134, 182f. Otto Michel had earlier made similar observations. He, too, connects Eleazar's speeches with Josephus's at Jotapata and sees there how Josephus emphasizes that the fight for freedom is a fight against a God-ordained world power. It thus leads to death. Otto Michel, "Die Rettung Israels und die Rolle Roms nach den Reden im 'Bellum Iudaicum,'" in *ANRW*, ed. Wolfgang Hasse (New York and Berlin: Walter de Gruyter, 1984), II.21.2,965. Similarly, Pierre Vidal-Naquet, "Flavius Josèph et Masada," *Revue Historique* 260 (1978): 15.

Jews' decision becomes obvious under examination, often torture; and (5) the execution is described.[84] Van Henten contends that those passages in Josephus that present a "noble death" are very similar to the traditional martyr text, and without elaboration he identifies the Masada and Alexandrian narratives of *War* 7 as examples. So, although he does not explicitly treat the Sicarii, his observations about this narrative device, if born out, would cast their deaths in a vastly more positive light.

Rajak makes similar observations about Jewish "martyr" texts from 2 and 4 Maccabees. Though there was no development of Jewish martyrology in ancient times, she says that stock characters run like a thread through a variety of Jewish literatures, establishing a "Jewish-Greek literary tradition." Among these are defense of the divine Law, a tyrannical oppressor, the threat to the Jewish nation, the heroic endurance by the ostensibly weak, a description of harrowing torture, the anonymity of the martyrs, and the inherence of victory in death itself.[85] She also adduces an expiatory power inherent in the martyr's blood.[86] She goes on to make connections both with Eleazar's speech at Masada and the value presented there of a religiously motivated suicide, and with the young Sicarii in the Alexandrian narrative "although he (Josephus) allows that their strength of mind may be madness."[87]

THE NEED FOR A NEW STUDY

In view of the scholarly studies of Josephus's Sicarii summarized above, a new study is justified at several points. In the first place, the literary studies described above demonstrate a disproportionate but understandable focus on Masada— understandable because there the Sicarii are so much more prominent, and the Masada narrative is replete with intriguing literary allusions, dramatic motifs, and seemingly contradictory elements. The upshot has been an almost complete neglect not only of those other places in *War* 7 where the Sicarii are protagonists—the Alexandrian narrative (7.410f.) and the Catullus narrative (7.437f.)— but also their several appearances in *War* 2 and 4. A complete study of Josephus's presentation of the Sicarii in *War* remains to be done.

Second, we have already seen above how scholars dismiss certain historical data about the Sicarii as nothing more than Josephus's rhetorical display. This

---

84. Jan Willem Van Henten, "Martyrion and Martyrdom. Some Remarks about Noble Death in Josephus," in *Internationales Josephus-Kolloquium Brüssel 1998*, ed. Jürgen Kalms and Folker Siegert (Münster: Lit Verlag, 1998), 131. For his earlier work, see *The Maccabean Martyrs as Saviors of the Jewish People* (Leiden: Brill, 1997).

85. Rajak, "Dying for the Law," in *The Jewish Dialogue with Greece and Rome* (Leiden: Brill, 2002), 100.

86. Ibid., 113f.

87. Ibid., 125.

reinforces the necessity of defining, as far as possible, the rhetorical elements that drive Josephus's presentation of the Sicarii before one can find firm ground for making a historical assessment. This point is pressed by Horst Moehring.

> It is entirely useless to make any attempts to separate in Josephus any supposedly "objective" passages from any "subjective" interpretations. Purely objective data are likely to be commonplace or uninstructive. When Josephus wrote, he had a practical purpose in mind, and that purpose was the reconciliation between Rome and the Jews. Everything he said, every story he told, every anecdote with which he enlivened his narrative, every document he quoted (or misquoted, or invented), and, above all, every speech he reported, every word had a purpose. Details in the huge corpus of his writings can be understood only if they are seen as parts of a totality which had a clear aim in mind.[88]

Of course Moehring is not denying the possibility of attaining factual information from this tendentious presentation of the *Judean War*. He is merely emphasizing the necessity of recognizing those elements. "It is unavoidable that his [Josephus's] narrative should raise some questions as to matters of fact. But before these can be discussed today, Josephus must be allowed to be heard on his own terms, he must be allowed to present and illustrate his own thesis."[89]

Steve Mason makes a similar observation in his work on the Pharisees, which has as its starting point that one can state nothing reliable about these characters from Josephus unless one has first embarked upon a literary analysis of those places where Josephus mentions them.[90] He presses the point home, however, in an article that calls into question the use of narrative contradiction as a method for isolating historical fact within and in opposition to the themes of Josephus. Jonathan Price, for example, employs narrative contradiction as a primary method of attaining historical realia from *War* about the Judean revolt. He says, "Omissions, mistaken inclusions, contradictions and other forms of carelessness are precisely what provide entry into the history that Josephus wanted to obscure or did not care about."[91] Mason responds:

---

88. Horst R. Moehring, "Joseph Ben Matthia and Flavius Josephus: The Jewish Prophet and Roman Historian," in *ANRW*, ed. Wolfgang Hasse (Berlin and New York: Walter de Gruyter, 1984), 868. Kraus and Woodman make a similar point about the importance of analyzing the shape of a narrative. "The *form* of a text can contribute as much to its meaning as does its content." See C. S. Kraus and A. J. Woodman, *Latin Historians* (Oxford: Oxford University Press, 1987), 2.

89. Ibid., 939.

90. Steve Mason, *Flavius Josephus on the Pharisees* (Leiden: Brill, 1991), 10ff.

91. Price, *Jerusalem under Siege: The Collapse of the Jewish State 66–70 C.E.* (Leiden: Brill, 1992), 182.

> Yet identifying contradictions presupposes an adequate assessment of the narra-
> tive's shape, themes, and rhetorical dimensions. Historical work, alas, too often
> depends upon reductive appraisals of Josephus' literary tendencies, and thus, of
> what counts as contradiction. When this happens, our rigorously rebuilt reality
> may turn out to be little more than our imaginative riffs on his grace notes.[92]

Again, the need is apparent for a careful literary/rhetorical analysis before one
can offer a historical assessment of the Sicarii. No complete analysis of Josephus's
narrative about the Sicarii has yet been done.

Now, in this regard Josephan studies have been changing rapidly, and among
those literary devices that have become apparent in *War* and guide the reader's
understanding of the Sicarii are chiasmus and irony. Josephus's employment of
chiasmus in his larger and second work, the *Judean Antiquities*, is well recognized.[93] Though a complete elaboration is yet to be published, Mason has isolated
such elements also in *War*. The history begins, for example, with the story of
how Onias, the high priest, left Jerusalem to build a temple in Egypt (1.31–33).
Josephus pointedly states he will return to this matter, yet does not until book
7 (7.420–36). Mason isolates this and other elements of a chiastic structure, and
identifies the narrative of how the rebels murdered Ananus and Jesus as the central panel.[94]

Now, as Welch has stated, at its most profound level chiasm becomes not
only an artful structure but also a literary device that shapes a text's meaning.

> Here the form becomes more than a skeleton upon which thoughts and words
> are attached. When chiasmus achieves the level of ordering the flow of thoughts
> throughout an entire pericope, or of a sustained unfolding of an artistic verbal
> expression, the character of the form itself merges with the message and mean-
> ing of the passage.[95]

Therefore, if we are intent upon a thorough understanding of how Josephus presents the Sicarii, we must also be attentive to any nuance these structural considerations might bring to their presentation. No scholars have placed the Sicarii
firmly within the structure of *War*.

---

92. Mason, "Contradiction or Counterpoint? Josephus and Historical Method," *Review
of Rabbinic Judaism* 6 (2003): 147. Such a "reductive" appraisal is apparent in Price. He says
Josephus "may have pretended to an overarching conception of the war, and he may have tried
to incorporate his learning about historical processes into his own history, but the genius
required to shape historical narrative so that its very form manifests the conception was lacking" (Price, *Jerusalem under Siege*, 182).

93. See Mason, "Introduction to the *Judean Antiquities*," in *Flavius Josephus: Judean
Antiquities 1–4. Translation and Commentary*, by Louis Feldman; ed. Steve Mason (Leiden:
Brill, 2001), xx–xxii.

94. Mason, *Josephus and the New Testament*, 66f.

95. John Welch, ed., *Chiasmus in Antiquity* (Hildesheim: Gerstenberg, 1981), 11.

A second literary device at work in *War*, the depth of which is only now becoming apparent, is irony. Mason had already identified this element in *Josephus and the New Testament*, but has recently established Josephus as an author completely at home with this technique.[96] Though Ladouceur recognizes this device, his analysis extends only to the Masada narrative and is elaborated exclusively from a Roman point of view. A reexamination of the narrative is in order if for no other reason than that Josephus did not write exclusively for Romans, and Josephus may have employed irony that would easily be understood by his Hellenistic Jewish readers as well. To this we might add the possible use of this narrative device for the Sicarii in all their contexts. Work yet remains to be done.

For all the above reasons a comprehensive study of the Sicarii is thoroughly justified. The scope of this study is an analysis of how Josephus presents the Sicarii in the *Judean War*. The procedure of the study will be as follows. We will first present the various contexts of *War* in chapter 2. There we will pay attention to the literary background of *War*, its thematic elements, its date and unity—paying special attention to the unity of *War* 7 with the prior six books—and finally Josephus's audience. With this groundwork in place, we will turn to an analysis of the Sicarii. The first step will be to isolate all those passages where Josephus mentions the Sicarii or where their presence is to be understood from context. The second step will be to perform a literary analysis of each passage. The steps we will follow in the analyses include an examination of the literary context, paying attention to how Josephus describes the activity of the Sicarii, the important words Josephus uses in the narrative, and how the narrative functions within the overall structure of *War*. Third, from these data we will draw conclusions about the thematic elements in Josephus's presentation of the Sicarii. Fourth and last, we will draw some preliminary historical conclusions about the Sicarii from Josephus's presentation.

---

96. Mason, *Josephus and the New Testament*, 81f. and esp. 85. But now see idem, "Figured Speech and Irony in T. Flavius Josephus," in *Flavius Josephus and Flavian Rome*, ed. Jonathan Edmondson, Steve Mason, James Rives (New York: Oxford University Press, 2005), 243–88. Mason's ideas find their appropriate place in chapter 2 below.

CHAPTER TWO

THE CONTEXTS OF *THE JUDEAN WAR*

Josephan studies focusing on *War* have advanced at an almost dizzying rate in the past few decades. Recent scholarship has transformed this author from a rather artless compiler of sources to one who not only rightfully takes his place in the rich Greco-Roman historiographical tradition, but is fully engaged in the finer elements of rhetoric such as the subtleties of irony. He has progressed from a mouthpiece of Flavian propaganda to an author who rather boldly insists on the nobility of the Jewish people and is not afraid to lay blame for the Judean revolt also at the feet of the Romans. He was thought at first to be writing to his own people on behalf of the Romans, warning them about the consequences of revolt, but is thought now to be writing more to Romans on behalf of his own people, defending them for their long history and nobility. In view of this rapidly changing field, this study of necessity begins by establishing the context of *War*, the foundation on which we might embark on an analysis of the Sicarii.

LITERARY BACKGROUND

War takes its place generally in the long tradition of Greco-Roman historiography. The commonplaces of the programmatic opening remarks, such as Josephus's claims about the importance of his subject matter, his unique authority as an author, and his impartiality place this work in the tradition of Thucydides.[1] Like its predecessors, *War* is punctuated by set-speeches, filled with digressions on matters of geography and culture, and is characterized by extended and

---

1. Harold Attridge, "Josephus and His Works," in *Jewish Writings of the Second Temple Period*, ed. Michael E. Stone (Philadelphia: Fortress, 1986), 195. See also Per Bilde, *Flavius Josephus between Jerusalem and Rome*, JSPSup 2 (Worcester: Sheffield Academic Press, 1988), 203f. For a more recent study on how Josephus's proem compares and contrasts with other ancient historians, see the wide-ranging work of John Marincola, *Authority and Tradition in Ancient Historiography* (Cambridge: Cambridge University Press, 1997). For a recent study on how Josephus employs the historiographical conventions of Thucydides in *War*, see Gottfried Mader, *Josephus and the Politics of Historiography: Apologetic and Impression Management in the Bellum Judaicum* (Leiden: Brill, 2000).

dramatic battles, acts of heroism, and sudden changes of fortune.[2] Like the works of Thucydides, Polybius, Livy, and Tacitus, *War,* according to Per Bilde, also has an "ideological and moralizing" element.[3] Moreover, Josephus wrote in a style of Greek that Steve Mason calls "a fine specimen of the developing Atticistic Greek so popular among the Greek revivalists of his time."[4]

Of particular note is the manner by which Josephus organizes his work around stock themes in Greco-Roman historiography, prominent among which is stasis (στάσις, "sedition"). As this concept, too, will become important in understanding how Josephus presents the Sicarii, it is worth pausing at this point to observe more carefully some of its features. Jonathan Price has demonstrated that Thucydides, the model historian which all others to some degree aspired to emulate, organized his *History* around this concept. Price analyzes stasis as a "pathology" that is presented by Thucydides in connection with the conflict at Corcyra in 3.81–83. This narrative in turn serves as a model for every stasis mentioned in the *History.*[5] Price further demonstrates how Thucydides organized his work around the concept.

> In what were highly original choices, he emphasized that the first casus belli and the first apparent incident of the war were στάσεις, he drew attention to στάσεις at critical junctures of the war, highlighting especially the cluster of

---

2. On tragic elements and enargeia in Thucydides, see Andrew D. Walker, "*Enargeia* and the Spectator in Greek Historiography," *TAPA* 123 (1993): 353–77. On the concept of "tragic-history," see F. W. Walbank, "History and Tragedy," in *Selected Papers: Studies in Greek and Roman History and Historiography* (Cambridge: Cambridge University Press, 1985). For an exploration of "dramatic" elements in Roman historiography, see Antoine Foucher, "Nature et Formes de L'histoire Tragique à Rome," *Latomus* 59 (2000): 773–801. For tragic elements in *War,* see Honora Howell Chapman, "Spectacle and Theater in Josephus' *Bellum Judaicum*" (Ph.D. diss., Stanford University, 1998).

3. Bilde, *Flavius Josephus,* 205. Bilde however detects a change of emphasis in that these historians "write for posterity, in particular for the benefit and enlightenment of politicians and statesmen" whereas Josephus "is engaged both in a political struggle on behalf of the Jewish people and in a vast cultural conflict between Judaism and the Hellenistic world."

4. Steve Mason, "Of Audience and Meaning: Reading Josephus' *Bellum Judaicum* in the Context of a Flavian Audience," in *Josephus and Jewish History in Flavian Rome and Beyond,* ed. Joseph Sievers and Gaia Lembi (Leiden: Brill, 2005), 75. As in so many areas of Josephan studies, here also more recent scholarly opinions give more credit to Josephus's abilities. In writing *War,* Josephus acknowledges the help of "assistants" in *Apion* 1.50 (χρησάμενός τισι πρὸς τὴν Ἑλληνίδα φωνὴν συνεργοῖς). Early on it was suspected that such helpers were in fact "ghost writers" of significant parts of *War* (so Thackeray, *Josephus the Man and the Historian,* New York: Jewish Institute of Religion, 1929). Rajak, however, allowed a far more limited role for these helpers, insisting that all such "fantastic" notions of ghost writers should be dispelled. See Rajak, *Josephus, the Historian and His Society,* 2nd ed. (London: Gerald Duckworth, 2002), 62–63.

5. Price, *Thucydides and Internal War* (Cambridge: Cambridge University Press, 2001), 11–78.

στάσεις around the Peace of Nicias, and he used the Athenian στάσις to organize the narrative after the Sicilian expedition. Not only did the larger war spawn στάσεις in the cities, but the war itself arose from and was fueled by smaller στάσεις. στάσις is ever before the reader's eyes and represents the very nature of the war.[6]

Thus, stasis becomes the means by which the war is framed and understood.

Significantly, Josephus analyzes and organizes his presentation of the Judean war in part around this same concept. As Mason points out, Josephus accents stasis in the proem (1.24, 25, 27) and then makes it the first word of the narrative proper (1.31). It becomes the interpretive term at the central panel of *War*, the murder of Ananus and Jesus (4.318–21). Subsequent to their deaths, when stasis breaks out in full force in Jerusalem, Josephus begins to label the various rebel groups.[7]

Mason observes that stasis was a convenient term for a number of reasons. It was a "hot-button" word filled with bad connotations from the time of Thucydides; it served to accent the ordinary problems faced by the Jewish leadership against any attempt to "demonize" them; and it served to place the Judean civil strife against its familiar counterpart in Rome itself.[8] Although Price contends that Josephus, who used the term for partisan polemic, did not truly understand Thucydides' employment of the term as a means of detached historical analysis,[9] the point here, in the first place, is to recognize the level at which Greek historiographic tradition permeated Josephus's presentation in *War*, and to be sensitive to how this also will color his presentation of the Sicarii. However, we will have more to say about stasis shortly when presenting Mason's arguments about Josephus's use of irony.

Josephus is further grounded in the Greek historiographic tradition by Arthur Eckstein. While recognizing those points where Josephus follows the tradition in a general way, Eckstein maintains that the nearest and most influential model for Josephus in all his writings was Polybius. He demonstrates this at several levels. Besides the points at which Josephus makes explicit reference to Polybius in his later works (*Ant.* 12.135–37, 358–59; *Apion* 2.84), Eckstein identifies several passages where Josephus's sequences of thought and vocabulary closely pattern Polybius. He points out that inasmuch as these are not commonplaces or clichés, they can only be explained by Josephus's direct modeling. One example would be Josephus's critical comments about Nicolaus of Damascus's treatment of Herod (*Ant.* 16.184–87), which display "not only precisely the same ideas, but

---

6. Ibid., 278.

7. Mason, *Josephus and the New Testament*, 2nd ed. (Peabody: Hendrickson, 2003), 67–68, 78–79.

8. Ibid., 80–81.

9. Price, "Josephus' Reading of Thucydides: A Test Case in the BJ." Online: http://pace. mcmaster.ca/media/pdf/sbl/price2003.pdf, 21–22.

in precisely the same *sequence*, and often expressed in the same language" as those found in Polybius's comments about other historians' treatment of Philip V (8.8.4–9).[10] Similarly, Eckstein finds "whole congeries of Polybian historiographical motifs" in the proem of *War*.[11]

In regard to *War*, Eckstein proposes three ways in which Josephus found Polybian motifs a useful "representational and/or interpretative tool" in presenting the Jewish revolt to his Greek-speaking audience. First, both Polybius and Josephus emphasize the foolhardiness of rebel behavior by presenting it as "irrational" (ἀλογία, ἀλόγιστος, ἀλογιστία, etc.) and "madness" (μανία).[12] Second, both emphasize the responsibility of the statesmen to control such irrational behavior. Eckstein points to the *Life* and two significant speeches in *War* (Agrippa, 2.346; Josephus, 5.364, 365, 367, 406, 419) as evidence of this theme in Josephus.[13] Third, Josephus attributes the Romans' supremacy, as Polybius, both to their practical training and skill and to the purposeful workings of "fate" (τύχη) to bring all things under their control.

This last point is especially telling for Eckstein inasmuch as Josephus, unlike Polybius, also attributes Roman supremacy to the will of God himself, and therefore the emphasis upon fate seems an "unnecessary complication."[14] "Indeed, one has to ask why a Jewish writer, who might well have been satisfied with an explanation for Roman supremacy anchored simply in Roman virtues and the favor of God, would have bothered to include Tyche in his narrative as an explanatory device in the first place."[15] The explanation can only be that even at the highest level of how Josephus presents and analyzes the Jewish revolt and defeat, he found Polybius's "interpretive tools" useful. But such a comparison also exposes Josephus's own and unique emphasis on the will of God in granting power to the Romans, something that Polybius did not do.[16] In the final analysis, then, both Polybius and Josephus emphasize "the brutal reality of Roman power, and the consequent necessity, in almost any situation, to make one's peace with it."[17] Eckstein's observations confirm Josephus's debt to the Greek historiographic tradition, but we will want to be alert also to how Polybius may have influenced his presentation of the Sicarii.

---

10. Arthur M. Eckstein, "Josephus and Polybius: A Reconsideration," *CQ* 9 (1990): 182. Emphasis his. For the explicit reference, see 176–77.

11. Ibid., 183.

12. Ibid., 190–91.

13. Ibid., 189–90.

14. Ibid., 202. Helgo Lindner attempted to connect this essentially Hellenistic term with the divine will of the Jewish deity (*Die Geschichtsauffassung des Flavius Josephus im Bellum Judaicum* [Leiden: Brill, 1972], 143–44), but Eckstein concluded that such a laborious connection would be lost on Josephus's Greek audience in any case.

15. Eckstein, "Josephus and Polybius," 199.

16. Ibid., 199.

17. Ibid., 208.

Returning now to Josephus's use of stasis as a narrative tool in *War*, Mason shows how Roman stasis and civil wars always lurk in the background of *War*. Josephus needs only to indicate the reference briefly and leave his Roman audience to ponder the parallels between their own recent experience of civil war and that of the Judeans. They should realize that "the Judean civil war, though it attracted Roman legions, is no different from their own common experience."[18] This Mason presents as an example of Josephus's employment of irony in a groundbreaking article on the topic.

Working off of D. C. Muecke's definition of irony, Mason first suggests two possible ways by which the observer of irony (here, the readers of a text) might be clued in to its presence. Either the author will have furnished within the text the information necessary so that the reader will detect the irony, a technique Mason calls "text-dependent" irony, or the author expects the reader to already possess sufficient knowledge, a technique Mason calls "audience-dependent" irony. The former is the "simpler and less risky" technique in that the author guides the reader's understanding by textual clues. For examples Mason points to New Comedy. Audience-dependent irony, Mason observes, "can be subtler and more effective" than the former, but it is "riskier" because there are no "authoritative guides" for the reader's understanding. Here the examples would be Old Comedy with its many allusions to current events, or the tragedies with undefined connections to epic poetry and myth.[19]

Turning to Quintilian's statements about the prevalence of "figured controversies" in the Flavian period as a starting point (*Inst.* 9.2.65), Mason illustrates the prevalence of irony in elite Roman discourse in a variety of settings.[20] For the purpose of his article, however, he demonstrates how Josephus also appears quite comfortable and adept at its use. Mason points out that one of the reasons Quintilian observed for the use of figured speech (*figuratae*) was that one might thus make a point when it was unsafe to speak frankly. Quintilian wrote:

> You can speak to good effect as openly as you wish against those tyrants as long as it can be understood otherwise because the danger (to you) and not the offense (to them) is then turned aside. And if it can be avoided by the ambiguity of expression, everyone will approve the trick.

> Quamlibet enim apertum, quod modo et aliter intelligi posit, in illus tyrannos bene dixeris, quia periculum tantum, non etiam offense vitatur. Quod si ambiguitate sententiae posit eludi, nemo non illi furto favet. (*Inst.* 9.2.66, 67)

---

18. Mason, "Figured Speech and Irony in T. Flavius Josephus," in *Flavius Josephus and Flavian Rome*, ed. Jonathan Edmondson, Steve Mason, and James Rives (New York: Oxford University Press, 2005), 268.

19. Ibid., 249–51.

20. Ibid., 252f.

Now *War* was written for an audience that assumed that the defeat of the Judeans and their God happened by virtue of Roman superiority and the blessings of Roman deities. However, "nothing could be clearer in Josephus's history than his claim that Jerusalem fell *not* because of any foreign power but because a *civil war* provoked divine punishment."[21] Beside his comments about stasis, summarized above, Mason demonstrates how Josephus employs irony to make this point safely. One example would be Josephus's repeated and ironic emphasis on Titus's clemency, to the point of "gullibility," as a means by which he might safely undermine Flavian power. Further evidence of "striking" irony by an author who was under obligation to praise the Flavians is detected in Josephus's "oily" description of Domitian's campaign in Gaul and Germany (*War* 7.85–86).[22] He makes similarly convincing presentations of Josephus's employment of irony in *Antiquities* and *Life*.

The subtleties of irony are often hard to detect and open to debate.[23] Some have hesitated to agree with all the examples of irony cited by Mason, and questions arise concerning authorial intent.[24] Frederick Ahl indicates this has been a problem encountered when interpreting classical texts of this period. Authors of the first century Rome displayed their artistry partially through figured speech, which was much preferred to direct statement. Not only were figures safer, they were also more effective. Classical rhetoricians assumed an inverse proportion to the force (*deinotes*) of an expression and its obvious intent. The more subtle the presentation, the more emphatic the statement.[25] Josephus's educated readers, Romans and Jews alike, would be sensitive to and looking for figured speech and irony in literary texts. This much is beyond doubt. It is also beyond doubt that Josephus possessed enough knowledge of the Greek language and literature to make figured presentations. To the evidence presented by Mason we might add that identified by Gottfried Mader. Though not about irony per se, Mader shows that Josephus was adept enough at textual manipulation to present what amounts to figured literary presentations as he deploys a "*color Thucydideus*" for apologetic purposes.[26] When we turn to our examina-

---

21. Ibid., 256. Emphasis his.

22. Ibid., 262–67 for Titus; 260–62 for Domitian. Mason makes these same points in *Josephus and the New Testament*, 81–88. There he states, "Josephus' over-the-top praise of Titus's kindheartedness, far from being obsequious flattery, is in fact spiked with irony," 83.

23. Muecke, for example, writes about "covert" irony, where the ironist, in playing the innocent, will attempt to avoid any "tone or manner or any stylistic indication that would immediately reveal his irony" (D. C. Muecke, *The Compass of Irony* [London: Methuen, 1969], 56).

24. See Joseph Sievers, "Reponse to Steve Mason, 'At Play Seriously': Irony and Humour in the *Vita* of Josephus." Online: http://pace.mcmaster.ca/media/pdf/sbl/sievers2001.pdf.

25. Frederick Ahl, "The Art of Safe Criticism in Greece and Rome," *AJP* 105 (1984): 192–95.

26. Gottfried Mader, *Josephus and the Politics of Historiography: Apologetic and Impression Management in the* Bellum Judaicum (Leiden: Brill, 2000), 149. "Josephus by evoking

tion of those passages about the Sicarii, we will, therefore, want to be alert to
the presence of figured speech and irony. But first, we note that the presence of
irony bears directly on our understanding of the thematic elements of *War*, and
it is to those themes that we now turn.

Thematic Elements

Until recent years it was part of the canonical view that Josephus wrote *War* as a
piece of imperial propaganda under the patronage of the Flavians to discourage
further Jewish unrest in the Parthian interior. This position was first proposed by
Richard Laqueur in his landmark study and echoed by H. St. John Thackeray.[27] It
was thought that such a theory would, among other things, explain *War*'s flattery
of the Flavians and its accent on the invincibility of Rome. The Parthian threat
was deduced from scattered references, such as Josephus's observation in *Ant.*
20.71 that king Vardanes in the forties was considering war against Rome, and
from Agrippa's statement in his speech to the Jews at Jerusalem that they should
not expect any help from their kinsmen in Abdiabene for "they will not entangle
themselves in such a war for a cause that is irrational."[28]

Yet cracks began to emerge in this theory. Rajak, for example, maintains that
War does not answer to the needs of such propaganda for the precise reason that
the evidence for a Parthian threat at this time to Rome is lacking. She adduces
evidence from Tacitus (*Ann.* 25.5), who reports that Vologaesus was determined
at this period to maintain peaceful relations with Rome. Moreover, "it is hardly
plausible that the news of Rome's effective suppression of a petty province in
revolt would have much impressed the ruler of a great empire like Parthia."[29]

Working from the major speeches (as noted above), Lindner concluded that
Josephus wished to emphasize how God himself had brought judgment against
the Jews for defiling His temple and that God had placed all things under "incontestable" Roman power. Thus, he also concluded that *War* could not be understood merely as a political-propaganda piece because Josephus so clearly connects
the will of God to the workings of fate and the rise of Rome.[30]

Scholars also began to notice other prominent themes that could not be

---

recognizable frames and models suggests analogies and parallels in a manner which would
engage his Greco-Roman readers in their own cultural terms, and which thus adds subtle
nuance to his narrative. From this perspective the 'Hellenizing glass' serves as a medium for
implied authorial comment, predisposing the reader to a particular interpretation of the historical data" (Mader, 9).

27. Richard Laqueur, *Der Jüdische Historiker Flavius Josephus* (Darmstadt: Wissenschaftliche Buchgesellschaft, 1920; repr., 1970); Thackeray, *Josephus*.

28. *War* 2.388–89, οἱ δ' οὔτε δι' αἰτίαν ἄλογον τηλικούτωι πολέμωι συνεμπλέξουσιν
ἑαυτούς.

29. Rajak, *Josephus*, 181.

30. Lindner, *Die Geschichtsauffassung*, 142–45.

reduced to mere imperial propaganda. Harold Attridge highlighted Josephus's tendency to blame the revolt on the revolutionary leaders, allegedly in the effort to absolve the Judean population as a whole of any responsibility for the war.[31] This view was echoed by Bilde, who added that Josephus also wished in particular to reject the militant nationalism and Messianism "as it was maintained and practiced by the rebellious groups before, during, and after the war."[32] Eckstein, on the basis of his comparison of Josephus with Polybius (see above), acknowledged that the power of God becomes "increasingly prominent" in the latter half of *War* even though he concluded that *War's* overall emphasis, from first to last, was the simple and inescapable fact of Roman power.[33]

In *Flavius Josephus on the Pharisees* Mason agrees with Rajak that *War* does not meet the needs of Flavian propaganda, adding to her statements that the imperial recognition of *War* does not imply a commissioning for this purpose.[34] Mason there emphasizes that the purpose of *War* should be worked out from its prologue. He expands upon this idea in an article about the aims and audience of *Antiquities*. Josephus, he states, did not intend this *magnum opus* as an apology for the statements he had earlier written against his own people in *War*, statements commonly understood as Roman propaganda. In that connection, Mason observes that *War* itself contains unabashedly defensive statements for the Jewish people. Again Mason cites the prologue, for there Josephus makes the following comments about others who are writing accounts of the Judean war:

> And those who were present misrepresent the facts, either out of flattery toward the Romans or hatred toward the Jews, and their writings present sometimes accusation, sometimes encomium, but nowhere the precision of history.... And yet they have the audacity to call these works histories, in which to my mind they appear to come short besides revealing no sound information. For they want to show how great the Romans were and alternatively always knock down and humiliate Jewish activities. (1.2, 7)

> οἱ παραγενόμενοι δὲ ἢ κολακείᾳ τῇ πρὸς Ῥωμαίους ἢ μίσει τῷ πρὸς Ἰουδαίους καταψεύδονται τῶν πραγμάτων περιέχει δὲ αὐτοῖς ὅπου μὲν κατηγορίαν ὅπου δὲ ἐγκώμιον τὰ συγγράμματα τὸ δ᾽ ἀκριβὲς τῆς ἱστορίας οὐδαμοῦ . . . καίτοι γε ἱστορίας αὐτὰς ἐπιγράφειν τολμῶσιν ἐν αἷς πρὸς τῷ μηδὲν ὑγιὲς δηλοῦν καὶ τοῦ σκοποῦ δοκοῦσιν ἔμοιγε διαμαρτάνειν βούλονται μὲν γὰρ μεγάλους τοὺς Ῥωμαίους ἀποδεικνύειν καταβάλλουσιν δὲ ἀεὶ τὰ Ἰουδαίων καὶ ταπεινοῦσιν.

31. Attridge, "Josephus and His Works," 195–96.
32. Bilde, *Flavius Josephus*, 77.
33. Eckstein, "Josephus and Polybius," 203f.
34. Mason, *Flavius Josephus on the Pharisees* (Leiden: Brill, 1991), 59.

Mason sees here an indicator that Josephus wants "to *challenge* the pro-Roman and anti-Jewish histories of the revolt that have already appeared."[35]

> Josephus dedicates his work to showing that, although the Judeans could rise to fight off an evil regime such as that of the Seleucids, they normally cooperate with the various world powers. They do so because they know that their God is in complete control of world history, and gives power even now to the Romans. The revolt was neither a characteristic expression of the Judean character nor a defeat of the Judean God. It arose, sadly, because a handful of would-be tyrants took advantage of the (admitted) egregious misrule of some Roman governors to incite sedition. In spite of its predictable flattery of Titus, then, the *War* is aimed at defending the surviving Jews against widespread post-war animosity, perhaps even reprisals.[36]

Thus, scholarly understanding of *War*'s purpose had changed considerably from thinking that it was a propaganda piece written under the patronage of the Flavians to concluding that it was an apologetic piece written on behalf of Jews to deflect popular resentment subsequent to the Roman victory over the Judean people.

Mason, however, soon used his analysis of *War*'s structure to refine and supplement his work on its themes, and as a result Josephus began to appear less on the defense and more on the offense in *War*. We have already noted above his work on the structure (chiasmus) and how it highlights the murders of Ananus and Jesus, two former high priests, as the central panel of *War*. In elaborating on Josephus's editorial comments at this central panel, Mason observes that Josephus not only offers a "moving eulogy" for these aristocratic leaders, but also states that the taking of the city began with their deaths (4.318–25).[37] In light of the emphasis on the nobility and honorable conduct of these two characters, Mason contends that it is too simplistic to conclude that Josephus is writing *War* either as Roman "lackey" or even, more honorably, to absolve the Jewish nobility for any responsibility in the rebellion.[38]

The central panel, part of a "sophisticated narrative, which has many dimensions, layers, internal tensions, and rhetorical tricks," suggests four overriding themes, all of which confronted the "triumphalist" attitude evident in Rome against the Jews when Josephus was authoring *War*. These are: (1) the Jewish nobility conducted themselves honorably both in relation to their own people and to the Romans; (2) the war was not a matter of the Jewish nation opposing

---

35. Mason, "'Should Any Wish to Enquire Further' (Ant. 1.25): The Aim and Audience of Josephus's *Judean Antiquities/Life*," in *Understanding Josephus: Seven Perspectives*, ed. Steve Mason (Sheffield: Sheffield Academic Press, 1998), 64–103, here 73. Emphasis his.

36. Ibid., 73

37. Mason, *Josephus and the New Testament*, 68.

38. Ibid., 68.

Rome but rather a civil war, also a problem for Romans, as Jews differed "about how to respond to nearly intolerable local provocations"; (3) Jerusalem's destruction was the work of the Jews' "discredited" God and not to be credited to the Romans; and (4) the "widely ridiculed Jews" fought with "brilliant" resourcefulness and courage, often to success, against the Roman legions.[39]

These ideas are furthered in an essay on the qualities of the Essenes as reported by Josephus (mainly *War* 2.119–61), and how it is highly implausible for them to be identified with those who wrote the Dead Sea Scrolls. Of significance here are Mason's observations that "manliness" was a valued character trait among Josephus's Greco-Roman audience, and it is precisely this quality that Josephus highlights among the Jewish rebels. As evidence, Mason adduces a comparison of *War* 3.98–107, where Josephus parades the martial skill of the Romans, with *War* 2.507–55, where these vaunted Romans are defeated by "Judean irregulars." *War*'s narrative here and elsewhere "systematically undermines any notion that the Romans were masters of warfare."[40] Josephus moreover regularly displays the manly characteristics of the Jews via words such as "contempt of death" (θανάτου καταφρονεῖν) and "endurance" (καρτερία), the latter being a "conspicuous" trait of the Spartans. He also dwells at length on his own role as general in the war (*War* 2–3).[41] In view of such highlights on Judean manliness, fighting character, and success in battle against the Romans, Mason concludes that the idea that Josephus wrote to defend the ruling class from taking part in the war "untenable." Josephus rather takes up a much more aggressive defense of Judean character, which "comes at some cost to the current Roman image."[42]

Mason emphasized many of these same points, although by a different path, in an essay on the audience of Josephus. He there points out many traits of *War* that point to a Roman readership. The narrative explains Judean realia and assumes knowledge of Roman history and the proem "conspicuously reaches out to a Roman audience." The consequence is that only by ignoring this intended Roman audience can one maintain the idea that *War* is imperial propaganda.[43]

> Now we can begin to take seriously Josephus' claim that he is writing to balance the record with a fair treatment of his people (1.1–3, 6–9). Now his ongoing emphases on Judean valor, toughness, and contempt for death, along with their talent for outwitting the famous legions, become more meaningful as a challenge to the dominant portrait. Now we may see his flattery of Vespasian and Titus, by contrast, as not more than *de rigueur*, and we may become more atten-

---

39. Ibid., 69f.
40. Mason, "Essenes and Lurking Spartans in Josephus' *Judean War*: From Story to History," in *Making History: Josephus and Historical Method*, ed. Zuleika Rodgers (Leiden: Brill, 2007), 219–61, here 230.
41. Ibid., 233–34.
42. Ibid., 230.
43. Mason, "Of Audience and Meaning," 91f., 95, 99.

tive to cracks in this portrait. These cracks are especially in the famous theme of Titus' clemency, which in fact makes the young emperor out to be rather gullible—deserving no *credit* for Jerusalem's fall.[44]

Thus we see how scholarly thinking about the themes of *War* has progressed; beginning with the understanding that Josephus was little more than a mouthpiece of Flavian propaganda, and then understanding that he was interested in defending his people. Now, particularly in light of Mason's work, Josephus appears not only to fend off negative images of the Jews current in Rome but also to present a positive image of his own people and how they are sometimes even superior to the Romans.

DATE AND UNITY

At several points above we have referred to some Roman attitudes toward the Jews to which *War* responds. This brings us to the date of *War*'s "publication" and its intended audience, and it is to the first of these matters that we now turn. We begin with the observation that "publication" in the ancient world, as Mason points out, involved a process of writing and circulating drafts among close associates, receiving criticism and suggestions, then rewriting and testing one's ideas. Thus, there was no clear line between writing and publication. The nearest equivalent to "publication" happened if an author finally surrendered control over the copying and distribution of his work, such as would happen if he were to deposit it in a public archive.[45] This point needs to be born in mind when we address here not only the date of "publication" but also the common scholarly suggestion that *War* 7 was "published" separately from the first six books. There is evidence that Josephus himself followed this procedure in writing *War*, sending volumes to King Agrippa for him to read and evaluate, for example, before the entire work was completed, which Titus ordered to be made public (*Life* 363–65).

The completion of the Temple of Peace in the sixth year of Vespasian (Dio 66.15), related in *War* 7.158, establishes 75 C.E. as the earliest date for the completion of the seven books. On the basis of Josephus's statements that he presented his "books" to Vespasian (*Life* 361, *Apion* 1.50), the latest date would seem to be before his death in 79 C.E., if indeed we should understand that Josephus was referring to all seven books. Yet it is precisely on this point that questions arise, and for a time the consensus of scholarship had *War* 7 issued at a later date than the prior six books. We need to pay attention to this matter, if for no other reason than this: the Sicarii figure prominently in *War* 7, and our understanding of Josephus's presentation will be altered if we think he is writing not to the time of

---

44. Ibid., 99–100. Emphasis his.

45. Ibid., 80, 82. See also R. M. Ogilvie, *Roman Literature and Society* (New York: Penguin Books, 1980), 11f.

Titus and Vespasian, but of Domitian or even of Trajan. The data adduced in this discussion may be divided into arguments about the style of Greek, a change of emphases in book 7 from the prior six, structural anomalies contained in book 7, historical data points, and statements that Josephus himself made about the process of publication. To these matters we now turn.

No less an authority than Thackeray first suggested that the last book shows a different style than the prior six. Although he did not elaborate in detail, he observed that "here another vocabulary, characteristic of the *Antiquities*, makes its appearance." Thackeray interpreted this as a signal that Josephus no longer had the advantage of his literary assistants and was therefore dependent more on his own capabilities with the Greek. He furthermore observed that the natural stopping point for the work was the destruction of Jerusalem, and that Josephus himself intended to write a "new edition" of *War*. For in *Ant.* 20.267 he writes:

> And if God permits, I will refer again in a running account both to the war and to the events that happened among us to the present day, which is the thirteenth year of the reign of Domitian Caesar.

> κἂν τὸ θεῖον ἐπιτρέπῃ κατὰ περιδρομὴν ὑπομνήσω πάλιν τοῦ τε πολέμου καὶ τῶν συμβεβηκότων ἡμῖν μέχρι τῆς νῦν ἐνεστώσης ἡμέρας ἥτις ἐστὶν τρισκαιδεκάτου μὲν ἔτους τῆς Δομετιανοῦ Καίσαρος ἀρχῆς.

These observations led Thackeray to conclude that book 7 was itself an appendix to the prior 6, with only the latter completed before the death of Vespasian.[46]

Speaking to this argument of style, that the Greek of book 7 is demonstrably different from the prior six, many scholars echo Thackeray's observation.[47] However, there is to my knowledge no extant elaboration of the data in support of this view. The closest exercise that might be brought to bear is the statistical analysis, performed by Morton and Michaelson, of elision to determine whether it is a reliable indicator of authorship. The authors chose elision and not some other element because it could be commonly avoided by a change of word order and therefore was to some degree subject to personal choice.[48] Here we might simplis-

---

46. Thackeray, "*Josephus*," 34–35, 105. Thackeray gives no date as to when this "appendix" may have been added.

47. See, for example, Louis H. Feldman. "But, as that excellent judge of Josephus' style, H. St. J. Thackeray . . . remarks, Book 7 of the *Bellum Judaicum*, of which the Masada episode forms a considerable portion, stands apart from the other books, especially in vocabulary, and it would seem that Josephus was thrown more upon his own resources, though we may conjecture that he simply had a different and more thorough assistant" (Feldman, "Masada: A Critique of Recent Scholarship," in *Christianity, Judaism and Other Greco-Roman Cults: Studies for Morton Smith*, ed. J. Neusner [Leiden: Brill, 1975], 218–48, here 236).

48. Andrew Morton and Sidney Michaelson, "Elision as an Indicator of Authorship," in *Revue—Organisation Internationale pour l'etude des Langues Anciennes par Ordinateur* (1973): 33–56, 33.

tically present as an analogy the difference between "are not" and "aren't." The study includes works of Thucydides, Herodotus, Isocrates, Lysias, Demosthenes, Xenophon, Diodorus Siculus, Josephus, Plutarch, Aristotle, Plato, and Homer. The authors concluded that the elision of ἀλλά and δέ and the modification of the negative particle οὐ seem to be "consistent habits" in Greek authors. "It would appear that as the basis for a test of authorship elision is likely to prove reliable but possibly rather insensitive."[49]

In regard to Josephus the authors tested the elision of δέ in *Life*, and its first one hundred occurrences in each of the following books: *War* 1, 5, 6, and 7; *Ant.* 1, 2, 3, and 4. According to the data, they concluded that *War* 7 shows a pattern that is significantly different from 1, 5, and 6 and that this pattern is similar to the books of *Antiquities*.[50] Thus it would seem that this data might support Thackeray's suggestion that *War* 7 was published independently of *War* 1–6.

We turn now to the different emphases of book 7, and here Shaye Cohen points to how Josephus alternately flatters Titus and Domitian. Titus receives the greatest amount of praise in books 1–6 while Domitian throughout this material is mentioned only three times in passing. At 7.85–88, however, Josephus extols Domitian's prowess. This Cohen interprets as evidence that Josephus completed book 7 when Domitian was emperor.[51] Not only the sons of Vespasian but also the Jewish tyrant John is judged by different standards in book 7. In the first six books Josephus condemns John for breaking the universal laws of "society and cult" whereas in 7.264 he is judged rather on the basis of the traditional Jewish laws of purity. Cohen accounts for this shift in Josephus's changing circumstance and conjectures that book 7 was written later when Josephus himself was currying favor with the emerging rabbinical authority and the discussions at Yavneh. Thus, halakhic considerations are only noticeable in *War* 7, "which, like [*Antiquities*], was completed under Domitian."[52]

Scholars also have detected what are thought to be structural anomalies that point to a later publication of *War* 7. We have seen, for example, that Thackeray suggested that *War* should have naturally ended with the destruction of Jerusalem in book 6. The assumption is that *War* 7 does not properly fit into the structure of the whole as it was originally conceived. Seth Schwartz elaborates on such issues and proposes that there is in fact no unity at all to book 7. Rather, he alleges three separate revisions, the last taking place as late as 96–117. On the basis of how Josephus sets forth the plan of his work in the prologue (1.29) and in particular how there is no reference there to Domitian nor to the disturbances in the diaspora, Schwartz states that book 7, which he calls the "Ur-book,"

---

49. Ibid., 43–44. This notwithstanding the "one real exception" encountered in the works of Aristotle, "which has a unique complication in the manuscript history" (43).

50. Ibid., 40f.

51. Cohen, *Josephus in Galilee and Rome* (Leiden: Brill, 1979), 85. So also Attridge, who notes the "prominence accorded Domitian" in book 7 ("Josephus and His Works," 193).

52. Cohen, *Josephus in Galilee and Rome*, 237–38.

must have originally excluded these episodes.[53] After Domitian's accession, when Titus could no longer be praised alone, Josephus made a revision to this work and added the "Domitianic book" (7:63–99), in which he extols Domitian.[54] The final revision added episodes about the annexation of Commagene, the disturbances at Alexandria, and those at Cyrene. The account of Antiochus, king of Commagene (7.219–43), mars *War* 7 inasmuch as it is "apparently irrelevant" to Jewish history. Schwartz states that this royal family was becoming conspicuous at Rome in the late 90s and early 100s, and this establishes a probable date for the addition of this part to *War* 7 though Schwartz can only speculate as to why Josephus might have wanted to include it.[55] As to the Alexandrian and Cyrenian episodes, Schwartz states that they form a "remarkably unsuitable ending to the book." He identifies the Catullus in the latter episode as Valerius Catullus Messalinus.[56] Since, according to Tacitus, Catullus was still alive in 93 (*Agr.* 45.1) and since it would be unlikely for Josephus to condemn him while two of his "closest friends, Domitian and Nerva," were still alive, this episode was likely added in Trajan's reign (98–117). Here again, Schwartz can only speculate about why Josephus would include such "unsuitable" episodes. He suggests that Josephus included the Alexandrian narrative because it would support a Jewish embassy from Alexandria sent in opposition to a Greek embassy at Rome, cited in *POxy* 1242, the *Acta Mermaisci*, which is dated early in Trajan's reign. Josephus perhaps included the Cyrene episode because he wished to defend the Jews as the situation heated up prior to the Jewish revolt in 115–117.[57]

Turning now to the historical data points that establish the date of *War* 7, recall that the completion of the Temple of Peace establishes 75 as the earliest date. Questions arise, however, in regard to Josephus's several statements about the completion of his work. In *Apion* 1.50–51 he says:

> Then when I had leisure time at Rome and when all my materials were ready, I composed my account of the events, making use of some helpers for the sake of the Greek. And I had so much confidence in its truthfulness that I expected the emperors, Vespasian and Titus, who were supreme commanders in the war, to be the first to testify to this. For I gave my volumes to them first.

> εἶτα σχολῆς ἐν τῇ Ῥώμῃ λαβόμενος πάσης μοι τῆς πραγματείας ἐν παρασκευῇ γεγενημένης χρησάμενός τισι πρὸς τὴν Ἑλληνίδα φωνὴν συνεργοῖς οὕτως ἐποιησάμην τῶν πράξεων τὴν παράδοσιν τοσοῦτον δέ μοι περιῆν θάρσος τῆς

---

53. Seth Schwartz, "The Composition and Publication of Josephus's Bellum Iudaicum Book 7," *HTR* 79 (1986): 377.

54. Ibid., 379.

55. Ibid., 374, 381–82.

56. Ibid., 375. So also, tentatively, E. Mary Smallwood, *The Jews under Roman Rule: From Pompey to Diocletian* (Leiden: Brill, 2001), 370 n. 50.

57. Schwartz, "Composition and Publication," 374–75, 383–84.

ἀληθείας ὥστε πρώτους πάντων τοὺς αὐτοκράτορας τοῦ πολέμου γενομένους Οὐεσπασιανὸν καὶ Τίτον ἠξίωσα λαβεῖν μάρτυρας πρώτοις γὰρ δέδωκα τὰ βιβλία.

Josephus makes similar statements in *Life* 361 and 363, where he responds to Justus and faults him for his inaccurate history. He writes:

> Indeed, I was not fearful in the same way about my writing. Instead I handed my volumes over to the emperors when the facts were still just about visible for I was aware that I had preserved the transmission of the truth, for which I was not disappointed in my expectation that I would find (them) as witnesses. . . . Indeed, the emperor Titus was so anxious that knowledge of the events should be handed down to people from these volumes alone that he affixed his signature to the volumes by his own hand and ordered them to be made public.

> οὐ μὴν ἐγώ σοι τὸν αὐτὸν τρόπον περὶ τῆς ἐμαυτοῦ γραφῆς ἔδεισα ἀλλ᾽ αὐτοῖς ἐπέδωκα τοῖς αὐτοκράτορσι τὰ βιβλία μόνον οὐ τῶν ἔργων ἔτι βλεπομένων συνῄδειν γὰρ ἐμαυτῷ τετηρηκότι τὴν τῆς ἀληθείας παράδοσιν ἐφ᾽ ᾗ μαρτυρίας τεύξεσθαι προσδοκήσας οὐ διήμαρτον. . . . ὁ μὲν γὰρ αὐτοκράτωρ Τίτος ἐκ μόνων αὐτῶν ἐβουλήθη τὴν γνῶσιν τοῖς ἀνθρώποις παραδοῦναι τῶν πράξεων ὥστε χαράξας τῇ ἑαυτοῦ χειρὶ τὰ βιβλία δημοσιῶσαι προσέταξεν.

Depending on how we are to understand these statements about the presentation of "volumes" (βιβλία) to the emperors, we might conclude that Josephus presented all the volumes prior to the death of Vespasian (*Apion* 1.50–51) resulting in a *terminus ante quem* of 79. But since Josephus only mentions Titus in *Life* 363, we might suppose that Vespasian received only *some* of the volumes and Titus alone the completed work.[58] The *terminus* would then be extended to 81. However, if Schwartz's argument concerning the identity of Catullus is sound, we would have to date the completion of book 7 to at least after 93. Moreover, if Thackeray is correct in his understanding that Josephus's statement at *Ant.* 20.267 is a reference to another edition of *War* and specifically to the addition of book 7, then the latter's completion would of necessity fall after 93, the accepted early date for the completion of *Antiquities*.

This evidence, taken all together, appeared convincing to many. However, let us weigh the evidence presented in each area and take up the historical references first. In a newly published article about Josephus's social contacts in Rome, Hannah Cotton and Werner Eck reject Schwartz's identification of Catullus in *War* 7 as L. Valerius Catullus Messalinus.[59] They begin with the observation that Jose-

---

58. See Mason, *Life of Josephus: Flavius Josephus. Translation and Commentary*, ed. Steve Mason (Boston and Leiden: Brill Academic Publishers, 2003), 148–49.

59. The identification had already been rejected by Edmond Groag in *Prosopographia Imperii Romani*, ed. Edmund Groag et al. (Berlin and Leipzig: Walter de Gruyter, 1933), 2:582;

phus himself arrived at Rome in early summer of 71; and to allow time for him to become acquainted with Catullus, the proconsulate of Josephus's Catullus cannot be dated before 72 or 73.[60] This timeline, however, does not work for L. Valerius Catullus, for he was *consul ordinarius* with Domitian in January of 73. This means that he would have had to enter the consulate *in absentia*. "No proconsul of a praetorian province like Crete and Cyrene is known ever to have entered the consulate *in absentia*." Moreover, a praetorian consulate was "far too low to serve as a stepping stone to the ordinary consulate." Additionally, Josephus's report that Catullus died "not long after" (οὐκ εἰς μακράν, 7.451) is not a fitting way to describe Valerius Catullus's death more than twenty years later after 93.[61]

We then turn to Josephus's notice at the end of *Antiquities* (20.267) of his intention to produce "a running account of the war and of our events to the present day." David Barish contends that this particular statement should be placed in parallel to that which immediately precedes it, statements Josephus makes about his own qualifications as an author and the circumstances of his life. Both Barish and Mason have convincingly shown that this statement at 267 is best understood as a reference to *Life* and not to some future addition to *War*.[62] Therefore, this notice does not serve to establish a late date for the completion of *War*.

This leaves Josephus's statements about his presentation of the volumes to the emperors as the only other external data point for the completion of *War*. Mason suggests that the reference in *Life* 362–63 to Titus alone probably means that Vespasian received only some of the volumes (*Apion* 1.50) and Titus the completed work.[63] Indeed, Josephus's references in his last-known writings, both to Titus's authorization of *War* (*Life* 362) and his presentation of the completed work to Vespasian, Titus, and other friends (*Apion* 1.50–52), imply a loss of authorial control over the work, which would make it difficult to imagine a much later supplement.

Turning to the arguments of structure and to the Alexandrian narrative in particular, Mason's work on the chiastic arrangement of *War* shows that Josephus had this ending in mind early in the composition of *War*.[64] Thackeray's observation that the destruction of Jerusalem is the natural stopping place for *War* does not take these structural considerations into account. As we will see

---

and more recently by Christopher Jones, "Towards a Chronology of Josephus," *Scripta Classica Israelica* 21 (2002): 113–31.

60. Hannah M. Cotton and Werner Eck, "Josephus' Roman Audience: Josephus and the Roman Elites," in *Flavius Josephus and Flavian Rome*, ed. Jonathan Edmondson, Steve Mason, and James Rives (New York: Oxford University Press, 2005), 37–52, here 46.

61. Ibid., 47–48.

62. David A. Barish, "The 'Autobiography' of Josephus and the Hypothesis of a Second Edition of His 'Antiquities,'" *HTR* (1978): 68. Mason, *Life of Josephus*, xiv–xv. So also Hans Petersen, "Real and Alleged Literary Projects of Josephus," *AJP* 79 (1958): 260.

63. Ibid., 148–49.

64. Mason, *Josephus and the New Testament*, 66f. See above.

below, the Alexandrian narrative presents the resolution of stasis and thus brings *War* to a neat and satisfying conclusion. Schwartz's conjectures about the reason for its inclusion and its date of composition are thus unnecessary. The Cyrenian narrative, which is the last episode that Josephus relates in *War*, admittedly does not show as tight a fit. Yet this alone does not provide compelling evidence for its addition subsequent to the reign of Domitian.

How are we to assess the data about the changing emphases of book 7? Let us begin with Domitian. Mary Beard connects the story of his campaign and his glorious return home with the overall triumphal structure and events of book 7. Here Josephus praises him also as he gradually brings together all the Flavians in the triumph, which was designed to display the inauguration of a new dynasty.[65] Thus, the narrative about Domitian would seem to be an integral part of the progress of book 7 and not a late addition. Barbara Levick also contends that the narrative harmonizes well with other evidence that shows how Vespasian and Titus would not allow serious advancement for Domitian.[66] For she calls Josephus's account of Domitian's expedition to Gaul a "masterpiece of ambiguity" which could be "safely" read by either brother when Vespasian was still alive. "Precocious or bumptious, it can be read either way."[67] The story thus need not be understood only as later praise for Domitian when he became emperor.

These same points should be borne in mind when assessing the arguments of emphasis as represented above by Cohen. The new note of praise for Domitian naturally fits into the structure of book 7 and is not out of place when Vespasian or even Titus was emperor. Concerning Cohen's contention that John is judged differently in the first six books than he is in book 7—for breaking laws of society and cult as opposed to Jewish laws of purity—we should note that even in the first six books the latter criteria are not entirely unknown, for purity extends throughout matters of society and cult. And so at 5.100 Josephus criticizes John for leading a band of followers, most of whom were "unclean" (οἱ πλείους ἦσαν ἄναγνοι), to invade the temple.

Of greater weight, however, is that Josephus's condemnation appears to be influenced by *War*'s narrative and not by Josephus's changing circumstance as an author. John was confined in the temple with his Zealot followers for a time by Simon (4.577) and later fought Eleazar for control there (5.9–11). Once the

---

65. Mary Beard, "The Triumph of Flavius Josephus," in *Flavian Rome: Culture, Text, Image*, ed. A. J. Boyle and W. J. Dominik (Leiden and Boston: Brill, 2003), 543–58, here 549–50. Beard calls the question about when exactly in the Flavian period *War* (or sections) was published a "predictably dead-end set of disputes" (547). "Tracking Domitianic revisions inserted into a Vespasianic substratum is a common sport (though generally based on the [preposterous] assumptions that explicit praise of Domitian indicates a Domitianic date)" (547 n. 13, brackets hers).

66. Barbara Levick, *Vespasian* (London and New York: Routledge, 1999), 191.

67. Ibid., 189f. Her statement here stands in line with Mason's analysis of this passage as irony. See above.

rebel tyrants unite against the imminent Roman threat, John joins them in their criminal activity against the populace (5.439f.). Therefore, it would be natural for Josephus to condemn John for breaking laws of society and cult in view of John's activity throughout the narrative of the first six books. When we arrive at book 7, John no longer takes his place in the narrative, of course, because the war in Jerusalem has ended. He is mentioned only twice, the first time in passing at 7.118 where we read that Titus had him and Simon conveyed to Rome for the triumph. Only at 7.263–64 does Josephus evaluate John at all, and there John takes his place beside all the other rebels in the Hall of Infamy (see below). There Josephus offers summary comments about John's conduct during the war. He faults him for breaking laws of society *precisely because* of his impious attitude toward God as *evidenced* by his abandonment of the laws of purity.[68] The connection is made clear by Josephus. "It should occasion no surprise if one who insanely committed acts of impiety towards God did not care about gentleness and fellowship toward men" (264). In other words, what we have here about John appears to be a typical summary statement—a connection of wicked *praxis* with corrupt *ethos*. In sum the evaluative comments about John's activity throughout the narrative are easily understood in light of the narrative's structure without any special appeal to the changing circumstances of the author.

That leaves the arguments of style. It would seem hazardous to press Morton's and Michaelson's arguments precisely because elision is subject to authorial control. This might explain why the data from Isocrates did not fit their conclusions as well as other authors.[69] Thackeray's statements are difficult to address and evaluate in the absence of anything but general observations from this admitted expert. Yet even if we were to decide that book 7 shows a different style of Greek than the first six, this does not speak directly to its date and unity. It would indicate only a change as Josephus worked on his manuscript over a period of time in the process of "publication." We might easily conjecture, as Thackeray himself has, that the literary collaborators for *War* 1–6 were no longer available, and we could imagine this happening all within the reign of Vespasian.

In sum, then, there is no compelling evidence to date *War* 7, in part or in whole, considerably later than the prior six books. The structure of *War* clearly includes all seven books. The arguments founded on the changing emphases of the narrative remain unconvincing, as do the arguments of style. We might easily conjecture, perhaps, a lapse of some time and a change of circumstance as would be normal in the process of its "publication," but finally Titus himself inscribed his name to the work and ordered it to be made public (δημοσιῶσαι, *Life* 363), which presupposes a loss of Josephus's control over his work. This latter point,

---

68. "He (John) filled the country with countless evils such as a man who had already committed insolent acts of impiety toward God would intend. For he both set a corrupt table, etc. (τὴν πατρίδα μυρίων ἐνέπλησε κακῶν οἷα πράξειν ἔμελλεν ἄνθρωπος ἤδη καὶ τὸν θεὸν ἀσεβεῖν τετολμηκώς. τράπεζάν τε γὰρ ἄθεσμον παρετίθετο κτλ.)."

69. Morton and Michaelson, "Elision," 41.

indeed, seems rather compelling. Surely we ought to conclude that by this time Josephus had completed *War* with its chiastic arrangement all intact—such as its notice in book 1 that particular issues will be addressed "later," which did not happen until book 7—than that he deposited six books only and left this carefully worked outline unresolved. In view of his complete lack of similar reference to any endorsement by Domitian (much less Trajan), it would therefore appear safest to conclude that prior to the end of Titus's reign, *War* in its entirety had been completed and made public as indeed the emperor had directed. Thus, *War* was completed between 75 and 81.

AUDIENCE

Some scholarly opinions about the type of audience Josephus envisioned for *War* have already surfaced when we examined its themes, for the two are inextricably linked. We could, for example, make little sense of Josephus's boasting in *War* about the nobility of Jewish fighting if Josephus wrote it as a piece of imperial propaganda aimed at discouraging a Jewish uprising in Parthia. We now turn our attention to complete our understanding of Josephus's intended audience. We might profitably begin by referring again to Mason's insistence that *War* envisions a Roman audience. Roman persons and events are highlighted in the proem whereas Jewish characters and events are omitted and await full explication in the narrative. Within the narrative itself, Jewish customs are explained whereas Roman events are merely referenced, sometimes with a statement such as "I may be excused from going into these matters because they are commonly known" (4.496). Mason summarizes:

> It seems rather carefully crafted to hook the audience in—a Roman audience—while reserving detailed reinterpretation of the war for the appropriate time. Josephus has already signaled that he will counter the prevailing jingoistic accounts with a balanced viewpoint (1.2–3, 6–10), but the force and consequence of his revisionist view must await careful articulation in the story itself.[70]

Mason supports these observations with others about the process of authoring in ancient Rome and concludes that Josephus wrote primarily for a non-Jewish and elite audience at Rome.

What attitudes, then, did the Romans hold about the Jews in general and the Judean revolt in particular that Josephus wished to address? If we were to back away from Rome for a moment to get a more general perspective, we might begin by noting that the Jews had been granted particular privileges by Julius Caesar, including the right to gather on the Sabbath and other holy days, to build synagogues, and to follow other Jewish regulations.[71] Josephus himself provides evidence that such

---

70. Mason, "Of Audience and Meaning," 96.
71. See Smallwood, *Jews under Roman Rule*, 128f.

rights were not curtailed after the war despite the urging of citizens at Antioch and Alexandria (*War* 7.100–111, *Ant.* 12.121–24). So there is no evidence that the civil rights of Jewish citizens changed subsequent to the Judean revolt.

Still, Jews in the empire were subject to suspicion, ridicule, and local acts of violence, although to what extent is a matter of scholarly debate. Peter Schäfer has recently made a fresh interpretation of what Greeks and Romans said about Jews and the degree to which what might be called "anti-Semitism" (Judeophobia) was in evidence in the empire. Among other things, he concludes that Roman attitudes toward the Jews were rather complicated, characterized by attraction as well as by hatred and alarm. Schäfer points out that even Tacitus, though writing somewhat later than Josephus, excoriates the Jews in unprecedented fashion and yet "appreciates on a philosophical level the Jewish belief in one God (*unum numen*) who is *summum et aeternum*."[72] The attraction is evident also when one considers the extent of Jewish proselytism. Schäfer traces its extent in how ancient authors became aware of and began to react against it. Tacitus refers to an expulsion of Jews from Rome in 19 C.E. (*Ann.* 2.85.4). Cassius Dio remarks on Domitian's banishment of Flavia Domitilla and the execution of Flavius Clemens for drifting into Jewish ways (67.14). Juvenal expresses alarm at Jewish proselytism because Jewish law is so foreign to Roman laws (*Satire* 15.9–11).[73]

Erich Gruen interprets the evidence slightly differently. The Romans, he maintains, showed little understanding of the Jews. Though the Jewish faith attracted harsh Roman labels such as "superstition" (*superstitio*), such comments were "snide and contemptuous, an expression of Roman disdain for practices that seemed meaningless or unintelligible." But there is no real evidence for Roman anxiety about the Jews. On the contrary, the Romans repeatedly defended Jewish practices.[74] The revolt did little to add or detract from the "sneers and caricatures" directed at the Jews. However, what it undoubtedly added was "disbelief and indignation." Gruen conjectures, "They must have felt outrage at the idea that this puny and insignificant *ethnos*, given to bizarre and contemptible practices, with a host of foolish and fatuous beliefs, would venture to challenge the power of Rome."[75]

---

72. Peter Schäfer, *Judeophobia: Attitudes toward the Jews in the Ancient World* (Cambridge, MA: Harvard University Press, 1997), 189, 193.

73. Ibid., 109f., 185. But now see Martin Goodman, "The *Fiscus Iudaicus* and Gentile Attitudes to Judaism in Flavian Rome," in *Flavius Josephus and Flavian Rome*, ed. Jonathan Edmondson, Steve Mason, and James Rives (New York: Oxford University Press, 2005), 165–77. Here Goodman suggests that this scholarly idea, that non-Jews in Flavian Rome were attracted to Judaism, is "not well founded" as to evidence and "deeply implausible" during the Flavian regime.

74. Erich S. Gruen, "Roman Perspectives on the Jews in the Age of the Great Revolt," in *The First Jewish Revolt: Archaeology, History, and Ideology*, ed. Andrea M. Berlin and J. Andrew Overman (London and New York: Routledge, 2002), 27–42, here 30f., 38.

75. Ibid., 38.

Returning our focus to attitudes at Rome specifically, Overman stresses how the Flavians used the revolt for their own political ends. In Flavian propaganda, the subjugation of Judea thus became an important component of a larger restoration of peace in the empire. This resulted in an "over-emphasis" and elevation of a "regional or parochial" conflict by means of the Judea Capta coins, the Jewish tax that funded the many Flavian building projects, and the hyperbole on the lost arch of Titus describing his victory.[76] The Arch of Titus on the Sacra Via, which portrayed the Jewish Temple relics carried in triumphal display, the Temple of Peace, which housed these same relics for public viewing, and the Flavian amphitheater, built by the spoils of war in Judea: all these advertised and enshrined the defeat of the Jewish people in public memory.[77] These combined with the *fiscus Iudaicus*, the triumphal display, and Vespasian's closing of the Temple of Janus invested the defeat of the Jews with a symbolic importance not seen since the defeat of Cleopatra.[78] Mason makes similar conclusions. Anti-Jewish sentiment, as expressed in the literature anyway, routinely accused the Jews of atheism and misanthropy. Such ill-will came to a head after the revolt. The Romans would interpret the Jewish defeat as a victory for the Roman gods and as an outgrowth of the reprehensible Jewish character.[79] Such was the environment at Rome when Josephus authored *War*.

Before we conclude this section we should bear in mind that although Josephus wrote primarily to a non-Jewish Roman audience, this should not be understood to mean that Josephus was unconcerned about Jewish readers as well, a point made by Mason at the beginning of his essay.[80] We might begin by turning to those references were Josephus indicates such an interest, starting with his reference to a prior edition of *War* in his own language.

> I planned to relate for those under Roman rule, by recasting into Greek, the things which I previously put together in my own language and sent to the Barbarians in the interior. . . . I thought it wrong that I allow the truth of such momentous events to be distorted and that the Parthians, Babylonians, distant

---

76. J. Andrew Overman, "The First Revolt and Flavian Politics," in *The First Jewish Revolt: Archaeology, History, and Ideology*, ed. Andrea M. Berlin and J. Andrew Overman (London and New York: Routledge, 2002), 211–20, here 214–18. As evidence of the "parochial" nature of the revolt, Overman observes that neither Vespasian nor Titus assumed the title "Judaicus" (215).

77. For a recent presentation on the "remarkable imprint" left by the Flavians upon the monuments of ancient Rome, see Fergus Millar, "Last Year in Jerusalem: Monuments of the Jewish War in Rome," in *Flavius Josephus and Flavian Rome*, ed. Jonathan Edmondson, Steve Mason, James Rives (New York: Oxford University Press, 2005), 101–28.

78. So T. D. Barnes, "The Sack of the Temple in Josephus and Tacitus," in *Flavius Josephus and Flavian Rome*, ed. Jonathan Edmondson, Steve Mason, James Rives (New York: Oxford University Press, 2005), 129–44.

79. Mason, "Essenes and Lurking Spartans," 225.

80. Mason, "Of Audience and Meaning," 73.

Arabians, my own people beyond the Euphrates, and the people of Adiabene to have accurate knowledge, due to my care, of how the war began and passed through so many calamities and ended, but that the Greeks and those Romans who were not involved in the campaign not know because they are surrounded by flattery and fictions. (*War* 1.3, 6)

προυθέμην ἐγὼ τοῖς κατὰ τὴν Ῥωμαίων ἡγεμονίαν Ἑλλάδι γλώσσῃ μεταβαλὼν ἃ τοῖς ἄνω βαρβάροις τῇ πατρίῳ συντάξας ἀνέπεμψα πρότερον ἀφηγήσασθαι. ... ἄτοπον ἡγησάμενος περιιδεῖν πλαζομένην ἐπὶ τηλικούτοις πράγμασι τὴν ἀλήθειαν καὶ Πάρθους μὲν καὶ Βαβυλωνίους Ἀράβων τε τοὺς πορρωτάτω καὶ τὸ ὑπὲρ Εὐφράτην ὁμόφυλον ἡμῖν Ἀδιαβηνούς τε γνῶναι διὰ τῆς ἐμῆς ἐπιμελείας ἀκριβῶς ὅθεν τε ἤρξατο καὶ δι᾽ ὅσων ἐχώρησεν παθῶν ὁ πόλεμος καὶ ὅπως κατέστρεψεν ἀγνοεῖν δὲ Ἕλληνας ταῦτα καὶ Ῥωμαίων τοὺς μὴ ἐπιστρατευσαμένους ἐντυγχάνοντας ἢ κολακείαις ἢ πλάσμασι.

Whatever we are to conclude about what this prior work may or may not have been, his interest in writing for fellow Jews is shown if for no other reason than that he wrote about the events of the Judean war for them first. He goes so far as to state that Jews of the eastern diaspora knew the truth about these events because of his careful attention. Even when he "recast" this work into Greek, he states he did so for "those under Roman rule" and not just for those in Rome. True, he does say that he is now writing for "Greeks and Romans," but this should not lead us to believe that Josephus was still not interested in a Hellenized Jewish readership also learning the facts of the war.

Evidence of such interest should not be missed in his statements about the integrity of *War*. In *Apion* 1.50–51 he says the following:

I expected to have the emperors, Vespasian and Titus, who were in the war, as witnesses (to *War*'s accuracy) for I gave my volumes to them first. And after them I sold the volumes to many Romans who had fought in the war and to many of my own countrymen who have education in Greek wisdom, among whom are Julius Archelaus, Herod, who was himself most dignified, and the most admirable king Agrippa.

πρώτους πάντων τοὺς αὐτοκράτορας τοῦ πολέμου γενομένους Οὐεσπασιανὸν καὶ Τίτον ἠξίωσα λαβεῖν μάρτυρας. πρώτοις γὰρ δέδωκα τὰ βιβλία καὶ μετ᾽ ἐκείνους πολλοῖς μὲν Ῥωμαίων τοῖς συμπεπολεμηκόσι, πολλοῖς δὲ τῶν ἡμετέρων ἐπίπρασκον, ἀνδράσι καὶ τῆς Ἑλληνικῆς σοφίας μετεσχηκόσιν, ὧν ἐστιν Ἰούλιος Ἀρχέλαος, Ἡρώδης ὁ σεμνότατος, αὐτὸς ὁ θαυμασιώτατος βασιλεὺς Ἀγρίππας.

Here Josephus states that he sold copies of *War* to "many of his own people who have education (μετεσχηκόσιν) in Greek wisdom." Who might these people be? He names several: Julius Archelaus, a brother-in-law to Agrippa II, King Agrippa himself, and Herod, an unknown person but undoubtedly also a noble (σεμνότατος). The others are unspecified, but we need not assume that they were all nobles even though they all had a certain amount of education in Greek wisdom, at least to the point where they would appreciate the effort that Josephus put into his language and style of presentation.[81] Josephus makes similar statements in *Life* 362, and for similar reasons.

> Right away I distributed my history to many others, some of whom were present in the war, such as King Agrippa and certain of his relatives.

> καὶ ἄλλοις δὲ πολλοῖς εὐθὺς ἐπέδωκα τὴν ἱστορίαν, ὧν ἔνιοι καὶ παρατετεύχεισαν τῷ πολέμῳ, καθάπερ βασιλεὺς Ἀγρίππας καί τινες αὐτοῦ τῶν συγγενῶν.

This statement does not provide much more information than *Apion* 1.51. As in the former passage, Josephus is here concerned to demonstrate the accuracy of *War*. After trotting out the endorsement of Vespasian and Titus (361), he again states that he distributed *War* to many. Once again Agrippa receives special mention along with some of his relatives, but Josephus does not otherwise specify who these others are.

Now Josephus made both these statements in defense of *War*'s integrity, but what we should not miss here is that not only was Josephus interested in a Jewish readership, but also that these same Jews were interested enough to purchase copies. This brings us to how *War* might have been distributed in Rome and other parts of the empire. William Harris states:

> An author at Rome who sought public attention normally put on a public reading, a *recitatio*. . . . There was no such thing as "popular literature" in the Roman Empire, if that means literature which became known to tens or hundreds of thousands of people by means of personal reading. Even the best known texts, those of Homer and Vergil (both of whom were very widely known), became familiar to schoolchildren through dictation and recitation, not through school editions. As for works written expressly for the masses, there were none.[82]

So it would be natural for Josephus, if he were interested in having Jews become aware of his work at Rome or even around the empire, to do so through personal contact. And we have seen above that this is precisely what he did.

We might assume that these Jewish contacts were all inhabitants of Rome, but there is no compelling reason to believe they could not be acquaintances from other parts of the empire. Rajak states that a necessary inference of the Cyrene episode in *War*, in which Josephus was himself to some degree involved to the point where he could be implicated for supplying arms to rebels (*Life* 424–25), is that Josephus is "visible and active in Jewish politics on an empire-wide scale at this period." If Josephus was not himself there at some stage, at least he was well known to the Jews of

---

81. Ibid., 75–76.
82. William V. Harris, *Ancient Literacy* (Cambridge, MA, and London: Harvard University Press, 1989), 225, 227.

that region.[83] However, even if we were to restrict the distribution of *War* to Rome, for which alone we have evidence, we might still ask who these associates were—these Roman Jews of some means and education who were interested enough in Josephus's account of the Judean war to buy a copy. Certainly there were enough Jewish people around. Gruen estimates that the Jewish population of Rome at this time was somewhere between 20,000 and 60,000.[84] Tomb inscriptions show that many were poor, but some were prosperous and educated.[85] These same inscriptions over a three century period attest to the literacy of the Jews at Rome. The data show that Greek was by far the preferred language (76 percent) with Latin a distant second (23 percent) and Hebrew or Aramaic hardly making an appearance (1 percent).[86] Of the inscriptions in Greek, some contain "glaring errors" in spelling and grammar; others were correct in language, and some written in an elegant style. Assessing the evidence, Leon concludes that "neither in the pronunciation of the Greek or Latin nor in their grammatical usage did the Jews of Rome differ in any demonstrable way from the other less educated Greek-speaking and Latin-speaking groups of the Mediterranean world of the second and third centuries."[87] In light of this data, we would reasonably conclude that the Jews of Rome interested in Josephus's work were a minority who were more literate and better educated than the majority of Jews.

Studies about the Jewish organization not only at Rome but also in the diaspora might help us say more. The center of Jewish life throughout the empire was the "ubiquitous" synagogue, which served as the center of Jewish community life where Jews engaged in instruction, worship, communal dining and festivities, record keeping, the storage of funds, the enacting of measures, and all other things designed to "entrench a sense of collective identity."[88] At this point, we might well bypass the scholarly debate about whether Jewish organization at Rome was unified or divided.[89] Of significance here is not only that Jewish communal life at Rome was to some degree regulated through the synagogue, but that

---

83. Rajak, "Josephus in the Diaspora," in *Flavius Josephus and Flavian Rome*, ed. Jonathan Edmondson, Steve Mason, and James Rives (New York: Oxford University Press, 2005), 88.

84. Gruen, *Diaspora: Jews amidst Greeks and Romans* (Cambridge, MA, and London: Harvard University Press, 2002), 16.

85. Harry J. Leon, *The Jews of Ancient Rome* (Peabody: Hendrickson, 1960; repr., 1995), 253f.

86. Ibid., 76.

87. Ibid., 92.

88. Gruen, *Diaspora*, 131.

89. See Leon for a historical sketch of the debate as to whether the Jews at Rome were organized in separate *collegia* or in a centralized *gerusia* (167f.). Leon concludes that the burden of proof lies with those who propose a centralized organization. For just such an argument, see Margaret Williams, "The Structure of the Jewish Community in Rome," in *Jews in a Graeco-Roman World*, ed. Martin Goodman (Oxford: Clarendon, 1998), 215–28.

Rome itself contained more synagogues than anywhere else besides Jerusalem.[90] Josephus had a large, organized, and interested audience right out his front door at Rome. Our understanding of the Jewish leadership at the various synagogues at Rome also has some importance for this discussion, for it would be difficult to imagine that many of the synagogue offices known to exist at Rome, such as *archisynagogus*, members of the *gerusia*, or *archon* could be occupied successfully by those who did not have a certain amount of philosophical education beyond basic literacy.[91] We might therefore understand that when Josephus reports that he distributed and sold copies of *War* to his Jewish associates, he is referring to Jewish leaders among the various synagogues.

What would he wish to say to these Roman Jews? Certainly, as Josephus himself states, he was concerned that the Jews knew the facts of the war in Judea. We might also emphasize here the apologetic themes that Mason detects in war as possibly motivating his interest in having his countrymen read his account of war. Rajak, however, would also press on to those internal purposes that stand "over and above apologetic." "These are concerned with clarifying, or even redefining, for himself and his circle, and for Jewish readers and sympathizers around the Roman world and across its boundaries, where they 'came from' and where they stood and could hope to stand." Josephus was interested in fostering, through his writings, "not only respect for Jews, but also their own self-respect and steadfastness in an atmosphere which could be difficult and uncertain, at both centre and periphery."[92] In other words, above and beyond the main apologetic themes of *War* aimed primarily at a non-Jewish Roman audience, we will want also to be aware of how Josephus might, in a secondary fashion, aim to bolster the "self-respect and steadfastness" of his own people. With these issues in mind, we may now turn to an analysis of how he presents the Sicarii.

---

90. Eleven different names of synagogues are known from inscriptions, and David Noy suggests that there may well have been others that were not recorded. See David Noy, *Foreigners at Rome: Citizens and Strangers* (London: Duckworth, 2000), 265.

91. See Leon, *Jews of Ancient Rome,* 171f. For a recent presentation of the archisynagogue as the representative of the Jewish communities to non-Jews, see Lee Levine, "Synagogue Leadership: The Case for the Archisynagogue," in *Jews in a Graeco-Roman World,* ed. Martin Goodman (Oxford: Clarendon, 1998), 195–213.

92. Rajak, "Josephus in the Diaspora," 96–97.

CHAPTER THREE

THE SICARII IN *WAR* 1–6

Josephus refers to the Sicarii fifteen times in eight separate contexts of *War*. These are:

- The Sicarii rise during the time of Felix (2.254)
- They join the rebels (2.425)
- They raid Engaddi (4.400)
- Mentioned in a passage about the Idumeans (4.516)
- The summary condemnation of Jewish rebels (7.253, 254, 262)
- Masada narrative (7.275, 297, 311)
- Activity in Egypt (7.410, 412, 415)
- In the cities around Cyrene/Catullus narrative (7.437, 444)

Moreover, in a number of passages the Sicarii are not mentioned, and yet their activity and/or presence is directly implied or may be legitimately inferred from the greater context of *War*. These passages are:

- Rise and activity of Judas in 6 C.E. (2.117–18)
- Capture of Masada (2.408)
- Rise and fall of Menahem (2.433–48)
- Joint activity with Simon ben Gioras—Part 1 (2.652–54)
- Joint activity with Simon ben Gioras—Part 2 (4.503–8)

Inasmuch as Josephus does not mention the Sicarii in any of these passages, the analysis of each one will begin with data to support its inclusion in Josephus's presentation of the Sicarii. It will be shown that the first passage (2.117–18), which is commonly referenced for the origins of the Sicarii, should be excluded from the analysis. This leaves twelve sections that one must examine closely for any study on how Josephus presents the Sicarii in *War*.

A complete analysis will address the following questions. (1) For those passages where Josephus does not name the Sicarii, what data may be brought to bear in showing that these passages should nevertheless be included in the study? (2) What is the context of the passage? That is, what immediately precedes the narrative, what immediately follows, and how does the narrative thus fit into the context? Moreover, as a profitable exercise in clarifying the narrative's connection with its immediate context, how might the context be outlined? (3) How does Josephus describe the Sicarii and their activity? (4) What important terms does Josephus use to describe their activity? (5) What is the book context? That is, are there any indicators of how the narrative serves the overall structure/outline of *War*? What intra-textual elements may be brought to bear? (6) What conclusions may be drawn from the passage in question? Thus, the analysis of each passage will follow this outline:

    I.   Evidence for including in the study (where applicable)
   II.   Immediate context
       a.   What immediately precedes the narrative?
       b.   What immediately follows the narrative?
       c.   How does the narrative fit into the context?
       d.   How might the immediate context be outlined?
  III.   Description of Sicarii activity
  IV.   Word studies
   V.   Book context
  VI.   Conclusions

    Chapter 3 will take up the passages of *War* 2 and 4, and chapter 4 will address the passages in *War* 7. Although from a compositional perspective these passages should not be rigidly separated, there are sound practical reasons for doing so. On the one hand, the Sicarii become much more prominent in book 7, which therefore merits a devoted treatment. On the other hand, this division yields two roughly equal amounts of material for analysis. The risk of such a division is that it might seem to imply an endorsement that *War* 7 was written at a significantly later date than the prior six books. We have seen, however, that the evidence for such a view is lacking, and I therefore wish to emphasize here that the arrangement of material in chapters 3 and 4 of this book should not be understood in any way as an endorsement of this view.

THE ACTIVITY OF JUDAS IN 6 C.E. (2.117–18)

EVIDENCE FOR INCLUDING IN THE STUDY

As we have seen in chapter 1 above, in this passage Josephus tells us that the territory that had fallen to Archelaus after the death of his father, Herod the Great, was reduced to a Roman province and that Augustus sent Coponius as procurator. At that time (6 C.E.), a certain Galilean named Judas arose and "was urging his countrymen to revolt, reproaching them if they would put up with the Roman tax and would tolerate mortal masters next to God." Josephus adds that Judas was a "teacher, not at all like the others, of his own sect" and then he proceeds

to describe the three legitimate sects—Pharisees, Sadducees, and Essenes.[1] Some
scholars would place the origins of the Sicarii during the time of Judas and under
his leadership on the basis of a family connection made by Josephus at 7.253f.
between Eleazar b. Yair at Masada and Judas. However, since Josephus makes
no mention of the Sicarii here and rather states that they arose at a later time, we
must examine the evidence in support of this conclusion and decide if this passage should be included in this study.

At *War* 7.253 Josephus has turned his attention to Masada, and there he says
the following:

> Now Eleazar, a powerful man and descendant of Judas, who persuaded many
> Jews (as I have stated earlier) not to participate in the census when Quirinius
> was sent to Judea as censor, was in command of those who had captured it. For
> at that time the Sicarii banded together against those who wanted to submit to
> the Romans and treated them in every way as enemies, plundering their posses-
> sions, driving away their livestock, and throwing fire into their homes, etc.

> προειστήκει δὲ τῶν κατειληφότων αὐτὸ σικαρίων δυνατὸς ἀνὴρ Ἐλεάζαρος,
> ἀπόγονος Ἰούδα τοῦ πείσαντος Ἰουδαίους οὐκ ὀλίγους, ὡς πρότερον
> δεδηλώκαμεν, μὴ ποιεῖσθαι τὰς ἀπογραφάς, ὅτε Κυρίνιος τιμητὴς εἰς τὴν
> Ἰουδαίαν ἐπέμφθη. τότε γὰρ οἱ σικάριοι συνέστησαν ἐπὶ τοὺς ὑπακούειν
> Ῥωμαίων θέλοντας καὶ πάντα τρόπον ὡς πολεμίοις προσεφέροντο, τὰς μὲν
> κτήσεις ἁρπάζοντες καὶ περιελαύνοντες, ταῖς δ᾽ οἰκήκεσιν αὐτῶν πῦρ ἐνιέντες·
> κτλ.

If we are to connect the Sicarii to Judas on the basis of this passage, two severe
difficulties arise. The first is that according to Josephus's own statement at 2.254,
the Sicarii arose as "a different form of bandit" (ἕτερον εἶδος λῃστῶν) during the
governorship of Felix. The natural reading is that the Sicarii were not active or
known as such in previous times, which would disallow the origin of the Sicarii
with Judas. The second difficulty is that *War* 7.253, as we will see below, comprises
the opening paragraph of what may be called the Hall of Infamy, the parade of
Jewish rebels and their criminal activities during the course of the war. Thus, the
criminal activities of the Sicarii described at 7.253, coordinated as they are with
the criminal activities of all the other rebel leaders during the course of the war,
should be understood also as ones they committed during the war and not as
those committed at the time of Judas. Indeed, Josephus tells us of no such crimi-

---

1. "At this time a certain Galilean man, Judas by name, urged his countrymen to revolt,
reproaching them if they would put up with paying taxes to Romans and would endure mortal masters next to God. Now this person was a teacher of his own sect, which was not at
all like the others" (ἐπὶ τούτου τις ἀνὴρ Γαλιλαῖος, Ἰούδας ὄνομα, εἰς ἀπόστασιν ἐνῆγε τοὺς
ἐπιχωρίους κακίζων εἰ φόρον τε Ῥωμαίοις τελεῖν ὑπομενοῦσιν καὶ μετὰ τὸν θεὸν οἴσουσι
θνητοὺς δεσπότας. ἦν δ᾽ οὗτος σοφιστὴς ἰδίας αἱρέσεως οὐδὲν τοῖς ἄλλοις προσεοικώς, *War*
2.118).

nal activity at all—robbery, plunder, and arson—during the time of Judas in 6 C.E., whereas we do read of the Sicarii committing precisely these crimes once they arise during the governorship of Felix.

These problems arise only when we connect the statements introduced by "for at that time" (τότε γὰρ) to the time when Quirinius was sent as censor to Judea. The text would thus read, "For at that time (when Quirinius was sent as censor to Judea) the Sicarii banded together, etc." But the statements introduced by τότε might as well connect to and elaborate on the activity of the Sicarii who followed Eleazar, in which case the comment about Judas would become parenthetical. "Eleazar, a powerful man and descendant of Judas (who, as I have previously indicated, persuaded many Jews not to participate in the census when Quirinius was sent as censor to Judea), was in command of the Sicarii who had captured it. For at that time the Sicarii banded together against those who desired to submit to the Romans, etc."

Indirect evidence might be brought to bear by a comparison of 2:118f. with the parallel material in *Ant.* 18.3–24. There Josephus links Judas with a Pharisee named Saddok, both of whom established a new "fourth" philosophy, and once again he places Judas's following alongside the three established Jewish philosophies. But his description is decidedly pejorative. Judas's philosophy was "alien" (ἐπείσακτον) to those of the traditional three, and it served as an example of how innovation to ancient tradition brought great harm (18.9). However, in neither *War* 2 nor in *Ant.* 18 does Josephus call Judas's followers "Sicarii," even though their attitudes and activities are in certain instances similar to those that are clearly associated with the Sicarii in *War*. These are their unconquerable passion for liberty, their idea that God alone is master, and their indifference to suffering and death.[2]

It would seem natural, if the Sicarii had been so identified at this early stage, for Josephus to label them as such. The absence of the label in *War*, however, is by no means conclusive evidence for the absence of a group's existence. Indeed, Josephus does not mention the Sicarii by name in *Ant.* 20:162, where they are undoubtedly in mind in view of the parallel material in *War* 2:254–57. Thus, considerations (negligence, irrelevance, thematic alteration, etc.) other than the group's existence might conceivably come into play in accounting for why Josephus employs such labels.

Of greater significance is that in neither section does Josephus attribute to Judas's following what he later describes as the distinctive trait of the Sicarii—their use of daggers in carrying out politically motivated assassination and murder (cf. 2.255 below). Indeed, there is no certain indication from either section that Judas's following embarked on violence of any sort at all, much less against their own countrymen.

If Josephus's purpose at 7.253 is not to say that the Sicarii originated during the time of Judas, then we might ask why he mentions Judas at all at this point.

---

2. For these qualities of the Sicarii, see *War* 7.323, 410, 411, 417–18.

That is, what is the connection between Judas and the Sicarii? Martin Hengel suggested that Josephus's connection between the Sicarii at Masada and Judas "was based on an ideal and at the same time on a dynastic and therefore also an organizational datum, namely that the leaders of the Sicarii, Menahem and Eleazar b. Ari, were descendants of Judas of Galilee."[3] That is, the point in mentioning Judas is to tell the readers that Eleazar, the leader of the Sicarii at Masada, had a rebel ancestry. Indeed, we will see below that Josephus makes this same connection also with Menahem, the first named leader of the Sicarii.

On balance, therefore, the evidence suggests that Josephus did not intend *War* 2.117–18 as an account of the origins of the Sicarii. This connection rests on a translation of 7.253 that is doubtful and in serious tension with both 2.117–18, which speaks only of Judas and tells of no Sicarii presence, violence, or activity at all, and 2.254, which presents the origins of the Sicarii at a much later date and at which point Josephus describes the distinctive form of violence that resulted in their name. Josephus's comments at 7.253 about the Sicarii's violence should not be understood as referring to the time of Judas, for their activities are coordinated there in the Hall of Infamy with those of all the other criminals during the course of the war. That the Sicarii did not exist as such during the time of Judas would also explain why Josephus makes no mention of them when describing Judas's following here or in *Ant.* 18. Therefore, this passage and its context should be omitted in assessing Josephus's presentation of the Sicarii in *War*. The passage, however, forms part of the context for Josephus's later introduction of the Sicarii in *War* 2.433–48 (below) and 7.253 (next chapter) and will thus be relevant at those places.

THE SICARII RISE DURING THE TIME OF FELIX (2.254–57)

Shortly after Josephus tells how Judea was made a Roman province, he turns his attention to several incidents of civil unrest among the Jews and how the Roman procurators, instead of restoring order, largely exacerbated the situation through some notable and provocative actions. All the while in the background of the narrative, banditry in Judea grows and spreads. In particular, Josephus tells of a new type of bandit, characterized by stealthy and high profile assassinations—the Sicarii. He writes:

> [254] Now when the country was cleared, a different type of bandit sprang up in Jerusalem, the so-called Sicarii, murdering people in the middle of the city in broad daylight. [255] Especially during the festivals they would mix with the crowd, hiding small daggers in their garments, and stab their opponents. Then when they fell dead, their murderers became part of those who cried out in indignation. Thus, by means of this air of plausibility they remained completely undiscovered. [256] And so Jonathan the high priest was the first to be slain by

---

3. Hengel, *The Zealots*, trans. David Smith, 2nd ed. (Edinburgh: T & T Clark: 1989), 49.

them, but after him many were done away with each day. The fear was worse than the misfortunes because hour by hour each person expected to die, just as in battle. [257] People were looking out for their enemies at a distance and had no trust in friends who approached. But in the midst of their suspicions and cautions they were killed; so great was the speed of the conspirators and their skill at remaining undetected.

[254] καθαρθείσης δὲ τῆς χώρας ἕτερον εἶδος λῃστῶν ἐν Ἱεροσολύμοις ἐπεφύετο, οἱ καλούμενοι σικάριοι, μεθ᾽ ἡμέραν καὶ ἐν μέσῃ τῇ πόλει φονεύοντες ἀνθρώπους. [255] μάλιστα [δὲ] ἐν ταῖς ἑορταῖς μισγόμενοι τῷ πλήθει καὶ ταῖς ἐσθῆσιν ὑποκρύπτοντες μικρὰ ξιφίδια, τούτοις ἔνυττον τοὺς διαφόρους, ἔπειτα πεσόντων μέρος ἐγίνοντο τῶν ἐπαγανακτούντων οἱ πεφονευκότες, διὸ καὶ παντάπασιν ὑπὸ ἀξιοπιστίας ἦσαν ἀνεύρετοι. [256] πρῶτος μὲν οὖν ὑπ᾽ αὐτῶν Ἰωνάθης ὁ ἀρχιερεὺς ἀποσφάττεται, μετὰ δ᾽ αὐτὸν καθ᾽ ἡμέραν ἀνῃροῦντο πολλοί· καὶ τῶν συμφορῶν ὁ φόβος ἦν χαλεπώτερος, ἑκάστου καθάπερ ἐν πολέμῳ καθ᾽ ὥραν τὸν θάνατον προσδεχομένου. [257] προεσκοποῦντο δὲ πόρρωθεν τοὺς διαφόρους, καὶ οὐδὲ τοῖς φίλοις προσιοῦσιν πίστις ἦν, ἐν μέσαις δὲ ταῖς ὑπονοίαις καὶ ταῖς φυλακαῖς ἀνῃροῦντο· τοσοῦτον τῶν ἐπιβουλευόντων τὸ τάχος ἦν καὶ τοῦ λαθεῖν ἡ τέχνη.

IMMEDIATE CONTEXT

Immediately preceding the narrative, Josephus describes how the maladministration of Cumanus, procurator in Judea (48–52 C.E.), led to his removal. During his tenure one of the soldiers in Jerusalem at Passover committed a lewd act, which enraged the assembled Jews and ultimately resulted in the death of more than 30,000 of them when Cumanus overreacted and his troops applied excessive force to quell the disturbance (2.224–27). Another soldier burned a copy of the Torah and was punished by Cumanus (2.228–31), but when a Jew was murdered by a Samaritan in Galilee, Cumanus declined to punish the offender. Certain Jews from Jerusalem then took matters in their own hands and began a massacre in areas of Samaria. Cumanus set off to defend the Samaritans. Josephus states that when the leaders from Jerusalem pled with their fellow Jews who had embarked on revenge to desist, the latter dispersed (2.232–39). Then both the Samaritans and the Jews took the affair to Ummidius Quadratus, governor of Syria (50–60 C.E.).

There the Jewish notables blamed Cumanus for allowing the situation to get out of hand. Quadratus punished some Jews and sent others with the high priests Jonathan and Ananias to Rome, directing Cumanus to go there also (2.239–44). The result of the hearing in Rome was that Claudius punished some prominent Samaritans, banished Cumanus, sent Felix as procurator, and enlarged Agrippa's kingdom (2.245–47). Josephus then tells how, when Claudius died, he was succeeded by Nero, whom Josephus declines to describe in detail in view of the audience's thorough knowledge (2.250–51). Back in Judea, Felix cleared the country of the bandits (2.253–54).

Immediately following the narrative, Josephus dwells on Jewish unrest, presented as a "sickness" during the rule of Felix (52–59 C.E.). False prophets arose who caused harm no less than the assassins (σφαγέων). Felix thought it was the beginning of an insurrection and slew many of them (2.258–60). Yet imposters and bandits looted and killed those who submitted to the Romans and filled all the countryside with their madness and war. In particular, a certain Egyptian "false prophet" led many into the desert and planned to force his way into Jerusalem. He was met by Felix, who killed or took captive the majority of his followers though the false prophet himself escaped (2.261–63). Josephus likens these events to a spreading sickness in a body (264–65).

Josephus then turns his attention to Caesarea, where Jews and Greeks fought each other and where efforts to control the unrest only provoked the parties to stasis (266–70). At this point Josephus directs our attention again to the malfeasance of the Judean procurators. Although Porcius Festus (59–61 C.E.), who succeeded Felix, attacked the bandits (2.271), his successor, Albinus (61–65 C.E.) plundered property and took ransoms (2.272–73). Then also the leaders in Jerusalem gathered mobs about themselves and began to act like "bandit chiefs or tyrants" (2.274–76). In this way Albinus fostered Jewish tyranny.

Josephus excoriates his successor, Gessius Florus (65–70 C.E.), upon introducing him (2.277–79). When the Syrian legate Cestius Gallus came to Jerusalem at Passover in 65 C.E., "three million" Jews complained about Florus. Florus then secretly planned to work at bringing about a revolt among the Jews to divert attention from his own crimes (280–83).

Viewing the narrative in its context, it becomes apparent that Josephus places it as the first item in a series that illustrates unrest among the Jews during the reign of Felix. Generally speaking, the text might be connected to the immediate context (following) through Josephus's summary statement at the beginning of 264:

> But even when these (the Sicarii, the false prophets, the Egyptian) were suppressed, still a different part was enflamed, just as in a sick body.
>
> κατεσταλμένων δὲ καὶ τούτων ὥσπερ ἐν νοσοῦντι σώματι πάλιν ἕτερον μέρος ἐφλέγμαινεν.

The text, the first in a series, illustrates this disease in the Jewish body—how Jews oppressed and murdered their own.

The text is connected to the surrounding context by the following accents. The Sicarii are called a different type (εἶδος) of bandit, thus connecting them generally to the banditry suppressed by Felix. Moreover, the Sicarii attack their own countrymen, thus working harm on them no less than the false prophets (2.258), the Egyptian, and the brigands who attack their own who support the Romans (2.264–65). An outline for the context might appear as follows:

I.   Felix's unsuccessfully attempt to suppress unrest among the Jews.
   a.   He suppresses the bandit chief Eleazar. (253)
   b.   But he is unable to check the "sickness" (264) of internal strife and murder among the Jews.
      i.   The Sicarii murder the high priest and by their murdering cause panic among the Jews. (254–57)
      ii.   The false prophets spread their ruin in Jerusalem. (258–60)
      iii. The Egyptian prophet leads Jews to their destruction outside the city. (261–63)
   c.   The sickness of the imposters and banditry afflicts Jews throughout the countryside. (264–65)
II. Civil unrest takes place between Jews and Gentiles in Caesarea (266f.). Stasis grows there.

Description of Sicarii Activity

Josephus states that the Sicarii committed stealthy murders via concealed daggers (μικρὰ ξιφίδια) in broad daylight, particularly during the Jewish festivals. The Sicarii were skilled and swift in murder such that their enemies, even though they were on guard, could not escape. The first murder attributed to them is that of Jonathan the high priest. Josephus offers no motive for the murder. His only other mention of Jonathan in *War* concerns the latter's defense of the Jews before Quadratus (2.240), who sent him with others up to Caesar (2.243). Josephus gives no account of Jonathan at Rome.

However, *Antiquities*, 20.162f. provides more information. There we read that Jonathan had requested Caesar to send Felix to replace Cumanus, and that Jonathan feared in consequence that the Jewish population might blame him for this. For Felix himself attempted to suppress unrest among the Jews and had in fact imprisoned and presumably crucified the bandit chief Eleazar (2.253). We might infer that for these reasons Jonathan became a victim of bandit hatred. But there is more. From *Antiquities* we learn that Jonathan had criticized Felix's administration and had therefore also made him an enemy, and so Felix subsequently bribed Doras, Jonathan's "most trusted" friend, to enlist "bandits" to kill Jonathan. Josephus goes on to record how these "bandits" (he at no time calls them Sicarii) were emboldened because Jonathan's murder went unpunished, and so they continued their murders, done exclusively for private or mercenary reasons. The summary conclusion of the narrative in *Antiquities* is that God himself brought the Romans to punish this impiety and to bring a purifying fire on the city, which summary falls in line with Josephus's themes in *Antiquities*.[4] Josephus omits all this information in *War*, drawing attention instead solely to the atrocities of the Sicarii. Numerous murders followed each day, and a panic as that in warfare ensued in Jerusalem.

---

4. See Steve Mason, *Josephus and the New Testament*, 2nd ed. (Peabody: Hendrickson, 2003), 99.

Other than Jonathan, Josephus does not stipulate the identity of the Sicarii's victims. However, the setting (the festivals in Jerusalem) and the immediate context (in which Jewish brigand chiefs, bandits, and false prophets bring destruction on their own people) leads to the natural conclusion that the Sicarii murdered their own people. Josephus does not explain the motive of the Sicarii. But here again the immediate context suggests that they, like the false prophets, were intent on revolutionary changes (259).[5]

Word Studies

Several words stand out in the narrative and its context that deserve careful attention. First and foremost is the noun *sicarii* (σικάριοι), an exceedingly rare word in Greek literature. The term is not found at all prior to Josephus. Only one contemporary, the author of Luke-Acts, employs the term, and he does so only once. In Acts 21:38 we read that Paul was arrested in a disturbance in Jerusalem. When Paul was escorted to the barracks, a tribune asked him if he was the Egyptian who led 4,000 Sicarii into the wilderness.[6] Outside of *War*, Josephus mentions the Sicarii in two separate contexts in *Antiquities*. At 20.186f. he tells how they became numerous after Festus arrived in Judea.

> And the so-called Sicarii (now these were bandits) were especially numerous at this time, making use of small daggers, very much in size like the Persian short curved sword, and resembling also the Roman *siccas,* as they were called. From these the bandits took the name for themselves, as they did away with many.

> καὶ οἱ σικάριοι δὲ καλούμενοι, λῃσταὶ δέ εἰσιν οὗτοι, τότε μάλιστα ἐπλήθυον χρώμενοι ξιφιδίοις παραπλησίοις μὲν τὸ μέγεθος τοῖς τῶν Περσῶν ἀκινάκαις, ἐπικαμπέσι δὲ καὶ ὁμοίαις ταῖς ὑπὸ Ῥωμαίων σίκαις καλουμέναις, ἀφ' ὧν καὶ τὴν προσηγορίαν οἱ λῃστεύοντες ἔλαβον πολλοὺς ἀναιροῦντες.

Josephus tells how these Sicarii, "bandits" who took this name for themselves in accordance with their weapons of choice, small daggers resembling the Roman *sicca,* would mingle with the crowds at festivals to slay their targets or how at other times they would arm themselves with weapons (μεθ' ὅπλων) and then plunder and set fire to the villages of their enemies. In a different context at *Ant.* 20.208f., Josephus tells how the Sicarii would kidnap members of Ananias's

---

5. Compare this with his explicit statements about the personal and mercenary motives of the nameless "bandits" and with his moralizing condemnation of their behavior in *Ant.* 20.162.

6. "Aren't you the Egyptian, who rebelled a while ago and led 4,000 of the Sicarii into the wilderness?" (οὐκ ἄρα σὺ εἶ ὁ Αἰγύπτιος ὁ πρὸ τούτων τῶν ἡμερῶν ἀναστατώσας καὶ ἐξαγαγὼν εἰς τὴν ἔρημον τοὺς τετρακισχιλίους ἄνδρας τῶν σικαρίων;) This incident probably corresponds to *War* 2.261–63, treated above.

house and hold them hostage until Ananias himself secured the release of Sicarii prisoners from Albinus. Other than these passages of Josephus and Luke-Acts, σικάριος is found nowhere else until much later in several church fathers.[7] Therefore, we must turn almost exclusively to Latin authors to discern how Josephus's readers would understand this loan word.

The place to begin, according to J. D. Cloud, is to examine its usage in literature contemporary to the *lex Cornelia de sicariis et veneficiis*, instituted as part of Sulla's reforms. Two places in particular he finds enlightening. Cicero's *De Inventione* (59–60) shows that "a member of an armed gang of which the purpose is *vis*, who commits an injury, is regarded as a person liable to be tried *inter sicarios*."[8] However, the most occurrences are in *Pro Roscio*, where the word is associated with cutthroats, gangs, and assassins (*sector, societas,* and *gladiatores*). Cloud states, "Despite the looseness of the language, Cicero makes it clear enough that *sic.* [i.e., *sicarius*] . . . is a gangster, forming part of a *societas*, who is a public nuisance, who kills or arranges killings for financial gain."[9]

In light of Cicero's usage, Cloud proposes that the *lex Cornelia* did not have to do primarily with murder but with public safety. Moreover, he adduces evidence that suggests that *sicarius* was used also to describe political violence. In this respect it overlaps with "bandit" (*latro*).[10] He concludes:

> The *sic.* at the period when the *lex Cornelia* came into force was not a murderer, but a gangster; there is some evidence to suggest that at times he operated as a member of a gang—words like *societas* and *collegium* occur in this connexion—and primarily in an urban context. Like his North American analogue, his operations were part economic, part political.[11]

However, in the Augustan era and later in the time of Quintilian, the term had changed from its usage in the time of Sulla and had come to denote murder in general.[12] Therefore, Cloud finds it remarkable that Josephus appears to use the

---

7. Hippolytus refers to them in a passage about the Essenes, and Origen tells how the Samaritans were thought to be Sicarii. See Otto Betz, "σικάριος," in *TDNT* 7:281–82.

8. J. D. Cloud, "The Primary Purpose of the *Lex Cornelia*," *Zeitschrift der Savigny-Stiftung für Rechtsgeschichte* 86 (1969): 271.

9. Ibid.. 271.

10. Ibid., 276–78. Cloud refers to the political violence of Catiline (*Pro Murena* 49), Clodius (*Pro Sestio* 53, 78, 81, 95), and Antony (*Philippics* 5.18). What makes *sicarius* distinct from *latro* is that the former is active primarily in an urban environment. For an alternative explanation of this law's intent, see Eric Gruen, *Roman Politics and the Criminal Courts: 149–78 B.C.* (Cambridge, MA: Harvard University Press, 1968), 261–62, where he states that the law amounts to Sulla's attempt to place previously existing procedures concerning murder (*de venificiis, sicariis,* and *parricidiis*) "under one piece of detailed legislation." That is, consolidation, not innovation, was the intent.

11. Cloud, "Primary Purpose," 280.

12. Quintilian states (*Inst.* 10.1.12), "We also loosely name 'sicarii' all who have commit-

word "almost exactly" as it was understood in the final days of the Republic. He says that the Sicarii in Josephus "are organized, they operate in the heart of the city, their aim is part political, part financial. The chief difference between the Roman and Jewish *sicarii* is the intense patriotism of the latter."[13] So far the background on *sicarius*.

Josephus uses another striking and known metaphor when he describes as a sickness the activity of Judean imposters and bandits who murder and pillage especially those Jews who submit to Rome (2.264). Summarizing as it does the immediate context, this word casts the rise and activity of the Sicarii in light of the "sickness" of internal unrest.

The group of words for sickness (νόσος, νοσέω, νόσημα, νοσηλεύω) occurs forty-one times in *War* and in ways that very much mirror other classical usage. There, besides its literal sense, the word group was used as a metaphor in describing political disturbances. Herodotus describes Miletus as "sickened in particular by stasis" (νοσήσασα ἐς τὰ μάλιστα στάσι 5.28). Sophocles has Teiresias famously confront Creon, stating that he is the source of the city's sickness (*Antigone* 1015). Similarly, Demosthenes enumerates those vices that "infect" Greece (9.39 *Philippic 3*). The word is similarly employed by Sallust (*Catiline* 36.5) and Tacitus (*Annals* 1.43.4; *Histories* 1.26.1).

In *War* Josephus normally uses the words in their literal sense. But in a few places besides the text in question, like his classical forebears, Josephus uses these words as metaphors for internal civil disorders such as in Rome (1.4) or in Agrippa's realm (3.443). Like Herodotus, Josephus links this word group to the στάσις word group in describing internal strife among the Jews. For example, Vespasian, in council with his commanders, decides not to attack Jerusalem immediately in part because the Jews were "infected" by domestic strife and the victory would be attributed not to the Romans but to the stasis (4.376).[14]

At several places, banditry and stasis together comprise a spreading sickness, as from Jerusalem whereby the entire countryside was affected (4.406-7). Similarly, the inhabitants of Gischala, who are otherwise inclined to peace, are afflicted by the sickness of the bandit gangs and are incited to rebel (4.84-85).

Josephus uses the verb as a summary term when introducing the Hall of Infamy at 7.260. The likes of John of Gischala, Simon b. Gioras, the Idumeans, and the Zealots illustrate a universal sickness in private and public affairs wherein people strove to outdo one another in impious acts toward God and crimes against neighbors. This "madness" of the Sicarii spread like a "sickness"

---

ted murder with a sword" (nam per abusionem sicarios etiam omnes vocamus, qui caedem telo quocumque commiserint).

13. Cloud, "Primary Purpose," 281-83.

14. "If greater fame from their success [was the consideration], they should not attack those who were infected by domestic strife, for the victory would be attributed with good reason not to them but to the stasis (ἐὰν εἴτε τὸ εὐκλεέστερον τοῦ κατορθώματος οὐ δεῖν τοῖς οἴκοι νοσοῦσιν ἐπιχειρεῖν ῥηθήσεσθαι γὰρ εὐλόγως οὐκ αὐτῶν τὴν νίκην ἀλλὰ τῆς στάσεως).

also to cities around Cyrene (7.437). In these ways Josephus links the Sicarii to a well-known metaphor.

He also describes the Sicarii as "bandits in different form" (ἕτερον εἶδος λῃστῶν). The noun λῃστής and its cognates (λῃστρικός, λῃστεία, λῃστεύω, λήζομαι) are found frequently in the first six books of *War*. There are no occurrences in the seventh book, though this is not surprising given that the guerrilla-like hostilities characteristic of the "bandits" have ceased with Jerusalem's destruction. "Bandits" and "banditry" were terms well known to Josephus's audience. In classical and Hellenistic authors, λῃστής commonly denotes one who devotes himself to robbery or piracy (Plato *Laws* 823e; Aristotle *Politics* 1256a36; et passim). Roman literature reflects the ubiquity of banditry in the empire.[15] Bandits might act alone but tended to work more in groups so as to become at times a threat not only to individual homes but also cities and governments. Thus the term was used to describe categories of warfare that were not legitimate or genuine (*iustum*).[16] Accordingly, such individuals fell outside the law, being classified neither as citizens nor as legitimate enemies of a foreign state. In support Shaw points to the *Digest* 50.16.118, which offers the following:

> Enemies are those who have publicly declared war against us, or we against them. The rest are "bandits" or "robbers."

> Hostes hi sunt, qui nobis aut quibus nos publice bellum decrevimus; ceteri "latrones" aut "praedones" sunt.

By extension the word came to be used by Cicero and Sallust as a "weapon of accusation" in the political combat of the late Republic. Shaw states:

> The fact is that once bandits had been defined as men who stood in a peculiar relation to the state, the label *latro* was available to be pasted on any "de-stated" person. It became a powerful metaphor in itself, used deliberately to cast doubt on hostile persons, principally political enemies. . . . Thereafter it was entrenched as part of political vocabulary and was commonly reverted to in times of central state crisis . . . to brand political enemies, particularly those who were competitors for local power and for the imperial throne.[17]

Shaw points to a similar usage of the terms to describe people who were claimed to be under Roman state control but who fought to remain "obstinately and rebelliously" outside it. Such were the bandit gangs of first-century Judea.[18]

Thomas Grünewald offers many similar ideas about banditry. He points to the specialized use of the terms by Cicero to describe Catiline's activities (1.9.23, 1.12.29, 1.13.31). "The constant elements in the Roman picture of the common,

---

15. See Brent Shaw, "Bandits in the Roman Empire," *Past and Present* 105 (1984): 3–52.
16. Ibid., 7.
17. Ibid., 23.
18. Ibid. 42–43.

contemptible bandit—poverty, need, an appetite for booty and violence, together with audacious courage and pride—were also used to designate bitter, political foes as *latrones*."[19] Like Shaw, Grünewald also points to *War* as an example of Josephus using the terminology to cast the activity of the rebels in a negative light. He says:

> The fact that Josephus categorises rebels from different social backgrounds, variously motivated and with a multiplicity of goals, globally as *leistai* is, *inter alia*, an expression of contempt, both Roman and his own, for their breed. . . . From his point of view, he was dealing with people who were acting illegally in attempting to win themselves a position of power, i.e. usurpers. For "usurper" Latin had *latro*, Greek *leistes*. In the many Jewish *leistai* we should see usurpers, great and small, a usage which is not peculiar to Josephus, but which was entirely normal in Antiquity.[20]

Grünewald notes especially how Josephus applies bandit terminology to John of Gischala, who was "neither a social bandit nor any sort of robber" but a "bitter political opponent of Josephus," and also to Simon b. Gioras, whom we will meet later in connection with the Sicarii. Grünewald says, "Josephus' account of the career of Simon 'the bandit' is so conventional that it is interchangeable with that of many another robber of the Roman period."[21]

These are examples of how Josephus employs bandit terminology according to established usage. He uses these terms to describe not only individuals, but also loosely organized bands in the country, often around a leader, which operate outside of the law and pillage districts, peoples, and towns (2.57). The size of their activity grew such that it necessitated intervention by Felix, and Josephus calls it "the principal plague of the country" during the time of Festus (2.253, 271). They were at times mercenary and could be recruited even by civil rulers (1.398f.). Josephus pointedly states that he recruited for war only elements of the population who abstained from banditry, for in his mind the bandits had not only the

---

19. Thomas Grünewald, *Bandits in the Roman Empire: Myth and Reality*, trans. John Drinkwater (London and New York: Routledge, 2004), 89.

20. Ibid., 98. Grünewald touches upon Masada in this context, saying that the deaths there "symbolise the indomitable bandit." He also follows the scholars above and places the episode alongside of Jotapata. "His [Josephus's] feelings of personal guilt and shame (for rigging the lot at Jotapata) could well explain the literary monument that he set up to the Sicarii of Masada. The myth of Masada owes its existence in one respect, therefore, to the 'Masada complex' of Flavius Josephus" (109).

21. Ibid., 100–104. Grünewald disagrees with Horsley's contention that the banditry in Judea exhibits the characteristics of social banditry, for this model does not fit well with what is known about Judea and the revolt. No bandits emerge as heroes of the peasantry as required by the model. Furthermore, only a small segment of the bandits were peasants. Third, their words and activities were highly politicized in a manner that does not sit well with the "undirected protests" of social bandits (see ibid., 92–95).

Romans but also God as their enemies (2.581). As the revolt gathers momentum in the narrative, Josephus uses the term to describe the followers of illegitimate rebel leaders such as Eleazar b. Deinaeus and Alexander (2.235), John of Gischala (2.587–93), and later Simon b. Gioras (4.510).

In his proem, Josephus begs indulgence for condemning such tyrants and their banditry (1.11). Bandit gangs constitute a "sickness" inasmuch as they pillage and murder fellow Jews under the banner of freedom from Rome. Bandit terminology is thus often found with the stasis word group. Bandit gangs afflict Gischala with the sickness of rebellion (ἀπόστασις, 4.48–85). Banditry spreads like an illness through the members of a body in part because of the stasis at Jerusalem (4.406). Eventually bandit gangs flood into and afflict Jerusalem itself, though at times Josephus appears to use the term in a rather more general and loose way to describe criminals (2.425ff.; 5.421, 448, 515; 6.195) or the rebels in Jerusalem as a whole in the absence of any legitimate leadership (5.524, 546). Once Jerusalem is destroyed, he drops the terminology.

Finally, we may briefly note that Josephus calls the activity of the Sicarii "murder" (φονεύοντες, οἱ πεφονευκότες), and the general panic he likens to that of warfare (καθάπερ ἐν πολέμῳ).

BOOK CONTEXT

We have already seen above that Mason makes stasis (στάσις) a structural concept in *War*, and we will want to be aware of its connections to the Sicarii.[22] Here we point out that the stasis word group (στασιάζω, στασιαστής, στάσις, στασιώδης) is largely absent from the immediate context, making its appearance only at the end in connection with the unrest at Caesarea. στασιαστής does not make a regular appearance until 2.267. The less frequent στασιάζω similarly makes an appearance in connection with Jewish unrest at 2.266. So also στάσις, which begins to appear regularly at 2.269. We will see, then, that Josephus connects the uncontrolled growth of stasis with the unrest at Caesarea (see below under "Capture of Masada"), which follows the text under consideration here.

στασιώδης alone appears prior to the text in the immediate context. At 2.225 Josephus tells us that "those who were less sober minded among the youth, with that part of the people who were rebellious by nature" (οἱ δὲ ἧττον νήφοντες τῶν νέων καὶ τὸ φύσει στασιῶδες ἐκ τοῦ ἔθνους) escalated the confrontation over the lewd act of the Roman soldier. At 2.235 Eleazar and Alexander lead rebels (στασιώδους) against the Samaritans.

The point here is that the Sicarii make their appearance before the uncontrolled outbreak of stasis. Indeed, their activity portends such an outbreak inasmuch as they embody that essential element of stasis as presented in Josephus—Jewish insurgents killing fellow Jews who do not share their political

---

22. See above under "Literary Background" in chapter 2.

agenda. The narrative thus illustrates the escalating internal strife among the Jews, here called a "sickness" in its immediate context.

It should be noted here also that the Sicarii arise before the Zealots as an identifiable group in the rebellion. The word for Zealot (ζηλωτής) does not appear until 2.444, and even there it does not appear to denote a party but the fanatical followers of Menahem.[23] Thus, it would be more accurate, at least within the narrative of *War*, to say that the Sicarii arose as an identifiable subgroup among the bandits (λῃσταί) than that they were an armed or murderous segment of the Zealots. And so in the Hall of Infamy at 7.262, Josephus states that the Sicarii were the first in their lawless behavior toward kinsmen.

Intra-textual connections exist between this narrative and 4:305–65, the central panel in the structure of *War*. There Josephus recounts the death of the high priests Ananus and Jesus, Ananus in particular being the last hope either for peace or skillful resistance against Rome (4.321).[24] Tyranny and internal butchery grow unabated subsequent to Ananus's death. The narrative about the Sicarii at 2.254–57 bears certain striking similarities to this central panel. These rebels murder the high priest Jonathan, and from that point murders and panic among the Jews grow. Josephus makes this murder, the first activity of the Sicarii, their introduction in the narrative. Josephus thus illustrates in the Sicarii those qualities that would lead ultimately to the irrevocable destruction of Jerusalem. Their activity thus presages the central panel at 4:305.

CONCLUSIONS

Josephus presents the Sicarii as a type of bandit gang. Such gangs operated in loose organizations outside the law and pillaged and killed their own people. They comprised a sickness in the body politic and were often connected with tyrant leaders and stasis. In Josephus's narrative, bandits were enemies not only of their own people and the Romans but also of God. What makes the Sicarii stand out from the rest of the bandits is the manner by which they employed violence: with small daggers. It is for this reason that they are called "Sicarii."

They stand out, also, because of their high-profile assassination of Jonathan, the high priest. Though we might infer a motive from *Antiquities*, that Jonathan incurred the Sicarii's anger because he encouraged Felix to suppress the ban-

---

23. Thus Solomon Zeitlin, "Zealots and Sicarii," *JBL* 81 (1962): 398; Morton Smith, "Zealots and Sicarii: Their Origins and Relation," *HTR* 64 (1971): 7–8; Tessa Rajak, *Josephus, the Historian and His Society*, 2nd ed. (London: Gerald Duckworth, 2002), 86. More on this below.

24. "In short, with Ananus alive to speak, they would undoubtedly have dispersed—for he was uncanny both in his speech and in persuading the people and he was already at work on those who opposed him—or they would have caused the Romans much trouble with him as their general" (καθόλου δ᾽ εἰπεῖν ζῶντος Ἀνάνου πάντως ἂν διελύθησαν, δεινὸς γὰρ ἦν εἰπεῖν τε καὶ πεῖσαι τὸν δῆμον ἤδη δὲ ἐχειροῦτο καὶ τοὺς ἐμποδίζοντας, ἢ πολεμοῦντες πλείστην ἂν τριβὴν Ῥωμαίοις παρέσχον ὑπὸ τοιούτῳ στρατηγῷ).

dits and that Jonathan had later run afoul of Felix and therefore was left isolated, Josephus in *War* comments on none of this. He rather directs our attention
solely to the Sicarii's murdering activity. This Josephus pointedly summarizes
as a sickness, a term he uses elsewhere to describe civil war and internal unrest.
Here Josephus states that such a sickness grew among the Jews because Felix was
unable to control it. By introducing the Sicarii via their murder of the high priest,
Josephus has them provide an early indication of the event that would bring the
battle to a point of no return—the murders of Ananus and Jesus.

The Capture of Masada (2.408)

Josephus continues the narrative of the uncontrolled growth of rebellion in Jerusalem. After making a long and impassioned speech, Agrippa urged the people
to submit to Florus until Caesar sent a replacement, at which advice the Jews
became exasperated and banished him from the city. At this point the rebellion
gained strength in Jerusalem. In this context Josephus writes at *War* 2.408:

> At this time some who were particularly inclined for battle gathered together
> and made a rush for a fortress called Masada. After capturing it by stealth, they
> slew the Roman guards and placed their own instead.

> κἀν τούτῳ τινὲς τῶν μάλιστα κινούντων τὸν πόλεμον συνελθόντες ὥρμησαν
> ἐπὶ φρούριόν τι καλούμενον Μασάδαν, καὶ καταλαβόντες αὐτὸ λάθρα τοὺς μὲν
> Ῥωμαίων φρουροὺς ἀπέσφαξαν, ἑτέρους δ᾽ ἐγκατέστησαν ἰδίους.

Evidence for Including in the Study

Although Josephus does not here mention the Sicarii, the link is established at
4.399–400, where he states that the Sicarii had already captured Masada when
rebellion broke out. Indeed, a review of how and when Josephus refers to Masada
in *War* reveals an emerging consistent connection between it and the Sicarii.

In book 1 Josephus introduces Masada in passing as the "strongest" of the
fortresses taken by the brother of Malichus, the enemy of Herod, but subsequently recaptured by Herod (237, 238). There Herod protected his family and
friends while fighting against the Parthians (264–66), and there they were later
besieged by Antigonus while Herod was at Rome, where he was made king (286).
Upon returning to Judea, Herod rescued Masada (292–94) and removed his family and friends (303)

In book 2 after the text in question, Josephus proceeds to tell how Menahem b. Judas armed himself and his compatriots at Masada before he returned
to Jerusalem as a king (433), where he became a leader of the stasis. When he was
killed, Menahem's followers escaped to Masada led by Eleazar b. Yair, a relative
of Menahem. There Eleazar became a tyrant (447). Later, we read how Simon
b. Gioras found refuge against Ananus among the bandits (λῃστάς) at Masada.

Simon remained there until Ananus's death. From this base he conducted raids in Idumea (653).

In book 4 Josephus introduces Masada again (φρούριον ἦν οὐ πόρρω Ἱεροσολύμων . . . ὃ ἐκαλεῖτο Μασάδα), this time as the repository and refuge built by "kings of old" (399). Previously taken by the Sicarii, it became the base of their raids (402–4). The narrative at 504 and 506, where Masada is mentioned, is an expansion of 2.653 about Simon b. Gioras, who was not at first completely welcomed by those at Masada. But he later gained their trust and accompanied them on their raids. The raids of the Sicarii from Masada compelled the Idumeans to protect themselves, and thus they could not oppose Simon in full force (516). Masada is listed as one of the three fortresses not subdued by Cerealius, Vespasian's officer, before the assault on Jerusalem (555). Finally, in book 7 Masada comes to center stage in connection with the subjugation of the last Sicarii rebels in Judea.

To summarize, then, we see that in book 1 Masada is consistently linked to the family and protection of Herod, but after the rebellion broke out, there is no indication that anyone other than the Sicarii held it. For the reader the connection between the Sicarii and Masada begins to emerge when Menahem, who arms himself from Masada, becomes a leader of the stasis in Jerusalem, which included the Sicarii. Josephus makes the connection clear for the reader at 4.400, and the connection is kept to the end of *War*. By virtue of the fact that there is no indicator that anyone other than the Sicarii occupied Masada in the narrative from 2.408 to the end, this passage as well as several to follow, where also the Sicarii are not mentioned by name, are included in this study.

LITERARY CONTEXT

Immediately preceding the text, Josephus describes the excesses of Gessius Florus, who allegedly planned to make the Jews revolt to cover his own crimes (2.282–83). Josephus states that the war began with a synagogue incident at Caesarea (2.284). There Florus refused to intervene in a dispute between Jewish and Greek Caesareans and instead left for Sebaste, giving the stasis free rein (288). Even when a riot broke out and the Jews left the city and appealed to Florus, he responded by having those who took the copies of the Law from Caesarea for protection arrested (2.291–92).

Florus then provoked those in Jerusalem, who had heard the news from Caesarea, by taking seventeen talents from the temple treasury and allowing his soldiers to plunder the market and kill those who resisted (2.293–303). The priests and ministers *en masse* urged the people of Jerusalem not to provoke the Romans (2.312–24), and the crowd was soothed. But when the cohorts of Florus arrived, the rebels (στασιασταί) provoked them to fall on the gathered Jews, a provocation that Josephus states was prearranged by Florus (2.325–26). The rebels responded by destroying the porticos adjoining the temple (2.330–31).

Florus then left Jerusalem, and Cestius Gallus sent Neapolitanus to investigate affairs there, which he did with Agrippa. The people pressed him for an embassy to Caesar in order to denounce Florus (2.336–44), and Agrippa made his long and impassioned speech against rebellion (2.345–401). The people responded by rebuilding the porticos, and the magistrates and council members collected the tribute that had fallen arrears. But when Agrippa ordered the people to submit to Florus until Caesar sent a replacement, the people became irritated and proclaimed his banishment from the city (2.402–7).

Immediately following the narrative in question, Josephus tells how the rebellion gained strength. Eleazar b. Ananus, "a very arrogant youth," persuaded the temple officials not to receive sacrifices for foreigners, including the Romans and Caesar. Josephus calls this the foundation (καταβολή) of war (2.409). The leading citizens, priests, and well-known Pharisees appealed to the rebels to desist this action, but they learned, when their arguments were rejected, that they themselves could not control the stasis (2.411–18). They appealed in vain to Florus, but received reinforcements from Agrippa and held the upper city while the rebel element (τὸ στασιάζον) held the lower city and temple (2.417–24).

Within this context, the capture of Masada does not receive much comment and therefore does not attract notice to itself per se. Rather, it serves as a signal, with the announced expulsion of Agrippa from Jerusalem and the more significant (in Josephus's narrative) cessation of sacrifice for Rome/Caesar, of rebel determination for war. The context might be outlined as follows:

I.   Florus works to bring about a revolt (ἀπόστασιν) among the Jews. (283)
   a. He gives stasis free rein at Caesarea (καταλείπει τὴν στάσιν αὐτεξούσιον 288), which grew around a synagogue riot and became the starting point of the war. (284–92)
   b. He provokes rebellion in Jerusalem. (293–344)
      i.   He takes the temple treasury.
      ii. He abuses people in the market, even crucifying Roman Jews of equestrian rank.
      iii. He turns a deaf ear to Bernice.
      iv. He reignites the flames of rebellion by prearranging a conflict between his cohorts and the Jews despite the efforts of the Jewish leaders to calm the rebels.
II. Agrippa delivers an impassioned speech against rebellion, here summarized to emphasize his main points. (345–401)
   a. "Your desire for revenge against procurators does not justify war."
   b. "Your desire for freedom is ill timed."
   c. "Consider all the peoples who submitted to Rome, all of which were greater than you."
   d. "No allies will help you, not from Parthia nor from God himself."
   e. "Expect no mercy from the Romans if you go to war!"
III. The Jews ultimately reject his appeal and rebel, they say, not so much against the Romans but against Florus. (402–7)

IV. The rebellion acquires a foundation. (καταβολή 409)
   a. Masada is taken. (408)
   b. Eleazar b. Ananias prevails in the cessation of sacrifice for Caesar/Rome. (409–10)
   c. Jewish leaders appeal to the rebels to desist, but their arguments are rejected. (411–17)
V. Reinforcements for the leaders arrive from Agrippa, and a standoff ensues. (418–24)

Description of Sicarii Activity

Josephus does not tell us much, although the slight details are significant. Those who are most inclined for battle captured Masada, slew the Roman garrison there, and placed their own instead.

Word Studies

The narrative is too brief to support word studies. But important concepts emerge from the book context particularly in light of stasis as a controlling theme.

Book Context

The stasis word group occurs five times in the proem. Josephus there states that stasis destroyed his country while the tyrants drew the unwilling Roman hands against the temple.[25] Josephus summarizes that stasis broke out when Vespasian went to restore order at Egypt (1.24) and it had reduced the city before Titus arrived (1.25), who desired to meet with the insurrectionists (στασιάζοντας) to save the city and temple (1.27). Josephus places stasis alongside war and famine as the source of the city's misfortunes (1.25). In this manner Josephus clearly accents stasis in the proem.

As Mason points out, Josephus signals his focus on this theme by making στάσις the first word of his narrative, where it broke out among the Jewish nobles at the time of Antiochus IV (1.31). Indeed, it was because of the growing stasis among the nobles that the Romans intervened in Jewish affairs to begin with.[26] The group of words is then applied in various contexts to describe insurrection

---

25. ὅτι γὰρ αὐτὴν στάσις οἰκεία καθεῖλεν καὶ τὰς Ῥωμαίων χεῖρας ἀκούσας καὶ τὸ πῦρ ἐπὶ τὸν ναὸν εἵλκυσαν οἱ Ἰουδαίων τύραννοι (1.10). This phrase is repeated almost verbatim at 5.257 when the war is in full swing and the Romans are encamped before the walls of Jerusalem. "For I say that the stasis captured the city, and the Romans the stasis, which was indeed far more stubborn than the city walls" (φημὶ γὰρ ὡς τὴν μὲν πόλιν ἡ στάσις Ῥωμαῖοι δ᾽ εἷλον τὴν στάσιν ἥπερ ἦν πολὺ τῶν τειχῶν ὀχυρωτέρα).

26. See 1.131–54, wherein this theme is sounded at 142. There Josephus states that when Pompey was besieging Jerusalem, "stasis broke out among those within, Aristobulus's party being willing to fight and rescue the king, Hycanus's party planning to open the gates to

or civil strife of the Jews against Herod (1.252), and early on especially within Herod's household (1.198, 254, 432, 460, 464, 467).

The word group, however, is first clustered together in the Caesarean narrative (2.266, 267, 269, 270, 274, 288, 289, 290, 291, 324), signaling this as the place were the Jewish revolt began. There insurgent groups among Jews and Greeks clashed in ways that the elder Jews and Felix found increasingly difficult to control (267, 270). Though Festus was more successful at controlling the stasis (271), Florus positively planned to provoke it; and so he embarked on those misdeeds reviewed above. Because of his provocations, the stasis among the Jews spread to Jerusalem, where Josephus portrays the Jewish leaders in opposition to stasis elements (419, 422). Thus, the irremediable outbreak of stasis began at Caesarea, where both Jews and Greeks bear some blame. Moreover, Josephus makes Florus responsible, inasmuch as the stasis results from his intention and provocative actions. Members of the Jewish nobility, by contrast, try to control the stasis, and when it appears they might succeed in their efforts, Florus stymies them with their arrest and with further provocative actions in Jerusalem. There is a note of irony here, for Josephus marks the outbreak of Jewish hostilities, via the controlling theme of stasis, not in Jerusalem but at the seat of Roman provincial government in Judea. One would think that there at least Roman procurators would have prevented its spread. Here we might suggest that Josephus is not too subtly reminding his Roman readers of their own recent experience with stasis at Rome. At the very least, by drawing attention to Florus's pro-war activities and the Jewish nobility's efforts to suppress the stasis, Josephus also blames the Romans for the Judean war.

The narrative in question, the implied Sicarii activity of 2.408, following as it does the speech of Agrippa, signals the rejection of submission to Rome. This much is obvious. However, in its context the narrative highlights the irreparable nature of the stasis that broke out in Caesarea and spread to Jerusalem. Therefore, the capture of Masada thus also presages, by its position, the stasis growing among the Jews. We will see that this connection between Masada and stasis is carried to the end of *War*.

CONCLUSIONS

The narrative here is brief, and, again, it must be admitted that the activity of the Sicarii is only implied. Yet on the basis of 4.399 and the clear connection between the Sicarii and Masada, the inference is sound.

Thus, the narrative in its context casts the Sicarii as those who are most inclined for war and, it might also be stated, the first to actually kill Roman soldiers although this latter point is not emphasized by Josephus. Their activ-

---

Pompey" (στάσις τοῖς ἔνδον ἐμπίπτει τῶν μὲν Ἀριστοβούλου πολεμεῖν ἀξιούντων καὶ ῥύεσθαι τὸν βασιλέα τῶν δὲ τὰ Ὑρκανοῦ φρονούντων ἀνοίγειν Πομπηΐῳ τὰς πύλας).

ity works in the background to highlight the growing stasis among the Jewish leaders.

In coming to a preliminary historical assessment, we would assume that when the Sicarii slew the Roman guards to capture Masada, they did not rely exclusively on concealed daggers. Thus we have in this narrative what will become fully apparent in later passages—evidence of how Josephus will apply the term Sicarii in a broader sense and not exclusively to those who commit stealthy assassinations with daggers in an urban environment.

They Join the Rebels (2.425)

Josephus continues his narrative about the growing rebellion and stasis in Jerusalem. The Jewish nobles and some leading priests largely opposed Eleazar's provocative gesture of not receiving sacrifices for Rome and Caesar, and so after receiving reinforcements from Agrippa, they took control of the upper city and were intent on expelling Eleazar and his compatriots from the temple. At this point Josephus tells how the Sicarii came to the temple and added their critical strength to the rebellion. Josephus writes:

> [425] Now the next day was the feast of wood gathering, when it was customary for all to bring wood to the altar so that fuel might never be lacking for the fire, for it always remained lit. On this day they excluded their opponents from this worship but welcomed many of the Sicarii (for this is what they called the bandits who had daggers in the folds of their garments), who flowed in with the weak people, and pressed their attack more boldly. [426] The royalists were defeated by the size and daring of the attack and gave way to those who forced them out of the upper city. Now they fell upon the house of Ananus the high priest and the palaces of Agrippa and Bernice and burned them, etc.

> [425] τῇ δ' ἑξῆς τῆς τῶν ξυλοφορίων ἑορτῆς οὔσης, ἐν ᾗ πᾶσιν ἔθος ἦν ὕλην τῷ βωμῷ προσφέρειν, ὅπως μήποτε τροφὴ τῷ πυρὶ λείποι, διαμένει γὰρ ἄσβεστον ἀεί, τοὺς μὲν διαφόρους τῆς θρησκείας ἐξέκλεισαν, τῷ δ' ἀσθενεῖ λαῷ συνεισρυέντας πολλοὺς τῶν σικαρίων, οὕτως γὰρ ἐκάλουν τοὺς λῃστὰς ἔχοντας ὑπὸ τοῖς κόλποις ξίφη, προσλαβόντες θαρραλεώτερον ἥπτοντο τῆς ἐπιχειρήσεως. [426] ἡττῶντο δ' οἱ βασιλικοὶ πλήθει τε καὶ τόλμῃ καὶ βιασαμένοις εἶκον ἐκ τῆς ἄνω πόλεως. οἱ δὲ ἐπιπεσόντες τήν τε Ἀνανίου τοῦ ἀρχιερέως οἰκίαν καὶ τὰ Ἀγρίππα καὶ Βερνίκης ὑποπιμπρᾶσιν βασίλεια· κτλ.

Literary context

The context for this passage is directly connected to the decision not to receive sacrifices for foreigners, including the Romans and Caesar, introduced above. At this point the leading citizens, priests, and well-known Pharisees appealed to the rebels to desist from this action (2.411–17). They expressed indignation at the "insolence" (τόλμαν) of the revolt and how it would bring war on the people and

attempted to show that Eleazar's prohibition contradicted ancient Jewish practice and sacred law. They insisted that the rebels were thus introducing a foreign
innovation, which not only courted war but also brought upon themselves the
charge of impiety. In support of their arguments they produced priests who were
experts in the ancestral tradition.

However, they learned when their arguments were rejected that they could
not themselves control the stasis (2.418), and so they appealed in vain to Florus
and received reinforcements from Agrippa. At this point Josephus indicates that
a struggle began. The leading citizens and priests held the upper city while the
rebel element (τὸ στασιάζον) controlled the lower city and temple (2.418–24).

After the text in question, Josephus recounts how Jerusalem was crippled.
The rebel element in the temple immediately captured the upper city and set fire
to the "tendons" (τὰ νεῦρα) of the city: the house of Ananias the high priest, the
palaces of Agrippa and Bernice, and the public archives (2.426–28). Some of the
leading citizens and chief priests escaped, but others such as Ananias, his brother
Ezechias, and the deputation to Agrippa locked themselves in the upper palace
(2.428–29). The rebels captured the Antonia, and continuous combat ensued at
the palace with neither side being able to gain the upper hand (2.430–32).

In its context, then, the addition of the Sicarii to the rebels in the temple
allowed the latter to capture the upper city. The context might be outlined in the
following manner:

I. The rebellion gains a foundation. (καταβολή 408–17)
   a. Masada is taken. (408)
   b. Eleazar b. Ananias prevails in the cessation of sacrifice for Caesar/Rome.
      (409–10)
   c. Jewish leaders appeal in vain to the rebels and are unable to control the
      stasis. (411–17)
II. Reinforcements for the leaders arrive from Agrippa, and a standoff ensues.
   (418–24)
III. The Sicarii strengthen the rebels. The city is weakened. (425–32)
   a. That which holds the city together is burnt. (τὰ νεῦρα τῆς πόλεως
      καταφλέξαντες)
   b. The rebels prevail over the leading citizens, chief priests, and those loyal
      to Rome in the upper city.
   c. They burn the chief priest's house, portions of the palace of Agrippa and
      Bernice, and the public archives.
IV. They capture part of the Antonia but are unable to take the entire palace,
   where Ananias in particular takes refuge.

Description of Sicarii Activity

The text tells how the Sicarii added their own strength to that of the rebels in the
temple. Josephus states that at the time of wood gathering, the Sicarii moved into
the temple with the "weaker" segments of the population. Thackeray translates

their movement (συνεισρυέντες) as "forced their way in." This is too polemical a translation. The word, rather, pictures how the Sicarii literally "flowed in with" the weaker element of the people to the temple at the time of wood gathering. A certain amount of stealth may be implied in the word, but not confrontation. Indeed, the rebels (τὸ στασιάζον) who held the temple welcomed (προσλαβόντες) the Sicarii. The rebels in the temple thus gained confidence and overpowered their Jewish royalist opposition. These latter could not match the size and the daring (πλήθει τε καὶ τόλμη) of the now-enlarged rebel force. We also see here that Josephus once again states how bandits who carried daggers in their garments were called Sicarii.

WORD STUDIES

Once again Josephus makes a connection between the Sicarii, the bandits, and stasis. For both these terms, λῃστής and στάσις, see above. Josephus adds a new term that occurs regularly throughout *War* when he says that with the addition of the Sicarii to the stasis element in the temple, the royalists were then outmatched in numbers and "daring" (τόλμη). Statistics in *War* (τόλμα—52 times; τολμάω—51 times; τόλμημα—10 times; τολμηρός—10 times; τολμητής—1 time) show that these words generally describe risky behavior that results from overstepping accepted boundaries in the social, military, or legal spheres. Inasmuch as this family of words in general Greek usage can have positive or negative connotations, depending on the context, it is important for us to examine exactly how Josephus employs them about the Sicarii.[27]

In most of its occurrences in *War*, the noun is used either in a neutral or negative way. In the latter sense it describes arrogance, audacity, or insolence such as of particular authors who presume to call their works "history" (1.7). The word thus becomes an oft-used pejorative label attached to the rebels. The Jewish leaders express indignation at the revolutionaries because of the audacity of their revolt (2.412). In Jerusalem after the subjugation of Galilee, the revolutionary party use youth and audacity to conquer age and self-control (νεότητι καὶ τόλμη γηραιῶν καὶ σωφρόνων 4.133). The words also describe criminal activity and attitudes. τόλμημα in particular, in at least nine of its ten occurrences in *War*, is used in this way.[28]

Josephus uses the words in a negative way to describe disorganized battle tactics, such as pillaging and burning (3.176). Titus in particular contrasts Jew-

---

27. Pindar, for example, praises Thearion for taking upon himself the courage to attempt noble things (τόλμαν τε καλῶν ἀρομένῳ, *Nemean* 7.59). The same word describes the recklessness shown by a robber (Aristophanes *Oedipus Tyrannus* 125).

28. Generally at 4.146, 171, 221, 245, 257; at 4.401 for the raid of the Sicarii at Passover; 7.89 for a Scythian rebellion against Rome; 7.257 to describe the crimes of the Sicarii; 7.393 for the evil of killing one's own; 7.405 the magnitude of the τόλμημα at Masada amazes the Romans. More on this next chapter.

ish "risk taking, rash behavior, and thoughtlessness" (τόλμα, θράσυς, ἀπόνοια) with Roman "skill, experience, and nobility" (ἀρετή, εὐπείθεια, τὸ γενναῖον). The former "passions" are vigorous in victory but quenched in defeat. The latter qualities do not fail in adversity (3.479).[29] However, when used to describe battle tactics, the same words often have a more neutral force, and this is how Josephus more often describes Jewish tactics. They are driven to risky behavior by injustice (1.35), necessity (3.149), and fear (6.143). Their "risky behavior" is nourished by fear and by innate fortitude under calamities (τόλμα δέει τρεφομένη καὶ τὸ φύσει καρτερικὸν ἐν συμφοραῖς). Though τόλμα contrasts to Roman experience and strength (5.306) and therefore often stands in contrast to military training and experience (3.22) and sometimes leads to defeat (3.24), Josephus pointedly states that John failed in his attacks because he was lacking those uniquely Jewish tactics in fighting. These include risk, sudden attack, a unified charge, and not turning back even under blows (6.17).[30]

Inasmuch as the lack of these qualities results in defeat, this summary statement of Josephus results in a more positive understanding of τόλμα. It is precisely these characteristics in battle that continually cause the Romans discomfort, as at Jotapata (3.152, 228). Vespasian must accordingly take measures to safeguard against this quality of the Jews (3.161). Although contrasted to strategy, it has a telling effect (5.280) and destroys Roman order (5.285).

Though Josephus uses the word group less frequently in a positive sense, the few examples are clear. Sometimes the words are synonymous with courage. Josephus reports that if he himself were to leave Jotapata, where he was in command, the inhabitants would lose courage and none would then dare face the enemy (μηδενὸς ἔτι τοῖς πολεμίοις τολμῶντος ἀνθίστασθαι 3.196). In another context, Titus himself urged his troops not to delay their attack on Tarichaeae, and he led the charge against the town. Fear seized all on the walls at his daring (πρὸς τὴν τόλμαν αὐτοῦ), and he took the town (3.498). Finally, the term on a few occasions describes individual acts of heroism, such as those done by the centurion Julianus (6.82) or Faustus Cornelius, the first Roman to cross the battle line (1.149).

For the text we are examining, there is no conclusive evidence for a negative or positive understanding of τόλμα. θαρραλεώτερον in the previous sentence would lead to a positive understanding of the word (as tantamount to courage).

---

29. "Risk taking, rash behavior, and thoughtlessness indeed lead on the Jews, passions which are vigorous in success but quenched in the smallest defeats; but skill and experience belong to us, and the nobility which is at its peak in good fortune and ultimately does not fail in losses" (Ἰουδαίων μὲν οὖν τόλμα καὶ θράσος ἡγεῖται καὶ ἀπόνοια πάθη κατὰ μὲν τὰς εὐπραγίας εὔτονα σβεννύμενα δὲ ἐν ἐλαχίστοις σφάλμασιν ἡμῶν δ᾽ ἀρετὴ καὶ εὐπείθεια καὶ τὸ γενναῖον ὃ κἂν τοῖς ἄλλοις εὐτυχήμασιν ἀκμάζει κἂν τοῖς πταίσμασιν οὐ μέχρι τέλους σφάλλεται).

30. "In short [he did not fight] like a Jew, for those unique qualities of the nation—risk, sudden attack, a unified charge, and not turning back even under blows—were lacking" (καθόλου τε εἰπεῖν οὐκ Ἰουδαϊκῶς· τὰ γὰρ ἴδια τοῦ ἔθνους ὑστέρητο ἅμα ἥ τόλμα καὶ ὁρμὴ καὶ δρόμος ὁμοῦ πάντων καὶ τὸ μηδὲ πταίοντας ἀναστρέφειν).

The context, however, casts a pejorative light on Sicarii activity. The stasis element holds and defiles the temple (μιαίνοντας τὸν ναόν 2.424), and any joint activity of the Sicarii with such reprobates is worthy of censure. Yet it would be incorrect to say that the royalists were defeated by the size and "insolence" of the rebels. So, "bravery" seems to be the connotation, which even those who defile the temple are capable of showing.

Finally, Josephus has the Sicarii join a group, the rebels (στασιάσται), who are "polluting" the sanctuary (τοὺς μιαίνοντας τὸν ναόν 424). This word group in *War* (μιαίνω—21 times; μιαρός—9 times; μίασμα—4 times; ἀμίαντος—1 time) describes ritual or sacred defilement. Pollution comes through such activities as the sacrifice of birds at the synagogue at Caesarea (2.289), or murder and sexual perversion in the city (4.562). More particularly, the temple itself is defiled by the entry of murderers (4.150) and by the killing within it (4.150, 5.10, et passim).

Josephus uses these terms on several occasions to describe the murder of one's own people. They thus cluster around the turmoil in Herod's house. Archelaus states that Alexander's wife was defiled by associating with her husband, who was implicated in a plot to murder his father, Herod (1.500; see also 1.506, 622, 624, 635). In another context, Josephus states that Roman civil war would defile the sacred precincts of the city (2.210). Similarly, Josephus told his fellow Jewish captives at Jotapata that he would not defile his hand by taking his compatriots' lives (3.391). Similarly, Ananus is anxious to spare the temple from defilement, and by that he means that no Jew should kill a fellow Jew within it (4.215).[31] For these same reasons, Titus on several occasions calls John and his followers "most defiled" (μιαρώτατοι, 6.124, 347).

The word group in this connection therefore becomes a means by which Josephus introduces into the narrative the notion of divine judgment. When the besieged Roman soldiers descend from the towers of Herod's former palace, under truce, and are treacherously killed by Eleazar's rebel followers, the citizens in consequence mourn inasmuch as the city, filled with such sacrilege, should expect some form of divine punishment (2:455).[32] Similarly, Simon of Scythopolis, upon realizing the crimes he committed in taking the lives of his fellow Jews, prays that his own life might serve as a fitting penalty for his sacrilege (2.473). Finally, Josephus, in his speech to the rebels, sarcastically states that they have "doubtless kept the holy place undefiled (ἀμίαντον 6.99)." On the contrary, "God himself is exterminating the city, which is full of sacrilege" (μιασμάτων γέμουσαν 6.110).

---

31. "For they were anxious not to defile the temple and that not one of their countrymen fall within it" (σπουδὴ τὸ παρ᾽ αὐτοῖς μὴ μιᾶναι τὸ ἱερὸν μηδέ τινα τῶν ὁμοφύλων ἐν αὐτῷ πεσεῖν).

32. "[Seeing] the city defiled with such sacrilege from which it was reasonable to expect some dreadful punishment" (τὴν δὲ πόλιν τηλικούτῳ μιάσματι πεφυρμένην ἐξ οὗ δαιμόνιόν τι μήνιμα προσδοκᾶν εἰκός).

BOOK CONTEXT

Within the structure of *War* this narrative illustrates the failure of the leading Jewish citizens and priests to control the stasis in Jerusalem. We have already seen how the Sicarii were instrumental in the outbreak of stasis there. Now we see that the Sicarii strengthen the stasis, and the city itself is crippled.

CONCLUSIONS

The Sicarii, who seem to be an identifiable group among the bandits, add their own pivotal strength to the rebel (stasis) contingent holding the temple. The Sicarii are so identified in part by their tactic of carrying daggers in their garments. The Sicarii are thus instrumental in a critical weakening (cf. "sinews") of the city. The Sicarii, by joining the rebels, are associated now with those who defile the temple and place themselves under divine judgment.

THE RISE AND FALL OF MENAHEM (2.433–48)

Josephus continues the narrative of *War* with the rise of the first tyrant among the Jewish rebels, Menahem b. Judas. This character armed himself from Masada and then, accompanied by his compatriots, preceded back to Jerusalem. There he took command of the siege of the palace, where the standoff between the royalists and the Romans on the one side and the rebels on the other continued, and soon captured it after allowing the royalists to go free and after the Roman soldiers had retired to the towers. But upon processing to the temple as a veritable king, Menahem himself was killed, and his compatriots, led by Eleazar b. Yair, went back to Masada, where they remained for the duration of the war. For the original text and translation of this section, see the appendix.

EVIDENCE FOR INCLUDING IN THE STUDY

Josephus does not refer explicitly to the Sicarii as associates of Menahem nor does he refer to them anywhere else in this episode. Yet the incident should be included in this study for two compelling reasons. In the first place, Josephus tells us that Menahem colluded briefly with the rebels at Masada, and these can only be the Sicarii (see above). In the second place, Josephus tells us that Eleazar b. Yair was not only a follower but also a relative of Menahem. After Menahem's death, this Eleazar returned to Masada, where he became the leader of the Sicarii until their death after the end of the war. For these two reasons the connection between Menahem and the Sicarii, though implicit, is clear.

LITERARY CONTEXT

The context continues from the previous section, where Josephus tells how with the addition of the Sicarii to the rebels in the temple area, the city itself was weakened (2.425–32). The rebels prevailed over the leading citizens, chief priests, and those loyal to Rome in the upper city (2.425–26); they burned the chief priest's house, portions of the palace of Agrippa and Bernice, and the public archives (2.426–29); and they captured part of the Antonia. They were unable, however, to take the entire palace, where Ananias in particular took refuge (2.430–32). Then Josephus proceeds to introduce Menahem.

Following this episode and against the hopes of the townspeople, the stasis element pressed the siege of the towers more energetically (2.449–50). The Roman soldiers there agreed to terms (2.450–51), but Eleazar b. Ananias and his followers broke their oath and killed them as they laid down their weapons (2.450–54). Josephus states that the city mourned this turn of events. It was now thought that the causes for war were incurable and that not only would the Romans bring vengeance on them, but God himself also would punish the city because it had become so polluted (455).

The arrival of Menahem serves several purposes in this context. For one thing, he enabled the rebels to capture the rest of the Antonia. But Menahem's activity also illustrates how the city became polluted with blood, and Josephus uses his death to illustrate further the split between the townspeople and the rebels. They both participated in his murder but for different reasons: the townspeople to do away with the stasis, the rebels to prosecute the war with greater freedom. We shall also see that Josephus takes the opportunity to illustrate in Menahem the blind folly of the Sicarii in particular and of stasis in general, for he, their first recognized leader, became the very thing against which they fought. The context might be outlined in the following manner:

I. The stasis gains strength.
   a. The Sicarii strengthen the rebels. The city is weakened. (425–32)
     i. The rebels prevail over the leading citizens, chief priests, and those loyal to Rome in the upper city.
     ii. They burn the chief priest's house, portions of the palace of Agrippa and Bernice, and the public archives.
   b. They capture part of the Antonia but are unable to take the entire palace, where Ananias in particular takes refuge.
II. Menahem illustrates the problem of stasis. (433–48)
   a. He directs the capture of the palace.
   b. He becomes that against which the rebels fight.
   c. He is therefore killed by the rebels.
III. Eleazar and the rebels treacherously press their attack, and the townspeople despair. (449–56)

DESCRIPTION OF SICARII ACTIVITY

Josephus states that Menahem became a "leader of the stasis" in Jerusalem. Indeed, the first thing Josephus emphasizes about Menahem is his rebel ancestry, pointing out that he was the son of Judas of Galilee, who organized a revolt against Rome and became the leader of an illegitimate sect in Judaism.[33] Josephus states that Menahem, like his father, was a teacher (2.445). But Josephus nowhere identifies the slogans or teachings of the son. Therefore, in the absence of any additional information, it is reasonable for the reader to associate Menahem with the qualities of the sect of Judas. In *War* these are the ideas that God alone is master and that the Jews should, therefore, not tolerate any other mortal masters or pay tribute to the Romans. See 2.118 above.

By introducing Menahem this way, Josephus immediately sets up "text-dependent" irony.[34] Previously he referred to Judas simply as a teacher (σοφι-στής 2.118); but now, when introducing his son, Josephus calls Judas an "uncanny teacher" (σοφιστὴς δεινότατος), who taught the Jews not to submit to the Romans after God. The stage for irony is set in part by "uncanny" (δεινός), an extraordinarily ambivalent term in Greek. On the one hand, it can denote something terrible, frightening, or shocking and, on the other, something wonderful, amazing, or ingenious. Josephus strengthens the irony by reminding his readers, when introducing the son, how the father had reproached the Jews for subjecting themselves to the Romans second to God (2.433). The irony then becomes apparent in the behavior of the descendant of this "uncanny teacher." He became the very thing his father hated—an insufferable tyrant (ἀφόρητος ἦν τύραννος 2.442).

Josephus states that Menahem armed himself at Masada, where he gained allies. Daniel Schwartz points out that he did not break into Masada, but only into the armory.[35] Josephus does not state how the Sicarii at Masada received Menahem, but we ought to presume that they welcomed him not only because he successfully armed himself from there but also because he returned with his "townsmen" and with "other bandits." That is, he gained allies at Masada.

Josephus tells that Menahem returned "just like a king" (οἷα δὴ βασιλεύς) to Jerusalem and became a leader of the stasis (434). Richard Horsley and John Hanson propose that this was a "climactic messianic episode" for the Sicarii in their long struggle against Rome.[36] Hengel had also identified this incident as a clear example of the messianic ambitions of the "Zealots."[37] However, with the possible exceptions of the term "king" (βασιλεύς) and the manner in which he describes how Menahem went to the temple in royal garb to pray (444), Josephus provides nothing in the context to lead the reader to understand Menahem as a messi-

---

33. See above under "Rise and Activity of Judas in 6 B.C.E."

34. Here I follow Mason's classification. For his study on irony in Josephus, see above in chapter 2, under "Literary Background."

35. Daniel R. Schwartz, "Once Again: Who Captured Masada? On Doublets, Reading against the Grain, and What Josephus Actually Wrote," *Scripta Classica Israelica* 24 (2005): 79.

36. Richard Horsley and John Hanson, *Bandits, Prophets, and Messiahs* (San Francisco: Harper & Row, 1985), 118–19. See also Horsley, "Menahem in Jerusalem: A Brief Messianic Episode among the Sicarii—Not 'Zealot Messianism,'" *NT* 27 (1985): 334–48.

37. Hengel, *Zealots*, 293–97.

anic pretender. It is plausible that this indeed may have been Menahem's intent, but Josephus's report necessitates no such conclusion. Josephus rather uses the term in its usual sense for earthly kings such as Herod or Agrippa, and barring any other indication from Josephus, this is the natural understanding here also. Such an understanding seems all the more likely in view of Josephus's controlling theme and literary intent. Menahem exemplifies growing stasis and tyranny at Jerusalem, and this, along with the manner in which Josephus introduces Menahem, stressing the irony of his ancestry, indicates that Josephus's focus has little to do with inappropriate messianic expectations. He, rather, wants to showcase the blindness of the rebels.

The narrative goes on to state that Menahem granted a truce to the besieged Jews but not to the Romans (2.437–38). The "bandits," however, treacherously killed Ananias, the high priest, and his brother Ezechias (2.441). Josephus does not identify these bandits, but the context would identify them as the followers of Menahem, some of whom he brought from Masada. At the least this would make the Sicarii from Masada party to the deaths of these Jewish leaders.

The death of the high priest and the reduction of the fortified places made the arrogance of Menahem swell to the point of violence, and he became an "insufferable tyrant" (2.442), as we have seen. Thereupon, the followers of Eleazar b. Ananias planned to kill Menahem (2.443). Their reasoning: "Why sacrifice our liberty to him after winning it from the Romans? Even if he were to abstain from violence, he comes from a lower class than we. Any leader would be better than he, if we must have a leader." Therefore, when Menahem went to the temple in pompous fashion and in royal attire, attended by armed fanatics (τοὺς ζηλωτὰς ἐνόπλους ἐφελκόμενος), Eleazar's followers killed him (2.443–48).

As noted above, the noun ζηλωταί appears here for the first time in *War*, and there has been some debate whether the term should be understood as a reference to the "fanatical followers" of Menahem or to the members of an identifiable party of Zealots. Outside of Josephus the former meaning is well attested in the literary tradition, where the word is often found with a qualifying genitive, and so Thackeray translates the phrase "suite of armed fanatics."[38] Morton Smith agrees with this translation, stating that the qualifying genitive is to be understood from the context (τοὺς ζηλωτὰς αὐτοῦ).[39] Alternatively, Hengel notes that in all but two of its fifty-five occurrences in *War*, the noun is used in its absolute sense, with no qualifying genitive, as the name of a party.[40] This, he insists, is the unambiguous meaning of the word for its third occurrence at 2.651, where

---

38. Josephus, *War* 2.444 (Thackeray, LCL) (Cambridge, MA, and London: Harvard University Press, 1929). See also Hans Drexler, "Untersuchungen zu Josephus und zur Geschichte des jüdischen Aufstandes," *Klio* 19 (1925): 286; and Gunther Baumbach, "Zeloten und Sikarier," *TLZ* 90 (1965): 733.

39. Smith, "Zealots and Sicarii," 7.

40. The two exceptions are at 5.314 and 6.59, where the term describes the Roman soldiers who are "emulators of bravery" (ζηλωταὶ τῆς ἀνδρείας).

Josephus draws attention to the noun to indicate the existence of an identifiable group, and next at 4.160, where Josephus further defines the characteristics of this self-identified group. Therefore, Hengel maintains not only that this is the natural understanding of the noun for those places in *War* that follow these passages but also that the first two occurrences of the noun, the passage in question and 2.564, do not deviate from Josephus's established usage.[41] As everywhere else in *War*, τοὺς ζηλωτάς here refers to an identifiable party of Zealots.

The question is this: are we to understand from this passage that Menahem was supported by the Zealots in his royal ambitions? If so, then this passage would supply evidence of the Sicarii and Zealots working together at some level during this early stage of the revolt. The problem with such an interpretation is that at this point in the narrative Josephus has given no indication that a party known as Zealots exists. It is not until the noun's third and fourth occurrences, at 2.651 and 4.160 that Josephus alters his Roman readers' natural incilnation, based on the noun's usage in the literary tradition, to interpret ζηλωταί as "admirers" or "fantical followers" so that when his readers see the word thereafter in the narrative, they will be alert to a party of Zealots. Therefore, in the absence of any such clarification at this point in the narrative, "fanatical followers" is the preferred translation. The result is that we have no certain evidence of Sicarii and Zealots banding together at this early stage of the revolt.

The citizens not attached to Eleazar also joined the attack, thinking that with the death of Menahem the stasis would also be crushed. At this point, Josephus introduces Eleazar b. Yair, Menahem's relative in the narrative. He along with a few others escaped to Masada after Menahem's death (2.447).

About the Sicarii, then, the text indicates that their first named leader was Menahem. Ironically, this leader exemplified that very thing the Sicarii opposed—tyranny. In this manner Josephus identifies not only the problems of stasis but also the blindness of the Sicarii in particular as they carry out their agenda of fighting against all who support Rome. Moreover, by their association with Menahem, they too were responsible for the death of the high priest Ananias. Finally, after the death of Menahem, the Sicarii gain a new leader: Eleazar, the relative of Menahem.

WORD STUDIES

Several important words used to describe Menahem and his followers have been addressed above. Among these are stasis, king, and uncanny teacher (στάσις, βασιλεύς, σοφιστὴς δεινότατος). To these Josephus adds a new note by calling Menahem a "tyrant." Beginning with Archilochus among the archaic Greek

---

41. Hengel, *Zealots*, 389f. At 2.564 Josephus states that those at Jerusalem did not trust Eleazar b. Simon because they saw that he was acting like a tryant, and his fantical followers were acting as his bodyguard (αὐτόν τε τυραννικὸν ὁρῶντες καὶ τοὺς ὑπ' αὐτῷ ζηλωτὰς δορυφόρων ἔθεσι χρωμένους).

authors, τύρραvoς did not at first acquire the negative connotations attributed to it by Plato and Aristotle. These latter, however, saw this degeneration of monarchy as the worst form of government.[42] According to Plato, tyrants kill all the most noble of the citizens because these are the greatest threats to their power. They alternatively elevate the base citizens and slaves for their support. Tyrants are hated by all and therefore must surround themselves with bodyguards. They give themselves over entirely to base desires (*Republic* 567–70). Among Roman authors, Livy devoted attention to the activities of tyrants, but Sallust's description of Catiline stands out (*Bell. Cat.* 5.4–6). Lechery, public murder, the need for money and subsequent plunder, the lust for power; these descriptors of tyranny also overlap with banditry, to which the word is often connected.[43]

Only a few years before Josephus authored *War*, Seneca addressed the issue in *De Clementia*, written for Nero at the beginning of his reign. After acknowledging the young emperor's power to liberate or enslave and to judge life and death over all people, Seneca urged Nero to use his power for good as a king (*rex*) and not for bad as a tyrant, who cruelly kills for pleasure and is therefore hated by all. The tyrant, therefore, "cannot trust his guards, his relatives, or anyone else—indeed, he dehumanizes his guards and soldiers by using them as instruments of torture."[44] These issues would undoubtedly have still been fresh in the memories of Josephus's readers, who lived through a period of civil war in the year of the four emperors.

Turning to Josephus, we see how he makes frequent use of this well-known pejorative term for people such as Trypho (1.49), Zeno (1.60), Hyrcanus (1.202), or Marion (1.238). The Jews came before Caesar and accused the dead Herod of having been a tyrant (2.84) and added that Archelaus was just the son of a tyrant (2.88). Josephus himself was accused by his enemies of being a tyrant (2.266). However, after Menahem, the figures that loom large as tyrants almost exclusively for the balance of *War* are Simon b. Gioras and John of Gischala. After the pivotal speeches of Ananus and Jesus, Josephus applies the term only three times to any other person—once to Eleazar (5.5) and twice in the same context to Vitellius (4.495, 496). Josephus, however, also makes this family of words, tyrant and tyranny, a controlling theme of *War*. To this matter we now turn.

BOOK CONTEXT

The connection between the Sicarii and stasis continues in this narrative. Menahem becomes a leader of the stasis after it breaks out at Caesarea and spreads to Jerusalem. To this now we need to add "tyrant" (τύραννoς) as another control-

---

42. Plato *Republic* 565–69; Aristotle *Politics* 1279b. Similarly, Polybius 6.4.8.

43. Matthew B. Roller, *Constructing Autocracy: Aristocrats and Emperors in Julio-Claudian Rome* (Princeton and Oxford: Princeton University Press: 2001), 75.

44. Ibid., 240–42.

ling theme, for this word also is emphasized in a number of places in the proem. There Josephus states:

> Stasis at home destroyed it (the capitol) and the Judean tyrants drew the unwilling Roman hands and fire against the temple. (1.10)
>
> αὐτὴν στάσις οἰκεία καθεῖλεν καὶ τὰς Ῥωμαίων χεῖρας ἀκούσας καὶ τὸ πῦρ ἐπὶ τὸν ναὸν εἵλκυσαν οἱ Ἰουδαίων τύραννοι.

Josephus accordingly begs indulgence for censuring the tyrants and their banditry (1.14). Moreover, in setting forth the plan of his work, Josephus states that he will relate how the tyrants rose in Vespasian's absence (1.24), how they brutally treated their own countrymen (1.22), and how they were captured (1.28). We conclude by his near exclusive use of this term for John and Simon that he primarily had these characters in mind when writing the proem.

Josephus begins to unwrap this theme in connection with the abusive reign of Albinus, who by his plunder and receiving of ransoms and bribes encouraged the emergence of bandit gangs with tyrant leaders (2.275). Josephus states that as a result of Albinus's behavior, tyranny spread everywhere and that from this time the "seeds of city's impending capture" (τὰ σπέρματα τῆς μελλούσης ἁλώσεως) were sown (2.276). The narrative in question illustrates how the seed sprouted in Menahem, the first identifiable tyrant among the Jewish rebels in *War*.

The problem of tyranny takes center stage later in the pivotal speech of Ananus. There he chastised the Jews for encouraging the tyrants by their inactivity and silence (4.166). He charged that the tyrants had made the temple a "fortified place of tyranny" (ἐπιτετειχισμένην τυραννίδα 4.172). In a telling comment later in the speech, Josephus had Ananus state:

> [178] If we will not endure the masters of the world, shall we put up with the tyrants of our own people? [179] Yet our yielding to foreigners someone might attribute to fate once it has beaten us, but to give in to evil men of one's own country is a freely chosen characteristic of low-minded people. (4:178–79)
>
> εἶτα τοὺς τῆς οἰκουμένης δεσπότας μὴ φέροντες τῶν ὁμοφύλων τυράννων ἀνεξόμεθα; [179] καίτοι τὸ μὲν τοῖς ἔξωθεν ὑπακούειν ἀνενέγκαι τις ἂν εἰς τὴν ἅπαξ ἡττήσασαν τύχην, τὸ δὲ τοῖς οἰκείοις εἴκειν πονηροῖς ἀγεννῶν ἐστι καὶ προαιρουμένων.

Similarly, Josephus presents Jesus in opposition to the tyrants, and it was against them that Jesus tried to enlist the Idumeans' help (4.258).

But John of Gischala had a "terrible desire for tyranny" (δεινὸν ἔρωτα τυραννίδος), and he became a traitor to Ananus (4.208). Both Ananus and Jesus were killed by the rebels (4.314–18). At this point Josephus editorialized that the downfall of the Jewish state began with their deaths (4.318). Indeed, the rebel leaders who quickly emerged, Simon and John, are frequently and consistently labeled "tyrants." Josephus thus summarizes at 4.397 that Jerusalem was buffeted by the three greatest evils: warfare, tyranny, and stasis.[45] In this way he reminds the reader of his controlling themes.

In this light, Menahem presages the tyranny that will dominate books 5 and 6, which Josephus anticipated in the prologue (1.10) as the cause of "unwilling" Roman intervention. Menahem exemplifies one of the primary causes for the downfall of the Jewish state.

CONCLUSIONS

Josephus would have the reader understand that Menahem and his followers exemplified that tyranny and stasis that would bring about the ruin of the Jewish state. This much is clear from the themes and structure of *War*. Both themes, stasis and tyranny, come to focus on this first named leader of the Sicarii. These terms, moreover, with their long-established and interconnected usage in Greco-Roman literature, remove Menahem and his followers from any legitimate claim to leadership.

In particular, the passage makes this point through the ironic presentation of Menahem's behavior. For the distinctive goal of both Judas and the Sicarii is that allegiance be paid to no one but God.[46] The irony is that the descendant of Judas and the first leader of the Sicarii becomes nothing more than a tyrant himself. Josephus thus not so subtly draws attention to the blindness of the rebels in general and the Sicarii, Menahem's compatriots from Masada, in particular. In fighting against those Jews who submitted to the Romans, they became the very things they vehemently opposed. We note here also how the narrative would resonate with a Hellenistic audience conversant with tragic themes. An otherwise admirable character trait, that one acknowledges the authority of God over all, is taken to excess and thus becomes much like the tragic flaws of many characters in Greek theater. This sets the stage for Eleazar's recognition speech at Masada, wherein he finally comes to acknowledge the monstrous crimes the Sicarii have committed against their own people.

The narrative, moreover, showcases how the Sicarii employed tactics that were inherently self-destructive. The self-destructive tendencies of stasis, which will be written large as it grows in Jerusalem, are portrayed early with Menahem's murder and portend how the Sicarii will finally and literally self-destruct at Masada. These issues will be explored in the next chapter.

---

45. ἡ πόλις τρισὶ τοῖς μεγίστοις κακοῖς ἐχειμάζετο πολέμῳ καὶ τυραννίδι καὶ στάσει.

46. See 2.118 above; also 7.323, where Eleazar opens his first speech at Masada with these words: "Good men, long ago we resolved to serve neither the Romans nor any other man but God, for He alone is the true and righteous master of men" (πάλαι διεγνωκότας ἡμᾶς ἄνδρες ἀγαθοί μήτε Ῥωμαίοις μήτ' ἄλλῳ τινὶ δουλεύειν ἢ θεῷ μόνος γὰρ οὗτος ἀληθής ἐστι καὶ δίκαιος ἀνθρώπων δεσπότης).

JOINT ACTIVITY WITH SIMON BEN GIORAS—PART 1 (2.652–54)

At the close of book 2 Josephus briefly spotlights the activity of Simon b. Gioras. Having just noted how he himself, as a general sent to make war preparations in Galilee, had mastered his opponents there and how Ananus was in charge of preparations at Jerusalem, Josephus's brief notice of Simon serves as an ominous portent. He writes:

[652] Now throughout the toparchy of Acrabetene, Simon b. Gioras got together many of those aiming at revolution and turned to robbery. Not only did he tear the houses of wealthy individuals to pieces, but also tormented their bodies and already back then was obviously beginning to act the tyrant. [653] And when an armed host was sent against him by Ananus and the rulers, he and those he had with him fled to the bandits at Masada and remaining there until Ananus and his other enemies were done away with, he joined them in plundering Idumea. [654] And so because of the amount of murders and the unending plunder, the rulers of that people raised an army and garrisoned the villages. Such was the state of affairs also throughout Idumea.

[652] κατὰ δὲ τὴν Ἀκραβετηνὴν τοπαρχίαν ὁ Γιώρα Σίμων πολλοὺς τῶν νεωτεριζόντων συστησάμενος ἐφ᾽ ἁρπαγὰς ἐτράπετο καὶ οὐ μόνον τὰς οἰκίας ἐσπάρασσεν τῶν πλουσίων, ἀλλὰ καὶ τὰ σώματα κατηκίζετο, δῆλός τε ἦν ἤδη πόρρωθεν ἀρχόμενος τυραννεῖν. [653] πεμφθείσης δ᾽ ἐπ᾽ αὐτὸν ὑπ᾽ Ἀνάνου καὶ τῶν ἀρχόντων στρατιᾶς, πρὸς τοὺς ἐν Μασάδα λῃστὰς μεθ᾽ ὧν εἶχεν κατέφυγεν, κἀκεῖ μέχρι τῆς Ἀνάνου καὶ τῆς τῶν ἄλλων ἐχθρῶν ἀναιρέσεως μένων συνελῄζετο τὴν Ἰδουμαίαν, [654] ὥστε τοὺς ἄρχοντας τοῦ ἔθνους διὰ τὸ πλῆθος τῶν φονευομένων καὶ τὰς συνεχεῖς ἁρπαγὰς στρατιὰν ἀθροίσαντας ἐμφρούρους τὰς κώμας ἔχειν. καὶ τὰ μὲν κατὰ τὴν Ἰδουμαίαν ἐν τούτοις ἦν.

EVIDENCE FOR INCLUDING IN THE STUDY

Once more we include a narrative wherein the Sicarii are not mentioned by name because the rebels at Masada, who welcome Simon, can only be the Sicarii. See above under "Capture of Masada."

LITERARY CONTEXT

Josephus had earlier been sent to Galilee to make preparations for war (2.569). There he successfully overcame opposition from John of Gischala (2.585ff.) as well as at Tarichaeae (2.595ff.) and Tiberias (2.608ff.). Josephus concludes the long narrative of these events with a summary statement (2.647):

So all the disturbances throughout Galilee were checked, and having stopped civil strife, they turned to making preparations against the Romans.

τὰ μὲν οὖν κατὰ Γαλιλαίαν ἐπέπαυτο κινήματα καὶ τῶν ἐμφυλίων παυσάμενοι θορύβων ἐπὶ τὰς πρὸς Ῥωμαίους ἐτράποντο παρασκευάς.

By contrast, Ananus's direction of affairs at Jerusalem merited a different kind of assessment. Those preparations were somewhat disordered, were lamented by the moderates, and took place under ill omens. All this, in Josephus's words, made Jerusalem appear to be doomed (2.648–50). Josephus observes, perhaps charitably, that Ananus intended to gradually abandon such preparations and turn the insurrectionists (στασιαστάς) and the Zealots to that which was more beneficial (2.651). Josephus indicates, however, that Ananus would be overcome by their violence (2.651).

Book 2 then closes with the narrative in question. By positioning this brief notice of Simon immediately after indicating how Ananus would fall to violence, the narrative introduces the opposition between the (future) tyrant Simon and Ananus, the legitimate Jewish leader. Josephus adds that Simon remained at Masada until the death of Ananus and his other opponents. Thus, the narrative foreshadows the violence that would soon overrun Jerusalem at the hands of the tyrants. Josephus picks up this narrative about Simon directly at 4.503 (see below). The context might thus be outlined:

    I.   Josephus brings civil strife to heel in Galilee. (569–646)
    II.   Ananus takes charge of preparations in Jerusalem. (647–51)
    III.   Simon portends the rise of tyranny. (652–54)

DESCRIPTION OF SICARII ACTIVITY

The Sicarii are denoted by the more general term "bandits." They receive Simon at Masada and go on raids with him to the point that the Idumeans are compelled to garrison their towns for protection. In this way they support someone who "already back then was obviously beginning to act the tyrant."

WORD STUDIES

Josephus employs a few words here that we have seen him attach to the Sicarii before. Josephus designates the Sicarii at Masada by the more general term "bandits" (λῃσταί) and he states that Simon, already at the time when he was welcomed at Masada, was beginning to act the tyrant (τυραννεῖν). For Josephus's use of these words, see above under "Rise during the Time of Felix" and "Rise and Fall of Menahem." We do note, however, that although Josephus had earlier associated the Sicarii with the high-profile assassination of Jonathan, he now describes the activities of the Sicarii with Simon as mere murder and plundering (φονευομένων καὶ τὰς συνεχεῖς ἁρπαγάς).

BOOK CONTEXT

This passage, which relates the rising power of Simon, is interrupted by Josephus's narrative and not resumed until 4:503–8. In between Josephus relates the battles in Galilee and its reduction, the deaths of Ananus and Jesus, the spreading stasis and tyranny in Jerusalem, and Vespasian's subsequent march there. The narrative then serves to keep the reader's eye on the rising tyranny that would overrun Jerusalem.

CONCLUSIONS

Josephus again connects Sicarii activity with the rise of tyrants. Their blindness, specified in their support of Menahem, continues in their support of Simon. Their activity, however, fails to rise above mere robbery and murder. The Sicarii here are no longer characterized by the one trait that Josephus uniquely attaches to them when explaining the origin of their name—the use of hidden daggers. Neither is there any notice in the narrative of any ideological terminology or concerns. That is, once they leave Jerusalem at the death of Menahem, for all intents and purposes within the narrative of *War*, the Sicarii recede into the political background of the nameless hordes of bandits infesting Judea. This point will be emphasized again in the next section.

THEY RAID ENGADDI (4.398–405)

In this passage Josephus tells us about one particular raid of the Sicarii from Masada—that upon Engaddi at Passover. He writes:

[398] Now a fourth evil set in motion for the dissolution of our people. [399] There was a very strong fortress built by kings of old not far from Jerusalem, a place prepared both for hiding possessions and for their own protection in the tides of war. It was called Masada. [400] The so-called Sicarii had captured it but up to this time did nothing more than make raids in the surrounding areas to get supplies. [401] For because they were afraid, they held back from wide-scale robbery. But when they learned that the Roman army was not moving and that the Jews in Jerusalem were divided by their own stasis and tyranny, they set upon greater crimes. [402] During the feast of Passover—when the Jews celebrate the saving deeds at that time when they put aside slavery to the Egyptians and came to their ancestral land—at night they slipped by those in the way and overran a small town called Engaddi. [403] They scattered and drove out of town those who were able to defend it before they could grab their weapons and gather together, but they killed those less able to flee, over 700 women and children. [404] Then, after plundering the homes and gathering the ripest of the crops, they took them back to Masada. [405] They plundered all the villages around the fortress and laid waste the entire area while many from every side were daily corrupted along with them.

[398] τέταρτον δὲ ἄλλο κακὸν ἐκινεῖτο πρὸς τὴν τοῦ ἔθνους κατάλυσιν. [399] φρούριον ἦν οὐ πόρρω Ἱεροσολύμων καρτερώτατον, ὑπὸ τῶν ἀρχαίων βασιλέων εἴς τε ὑπέκθεσιν κτήσεως ἐν πολέμου ῥοπαῖς καὶ σωμάτων

ἀσφάλειαν κατεσκευασμένον, ὃ ἐκαλεῖτο Μασάδα. [400] τοῦτο κατειληφότες οἱ προσαγορευόμενοι σικάριοι τέως μὲν τὰς πλησίον χώρας κατέτρεχον οὐδὲν πλέον τῶν ἐπιτηδείων ποριζόμενοι· [401] δέει γὰρ ἀνεστέλλοντο τῆς πλείονος ἁρπαγῆς· ὡς [δὲ] τὴν Ῥωμαίων στρατιὰν ἠρεμοῦσαν, στάσει δὲ καὶ τυραννίδι ἰδίᾳ τοὺς ἐν Ἱεροσολύμοις Ἰουδαίους ἐπύθοντο διῃρημένους, ἁδροτέρων ἥπτοντο τολμημάτων. [402] καὶ κατὰ τὴν ἑορτὴν τῶν ἀζύμων, ἣν ἄγουσιν Ἰουδαῖοι σωτήρια ἐξ οὗ τῆς ὑπ᾽ Αἰγυπτίοις δουλείας ἀνεθέντες εἰς τὴν πάτριον γῆν κατῆλθον, νύκτωρ τοὺς ἐμποδὼν ὄντας διαλαθόντες πολίχνην τινὰ κατατρέχουσιν καλουμένην Ἐνγαδδί, [403] ἐν ᾗ τὸ μὲν ἀμύνεσθαι δυνάμενον πρὶν ὅπλων ἅψασθαι καὶ συνελθεῖν, φθάσαντες ἐσκέδασαν καὶ τῆς πόλεως ἐξέβαλον, τὸ δὲ φυγεῖν ἧττον, ὅν γύναιά τε καὶ παῖδας, ὑπὲρ ἑπτακοσίους ἀναιροῦσιν. [404] ἔπειτα τούς τε οἴκους ἐξεσκευασμένοι καὶ τῶν καρπῶν τοὺς ἀκμαιοτάτους ἁρπάσαντες ἀνήνεγκαν εἰς τὴν Μασάδαν. [405] καὶ οἱ μὲν ἐλήιζοντο πάσας τὰς περὶ τὸ φρούριον κώμας καὶ τὴν χώραν ἐπόρθουν ἅπασαν, προσδιαφθειρομένων αὐτοῖς καθ᾽ ἡμέραν ἑκασταχόθεν οὐκ ὀλίγων·

LITERARY CONTEXT

The high priest Ananus, whom Josephus calls a man of "highest integrity" (δικαιότατος), and who, in Josephus's words, would have led the Jews either to come quickly to terms or to present a skilled defense, has been killed along with Jesus. Josephus pointedly states that the Zealots and Idumeans then tortured and butchered the people in Israel as if they were "unclean animals." Twelve thousand young nobles died (4.326–33).

Josephus also claims that the Zealots held mock trials. One defendant in particular, Zacharias by name, a wealthy man who hated evil and loved liberty, was acquitted by seventy jurors. Josephus states that the jurors did not understand their expected part in the play (ἐπὶ σκηνῆς σχῆμα), and so two Zealots slew Zacharias while the rest drove out the jurors with swords to set an example to the rest of the city (4.334–44).

The Idumeans, who had come earlier to defend Jerusalem against the Romans, took offense at these proceedings, especially after meeting with a Zealot informant (4.345–52). Releasing their prisoners, who went over to Simon, the Idumeans left (4.353). This, however, only spurred the Zealots on to commit greater atrocities (4.354–57).

In describing these events, Josephus at several points reminds his readers that God himself was punishing the Jews for their crimes. In the first instance, he tells how the Zealots killed Gurion and Niger, the latter in particular having pronounced a curse that the Jews would turn on one another. Josephus states that God ratified this curse in a "most righteous way in that as they rebelled, they were soon about to taste of each other's madness" (4.362–65).[47] Vespasian, who delayed

---

47. ἃ δὴ πάντα κατὰ τῶν ἀσεβῶν ἐκύρωσεν ὁ θεός καὶ τὸ δικαιότατον ὅτι γεύσασθαι τῆς ἀλλήλων ἀπονοίας ἔμελλον οὐκ εἰς μακρὰν στασιάσαντες.

his attack, expressed nearly the same ideas to his troops: God is punishing the Jews by turning them against one another in the worst of calamities—stasis (4.366–76). Many wealthy people fled from the Zealots to the Romans. Those of lesser means, however, unable to produce the bribe, were slaughtered (4.377–80). Josephus then for a third time emphasizes divine retribution, stating that such barbarity fulfilled an ancient prophecy that the temple would be destroyed by stasis and polluted by murder carried out by its own people (381–88).

After telling how John aspired to power so that a split formed among the Zealots (389–96), Josephus summarizes:

> The city was buffeted by the three greatest evils—warfare, tyranny, and stasis. Of these, warfare seemed milder to the citizens. (4.397)

> ἐπεὶ δὲ ἡ πόλις τρισὶ τοῖς μεγίστοις κακοῖς ἐχειμάζετο, πολέμῳ καὶ τυραννίδι καὶ στάσει, κατὰ σύγκρισιν μετριώτερον ἦν τοῖς δημοτικοῖς ὁ πόλεμος.

In fact, many took refuge with the Romans. This statement leads directly into the passage in question, after which Josephus states that ruin spread throughout the countryside (4.406–9). At the pleading of those who had deserted from Jerusalem, Vespasian became active again (4.410–12).

Josephus introduces the narrative by drawing attention to a "fourth evil." This connects the narrative directly to the preceding context, where the previous three evils are clearly labeled—warfare, tyranny, and stasis. The fourth evil has no such label, but its nature is made clear by the summary statements of Josephus that follow the narrative, beginning at 4.406. There we see that the activity of the Sicarii at Masada illustrated how "banditry, formerly quiet, set in motion throughout the other districts of Judea." Josephus connects this spreading evil to the stasis in the capital at 407.

> At any rate, because of the stasis and political unrest in the mother city, wicked men throughout the countryside among those who were plundering had no fear of punishment.

> διὰ γοῦν τὴν ἐν τῇ μητροπόλει στάσιν καὶ ταραχὴν ἄδειαν ἔσχον οἱ κατὰ τὴν χώραν πονηροὶ τῶν ἁρπαγῶν.

Josephus likens this spreading evil to a disease (4.406), a metaphor he uses for internal disorder and unrest.[48] He thus concludes the summary:

---

48. See above under "Rise during the Time of Felix." Note especially the similar situation and terminology at 2.264, where Josephus applies the metaphor to the activity of Judean imposters and bandits, who go throughout the country to murder and pillage especially those Jews who submit to Rome. "Just as in a sick body, another part became inflamed again. For the imposters and bandits gathered together and were urging many to revolt and encouraged them

And there was no part of Judea that was not destroyed along with the capital, which set the example. (409)

οὐδὲν δὲ μέρος ἦν τῆς Ἰουδαίας ὃ μὴ τῇ προανεχούσῃ πόλει συναπώλλυτο.

The fourth evil, therefore, is the spreading activity of bandit gangs in general, and the narrative, the activity of the Sicarii from Masada, thus serves as an example of this spreading disease. The context may be outlined in the following manner:

I. Jerusalem is buffeted by evils (subsequent to the deaths of Ananus and Jesus).
    a. Prominent citizens are killed. (334–61)
       i. Mock trial of Zacharias.
       ii. The Idumeans leave.
       iii. Gurion and Niger are killed.
    b. Stasis as divine punishment among the rebels. (362–96)
       i. God honors Niger's curse.
       ii. Vespasian delays his attack in view of the stasis. "God is punishing the rebels."
       iii. Zealot barbarity fulfills ancient prophecy about stasis and murder.
    c. Summary: the ship of state buffeted by stasis, tyranny, warfare. (397)
II. A fourth evil: banditry spreads throughout the countryside. (398–409)
    a. The Sicarii raid Engaddi.
    b. This disease spreads from Jerusalem.
III. Vespasian becomes active against the stasis. (410–12)

Description of Sicarii Activity

Josephus states that the Sicarii, who had taken Masada and had previously conducted raids for supplies only, now embarked upon "more violent crimes" (ἁδροτέρων ἥπτοντο τολμημάτων) when they learned that the Roman army was inactive and Jerusalem was divided in stasis and tyranny. And so they made a raid on Engaddi during Passover, driving out those who could resist and killing over 700 women and children who could not.

Josephus nowhere specifies why the Sicarii chose this particular time, place, and method for the attack. He has already indicated that the Sicarii arose as a type of bandit gang (see above under 2.254f.). Here he presents their activity as an example of the banditry that spread throughout the Judean countryside (4.406). One might suggest, therefore, that no clarification is needed for their motivation. They are doing what bandit gangs do—plundering and killing for their own profit.

---

for freedom, placing a death sentence on those who were obedient to the Roman hegemony and saying that those who preferred to be willing slaves should be deprived of their desire, to the point of violence" (ὥσπερ ἐν νοσοῦντι σώματι πάλιν ἕτερον μέρος ἐφλέγμαινεν οἱ γὰρ γόητες καὶ λῃστρικοὶ συναχθέντες πολλοὺς εἰς ἀπόστασιν ἐνῆγον καὶ πρὸς ἐλευθερίαν παρεκρότουν θάνατον ἐπιτιμῶντες τοῖς πειθαρχοῦσιν τῇ Ῥωμαίων ἡγεμονίᾳ καὶ πρὸς βίαν ἀφαιρήσεσθαι λέγοντες τοὺς ἑκουσίως δουλεύειν προαιρουμένους).

But Josephus also has connected the Sicarii to the person of Menahem, and we might therefore also legitimately infer other reasons for the time, place, and method of attack. Josephus associated Menahem with the teaching of Judas that Jews should claim only God as master. Menahem himself fought the Romans, the royalists, and other citizens who favored peace with Rome. Presumably, the Sicarii who followed Menahem held the same views. We might suspect that some of these ideas also furnished motivation for the attack. Inasmuch as Engaddi served as a location for a Roman garrison, it may have been viewed by the Sicarii as a symbol of Roman support.[49] As they did in Jerusalem, so also at Engaddi they are attacking those who favor peace with Rome.

Passover also may furnish a clue to the motive. Josephus reminds his readers that this feast commemorated Jewish deliverance, which the Jews celebrated from the time they put away their slavery under the Egyptians and came to their homeland (4.402). From this bit of information we may conjecture that the Sicarii conducted the raid on a Roman outpost at Passover as a blow against foreign enslavement, a reenactment in the minds of the Sicarii of the original acts of divine judgment against the Egyptians.

In this way, Josephus sets up another piece of text-dependent (and also for Josephus's Jewish readers, audience-dependent) irony. On a day when Jews celebrated salvation and freedom from slavery in their homeland, they turned on one another. The irony becomes all the sharper if we infer that the Sicarii attacked Engaddi because its Jewish inhabitants favored peace with Rome. Once again, in fighting against those Jews who support "enslavement" to a foreign oppressor, the Sicarii themselves become far worse oppressors. Josephus concludes the narrative by saying that the Sicarii laid waste the whole district with similar raids.

WORD STUDIES

The words by which Josephus describes the Sicarii and their activity we have already encountered above. We note stasis, tyranny, and sickness (στάσει, τυραννίδι, συνενόσει 4.401, 406). To these Josephus adds "inflame" (φλεγμαίνω), a rare word in *War*. The verb occurs only four times and the noun (φλεγμονή) twice. The words generally mean "to swell." When connected as it is in the context to sickness (συνενόσει), "inflammation" is undoubtedly the meaning, a metaphor for the spread of stasis and civil unrest from the capital.

BOOK CONTEXT

The text serves to highlight two of Josephus's controlling themes: stasis and tyranny. These are brought to the reader's attention at 4.397. More particularly, Josephus states at 4.318 that the downfall of the Jewish state began with the deaths of

---

49. See S. Appelbaum, "The Zealots: The Case for Revaluation," *JRS* 61 (1971): 165.

Ananus and Jesus. The text is part of the narrative that immediately illustrates that fate.

CONCLUSIONS

The legitimate rulers in Jerusalem, Ananus and Jesus, are dead. Stasis now spreads unabated throughout the country. The Sicarii are emblematic of the spread of this disease. Second, we see here once again evidence that Josephus uses the term *sicarii* more broadly, for these Sicarii of the narrative, at least in regard to their tactics, are hardly distinguishable from a more general "bandit" gang. Although Josephus does not make the point, we may observe that the Sicarii are no longer confining themselves to the use of the dagger. Indeed, we might legitimately question whether daggers are at all appropriate weapons for the raid on Engaddi and for laying waste the entire district. Third, Josephus here also reminds his readers of the motivation of the Sicarii, but more subtly this time. The point comes by way of irony (audience- and text-dependent) in having the Sicarii at Passover attack Jews who inhabit a Roman outpost. Thus, Josephus presents again the self-destructive nature of the Sicarii's values and activities.

JOINT ACTIVITY WITH SIMON BEN GIORAS—PART 2 (4.503-8)

In some respects, this episode repeats that at 2.652-54, where Josephus has already indicated how the "bandits" at Masada welcomed Simon and accompanied him on raids. In its context, the narrative there served as a portent of the tyranny that would overrun Jerusalem. After a lengthy interruption wherein Josephus recounts the war in Galilee, the deaths of Ananus and Jesus, and the spreading stasis and tyranny in Jerusalem, here Josephus picks up this thread ultimately to bring Simon to Jerusalem. In doing so, he also reminds the reader of stasis in Rome. He writes:

> [503] Now another battle rose against the people of Jerusalem. There was a son of Gioras, Simon, by birth from Gerasa, a young man less crafty than John, who had already captured the city. But Simon stood out in bodily strength and daring spirit. [504] Therefore when he was banished by Ananus the high priest from the toparchy of Acrabetene, which he once held, he came to the bandits who had captured Masada. [505] At first they were suspicious of him. So they allowed him to come with the women he brought to the lower part of the fortress while they themselves inhabited the upper part. [506] But later due to his familiar disposition and because he seemed trustworthy, he joined them in their plundering activity, going out with them and ravaging the area around Masada. [507] But even though he encouraged them, he was unable to persuade them to greater enterprises. For since they were accustomed to the fortress, [508] they were afraid to go far from their lair, as it were. But showing the qualities of a tyrant and aiming for great enterprises, he left for the hill country when he heard about the death

of Ananus, and gathered together wicked men from everywhere by proclaiming freedom to slaves and a reward to the free.

[503] ἐπανίσταται δὲ ἄλλος τοῖς Ἱεροσολύμοις πόλεμος υἱὸς ἦν Γιώρα Σίμων τις Γερασηνὸς τὸ γένος, νεανίας πανουργίᾳ μὲν ἡττώμενος Ἰωάννου τοῦ προκατέχοντος ἤδη τὴν πόλιν, ἀλκῇ δὲ σώματος καὶ τόλμῃ διαφέρων, [504] δι᾽ ἣν καὶ ὑπὸ Ἀνάνου τοῦ ἀρχιερέως φυγαδευθεὶς ἐξ ἧς εἶχε τοπαρχίας Ἀκραβετηνῆς πρὸς τοὺς κατειληφότας τὴν Μασάδαν λῃστὰς παραγίνεται. [505] τὸ μὲν οὖν πρῶτον ἦν αὐτοῖς δι᾽ ὑποψίας· εἰς τὸ κατωτέρω γοῦν φρούριον ἐπέτρεψαν αὐτῷ παρελθεῖν ἅμα ταῖς γυναιξίν, ἃς ἄγων ἧκεν, αὐτοὶ τὸ ὑψηλότερον οἰκοῦντες· [506] αὖθις δὲ διὰ συγγένειαν ἠθῶν καὶ ὅτι πιστὸς ἐδόκει, συμπροενόμευε γοῦν αὐτοῖς ἐξιὼν καὶ συνεπόρθει τὰ περὶ τὴν Μασάδαν. [507] οὐ μὴν ἐπὶ τὰ μείζω παρακαλῶν ἔπεισεν· οἱ μὲν γὰρ ἐν ἔθει ὄντες τῷ φρουρίῳ, [508] καθάπερ φωλεοῦ χωρίζεσθαι μακρὰν ἐδεδοίκεσαν, ὁ δὲ τυραννιῶν καὶ μεγάλων ἐφιέμενος ἐπειδὴ καὶ τὴν Ἀνάνου τελευτὴν ἤκουσεν, εἰς τὴν ὀρεινὴν ἀφίσταται, καὶ προκηρύξας δούλοις μὲν ἐλευθερίαν, γέρας δὲ ἐλευθέροις, τοὺς πανταχόθεν πονηροὺς συνήθροιζεν.

EVIDENCE FOR INCLUDING IN THE STUDY

The rebels at Masada, mentioned in both passages, can only be the Sicarii. See above.

LITERARY CONTEXT

Immediately prior to the passage in question, Josephus relates that Vespasian learned of Nero's death (4.491). In a somewhat lengthy passage, Josephus describes what he will refuse to treat in his present work—the intrigues and fighting of Otho, Galba, and Vitellius. He states that such events are well known and rehearsing them would break his narrative (4.492–96).[50] Vespasian, on hearing the news of Nero's death, postponed his campaign against Jerusalem (4.497–501).

After the narrative in question, Josephus details how Simon gathered strength from the surrounding countryside (4.509–13), repelled a preemptive attack of the Zealots from Jerusalem (4.514), devastated Idumea (4.515–37), and recovered his kidnapped wife (4.538–44). Meanwhile, with civil war spreading in Italy, Vespasian resumed his campaign in Judea. Cerealius, one of Vespasian's officers, reduced all of southern Judea except the fortresses Herodion, Masada, and Machaerus. The Romans then turned to Jerusalem (4.545–55), which Simon surrounded (4.556–57).

Josephus introduces the narrative in this context as "another battle" that

---

50. The passage sounds like a typical *recusatio*, a topos of Horace, as in *Odes* 1.6 or 2.12, in this respect; by his lengthy description of what he declines to address, Josephus demonstrates that he is fully capable of treating these topics. The passage also serves as evidence that Josephus is writing for a Roman audience. See above in chapter two, "Audience."

turned against the people in Jerusalem. In this way he connects Simon's advance with Vespasian's suspended campaign. In the absence of a foreign enemy, another arises. This enemy is Simon b. Gioras, who will eventually become one of the two feuding tyrants in Jerusalem. The context might be outlined as follows:

I.   Warfare on two fronts
     a.   The foreign enemy withdraws because of a civil war at home. (491–502).
     b.   The household enemy arises and strengthens a civil war at home. (503–44).

DESCRIPTION OF SICARII ACTIVITY

Josephus had previously stated that the bandits at Masada "welcomed" Simon. Here, however, he notes the initial reservation of the Sicarii, who eventually allowed him to accompany them in plundering and destroying the area around Masada (4.506). Josephus states that Simon "showed the qualities of a tyrant and was aiming at great enterprises" (4.508). The Sicarii, on the other hand, were merely content with conducting raids from the safety of Masada and were afraid to attempt anything greater.

WORD STUDIES

We note here that Josephus identifies the Sicarii by his more general term "bandits" (λῃσταί). To that he adds a new metaphor, saying that the Sicarii "had become afraid to go far from their lair, as it were." This term, "lair" (φωλεός), describes a den or cave—a place where dangerous wild animals lurk. Thus, the raids from Masada amount to little more than animal savagery, and the ignobility of such raids is emphasized by the fear of the Sicarii to venture on to anything greater.

BOOK CONTEXT

As stated above, this passage resumes the narrative already begun by Josephus at 2.652–54. Simon personifies the problem of tyranny, a controlling theme of *War*. But there is an apologetic note here. By dwelling on the civil unrest at Rome while accounting for the rising strength of the tyrant Simon, the passage serves as evidence for the way in which, as Mason observes, Josephus attempts to demonstrate to his Roman readers how the Jewish civil problems were not so different from those that the Romans themselves experienced.[51] Rome, too, had its share of savagery in the civil unrest subsequent to Nero's death.

---

51. See above in chapter 2 under "Thematic Elements" and "Audience."

CONCLUSIONS

There is not much new here that Josephus has not already stated about the Sicarii. Their link to civil unrest and tyranny continues in the person of Simon, and their activity does not rise above mere banditry. However, Josephus adds two riff notes that are not present in the prior narrative about the Sicarii activity with Simon. First, he highlights the ignoble savagery of the Sicarii by comparing their activity to those of a savage and fearful animal. Simultaneously, however, Josephus frames the narrative about the Sicarii in a manner he intends the Romans to recognize and with which he wants them to sympathize. The entire episode thus takes on an ironic twist.

Finally, before turning to book 7 we note one more bit of information given about the Sicarii at 4.516, which does not merit separate treatment inasmuch as it amounts to little more than a passing detail. The context presents Simon's conflict with Idumea as he increased in power. We read that before going out to meet Simon, the Idumeans left the bulk of their population to protect against raids on their property by the Sicarii. Josephus writes:

> The Idumean leaders quickly gathered together a fighting force of about 25,000 from the country, and after leaving many to garrison their own because of the raids of the Sicarii at Masada, they met Simon at their borders.

> οἱ δὲ ἄρχοντες τῆς Ἰδουμαίας κατὰ τάχος ἀθροίσαντες ἐκ τῆς χώρας τὸ μαχιμώτατον περὶ πεντακισχιλίους καὶ δισμυρίους, τοὺς δὲ πολλοὺς ἐάσαντες φρουρεῖν τὰ σφέτερα διὰ τὰς τῶν ἐν Μασάδᾳ σικαρίων καταδρομὰς ἐδέχοντο τὸν Σίμωνα πρὸς τοῖς ὅροις.

Thus, Josephus emphasizes how the Sicarii were powerful enough to be a scourge to the Idumeans.

CHAPTER FOUR

THE SICARII IN *WAR* 7

Turning now to Josephus's presentation of the Sicarii in the last book of *War*, we begin by noting how much space he devotes to these characters. In the first six books they feature in only a few, admittedly critical, episodes. By contrast they come center stage as the major protagonists of *War* 7. It might seem surprising that Josephus would pay them so much attention in view of his obligation to present an account of the triumph in all its glory, and indeed Josephus does not disappoint his patrons. However, the structure of book 7 reveals that episodes about the Sicarii displace the Flavians and their triumph.

The Structure of *War* 7

The book opens with an account of Titus's gradual return to Rome and the Triumph, which Mary Beard has convincingly shown stands as a unified narrative, marked as it is by "triumphal" events throughout.[1] As Mason indicates, at the conclusion of this narrative there is a culminating statement at 157–58 which sounds the resolution of Roman civil war, which is "constantly" in the background of book 1.[2] There Josephus says:

> [157] For the city of Rome feasted this day as a victory in a campaign against enemies, as an end to its own civil unrest, and as the beginning of its hopes for happiness. [158] Now after the triumph and the establishment of Roman rule on the firmest foundation, Vespasian determined to build the Temple of Peace.

---

1. Beard, "The Triumph of Flavius Josephus," in *Flavian Rome: Culture, Image, Text*, ed. A. J. Boyle and W. J. Dominik (Leiden and Boston: Brill, 2003), 543–58, here 556. Beard thus places the triumph as the centerpiece of the whole book. It portrays the legitimization of the Flavians, whose accession begins with Titus's gradual return. She maintains that the episodes told by Josephus after the triumph's culmination serve this same strategy, displaying the fate of the Jewish rebels and charting the progress—"political, geographical, and royal"—of the new dynasty (549).

2. Steve Mason, *Josephus and the New Testament*, 2nd ed. (Peabody: Hendrickson, 2003), 67.

[157] ταύτην γὰρ τὴν ἡμέραν ἡ Ῥωμαίων πόλις ἑώρταζεν ἐπινίκιον μὲν τῆς κατὰ τῶν πολεμίων στρατείας πέρας δὲ τῶν ἐμφυλίων κακῶν, ἀρχὴν δὲ τῶν ὑπὲρ τῆς εὐδαιμονίας ἐλπίδων. [158] Μετὰ δὲ τοὺς θριάμβους καὶ τὴν βεβαιοτάτην τῆς Ῥωμαίων ἡγεμονίας κατάστασιν Οὐεσπασιανὸς ἔγνω τέμενος Εἰρήνης κατασκευάσαι.

While Mason presents this passage as evidence of large-scale chiasmus in *War*, we should also here note, focusing more narrowly, that this statement amounts to a transitional point in book 7. Thus, after a brief description of the Temple of Peace (159–62), the next section begins at 163 with a shift back to Judea.

> Now when Lucillius Bassus had been sent out as procurator to Judea and had received the army from Cerialius Vitellianus . . . .
>
> εἰς δὲ τὴν Ἰουδαίαν πρεσβευτὴς Λουκίλιος Βάσσος ἐκπεμφθεὶς καὶ τὴν στρατιὰν παρὰ Κερεαλίου Οὐετιλιανοῦ παραλαβών, κτλ.

Josephus then recounts how Bassus proceeded against the remaining Jewish resistance including that at Machaerus and in the Jardean forest. These two episodes end with Josephus's account of the imposition of a tax upon the Jews, which happened "about the same time." Then Josephus briefly turns his attention from Judea to the fortunes of Antiochus, king of Commagene, and a segment about the Alani. These last events are perhaps meant to provide a contrast to the affairs of Antiochus.

Josephus follows with another transitional statement at 252, which introduces the Masada narrative.

> Now after Bassus died, Flavius Silva became procurator over Judea, and when he saw that all the rest of it had been reduced and that one fortress only still remained, he gathered together his entire scattered force to this place. Now the fortress was called Masada.
>
> ἐπὶ δὲ τῆς Ἰουδαίας Βάσσου τελευτήσαντος Φλάυιος Σίλβας διαδέχεται τὴν ἡγεμονίαν, καὶ τὴν μὲν ἄλλην ὁρῶν ἅπασαν τῷ πολέμῳ κεχειρωμένην, ἓν δὲ μόνον ἔτι φρούριον ἀφεστηκός, ἐστράτευσεν ἐπὶ τοῦτο πᾶσαν τὴν ἐν τοῖς τόποις δύναμιν συναγαγών· καλεῖται δὲ τὸ φρούριον Μασάδα.

This statement achieves several purposes. It introduces Flavius Silva as procurator of Judea, alerts the reader to the one remaining rebel fortress, and focuses the reader's attention there much as Silva focused all his forces there. The Masada narrative is brought to a conclusion with another summary statement at 407–8.

> [407] After this conquest, such as it was, the general left a garrison at the fortress and he himself departed for Caesarea with his forces. [408] For there no longer remained any enemy throughout the country. On the contrary, it had been entirely reduced through a lengthy war, which came to the awareness of many who dwelled far off and brought a risk of disturbance.

⁴⁰⁷ τοιαύτης δὲ τῆς ἁλώσεως γενομένης ἐπὶ μὲν τοῦ φρουρίου καταλείπει φυλακὴν ὁ στρατηγός, αὐτὸς δὲ μετὰ τῆς δυνάμεως ἀπῆλθεν εἰς Καισάρειαν. ⁴⁰⁸ οὐδὲ γὰρ ὑπελείπετό τις τῶν κατὰ τὴν χώραν πολεμίων, ἀλλ᾿ ἤδη πᾶσα διὰ μακροῦ τοῦ πολέμου κατέστραπτο πολλοῖς καὶ τῶν ἀπωτάτω κατοικούντων αἴσθησιν καὶ κίνδυνον ταραχῆς παρασχόντος.

Immediately following at 409 is another transitional statement designed to introduce the disturbances of the Sicarii in Egypt.

But still also around Alexandria in Egypt it happened that many of the Jews died.

ἔτι δὲ καὶ περὶ Ἀλεξάνδρειαν τὴν ἐν Αἰγύπτῳ μετὰ ταῦτα συνέβη πολλοὺς Ἰουδαίων ἀποθανεῖν.

Following this episode is one smaller, which took place at Cyrene and which also dwells on the remaining vestiges of Sicarii criminal behavior, introduced at 437 by the statement:

Now the madness of the Sicarii, just like a disease, affected the cities around Cyrene.

ἥψατο δὲ καὶ τῶν περὶ Κυρήνην πόλεων ἡ τῶν σικαρίων ἀπόνοια καθάπερ νόσος.

Then Josephus brings *War* to a close with a short epilogue.

If the contents of *War* 7 were to be outlined accordingly, it would look as follows:

    I.   Titus's gradual return to Rome and the Flavian triumph
        (Allocation of space: 1–162, 4,481 words, 36.5 percent of book 7)
    II. Machaerus, Jardean forest, imposition of Jewish tax
        (Allocation of space: 163–218, 1,534 words, 12.5 percent of book 7)
    III. Antiochus of Commagene and the Alani
        (Allocation of space: 219–51, 798 words, 6.5 percent of book 7)
    IV. Masada
        (Allocation of space: 252–406, 4,209 words, 34.3 percent of book 7)
    V. Remnants of Jewish stasis
        (Allocation of space: 407–53, 1,213 words, 9.9 percent of book 7)
    VI. Epilogue
        (Allocation of space: 454–55, 50 words, .3 percent of book 7)

Immediately apparent here is the prominent position Josephus accords the Sicarii. The narratives about Masada and the remnants of Jewish stasis in Alexandria and Cyrene, in which episodes the Sicarii are prominent, amount to about 44 percent of book 7. Compare this with the amount of space Josephus allocates to the Flavians, just over 36 percent. We will see below that there are compelling structural and thematic reasons why Josephus ends *War* with such a focus. We simply note here how the net effect of this allocation is that what Josephus *wants* to tell us in connection with the Sicarii upstages what he *is obligated* to tell in connection with his patrons. Quantity has a certain quality all its own. With these matters in mind, we turn now to the first passage.

THE SUMMARY CONDEMNATION OF JEWISH REBELS (7.253–62)

Josephus begins the Masada narrative with what may be called the Hall of Infamy, a summary condemnation of the main Jewish rebels already featured in *War*. First on the list are the Sicarii, who are prominent throughout the rest of the book.

> [253] Now Eleazar, a powerful man and descendant of Judas, who persuaded many Jews (as I have stated earlier) not to participate in the census when Quirinius was sent to Judea as censor, was in command of those who had captured it. [254] For at that time the Sicarii banded together against those who wanted to submit to the Romans and treated them in every way as enemies, plundering their possessions, driving away their livestock, and throwing fire into their homes. [255] For they claimed that they were no different than foreigners by so ignobly throwing away their freedom, for which the Jews had fought, and by agreeing to choose slavery under the Romans. [256] But this statement was a pretext which they used as a cover for their violence and greed. They made this clear through their activities. [257] For some joined with them in revolt and took up the battle against the Romans, but they suffered worse crimes from those with whom they joined. [258] And when they were convicted about lying with this pretext, they mistreated all the more those who formally reproached them about their wickedness.

> [253] προειστήκει δὲ τῶν κατειληφότων αὐτὸ σικαρίων δυνατὸς ἀνὴρ Ἐλεάζαρος, ἀπόγονος Ἰούδα τοῦ πείσαντος Ἰουδαίους οὐκ ὀλίγους, ὡς πρότερον δεδηλώκαμεν, μὴ ποιεῖσθαι τὰς ἀπογραφάς, ὅτε Κυρίνιος τιμητὴς εἰς τὴν Ἰουδαίαν ἐπέμφθη. [254] τότε γὰρ οἱ σικάριοι συνέστησαν ἐπὶ τοὺς ὑπακούειν Ῥωμαίων θέλοντας καὶ πάντα τρόπον ὡς πολεμίοις προσεφέροντο, τὰς μὲν κτήσεις ἁρπάζοντες καὶ περιελαύνοντες, ταῖς δ' οἰκήκεσιν αὐτῶν πῦρ ἐνιέντες. [255] οὐδὲν γὰρ ἀλλοφύλων αὐτοὺς ἔφασκον διαφέρειν, οὕτως ἀγεννῶς τὴν περιμάχητον Ἰουδαίοις ἐλευθερίαν προεμένους καὶ δουλείαν αἱρεῖσθαι τὴν ὑπὸ Ῥωμαίοις ἀνωμολογηκότας. [256] ἦν δ' ἄρα τοῦτο πρόφασις εἰς παρακάλυμμα τῆς ὠμότητος καὶ τῆς πλεονεξίας ὑπ' αὐτῶν λεγόμενον· σαφὲς δὲ διὰ τῶν ἔργων ἐποίησαν. [257] οἱ μὲν γὰρ αὐτοῖς τῆς ἀποστάσεως ἐκοινώνησαν καὶ τοῦ πρὸς Ῥωμαίους συνήραντο πολέμου, καὶ παρ' ἐκείνων δὲ τολμήματα χείρω πρὸς αὐτοὺς ἐγένετο, [258] κἀπὶ τῷ ψεύδεσθαι πάλιν τὴν πρόφασιν ἐξελεγχόμενοι μᾶλλον ἐκάκουν τοὺς τὴν πονηρίαν αὐτῶν διὰ τῆς δικαιολογίας ὀνειδίζοντας.

Though, properly speaking, the passage in question serves as an introduction to Masada and is therefore part of that larger narrative, we give it independent treatment in view of how it summarizes past behavior. That is, the passage does not describe Eleazar and his compatriots directly.

LITERARY CONTEXT

We have already noted the overall arrangement of book 7. Here we might profitably give an account of the episodes that follow the triumph in order to see more clearly both their connections with and their independence from the Masada narrative. After concluding his narrative about the triumph, Josephus tells of the battle at Machaerus, one of the last places of rebellion. Close inspection also reveals its presence here for structural reasons. Josephus had introduced the place in the narrative concerning Alexander's revolt against Gabinius, governor of Syria. Alexander fortified the place but later, while besieged in Alexandrion, surrendered it to Gabinius (1.161–67). His father, Aristobulus, upon escaping from Rome, attempted to fortify the place in revolt, but was defeated (1.171–72). When we compare that episode to the one at hand in book 7, clear features of chiasm emerge. Josephus introduces Machaerus in *War* as a fortified place of Jewish revolt against Rome in book 1 and treats the final reduction of this fortified place of rebellion in book 7. Note also that both at the beginning and the end Machaerus is given over to the Romans through surrender.

Bassus then gets a victory in a battle at the forest of Jardes. This place is mentioned only here in *War*. Among the slain rebels, who originally came from Jerusalem and Machaerus, Josephus mentions Judas b. Ari, a Zealot leader distinguished earlier in battle at Jerusalem (6.92). The story thus illustrates, among other things, a theme sounded at the beginning of book 7 (7.34). There, after Simon was found by the Romans, Josephus editorializes that God himself had delivered Simon into the hands of his enemies as a fitting punishment for his crimes.

> For wickedness does not escape God's wrath, nor is justice weak, but in time He comes upon those who made transgressions against it and brings upon the wicked a worse punishment because they also supposed that they had gotten away with it when they were not punished immediately. (7.34)
>
> οὐδὲ γὰρ διαφεύγει πονηρία θεοῦ χόλον, οὐδὲ ἀσθενὴς ἡ δίκη, χρόνῳ δὲ μέτεισι τοὺς εἰς αὐτὴν παρανομήσαντας καὶ χείρω τὴν τιμωρίαν ἐπιφέρει τοῖς πονηροῖς, ὅτι καὶ προσεδόκησαν αὐτῆς ἀπηλλάχθαι μὴ παραυτίκα κολασθέντες.

This theme stands out all the more in view of the similar statement about Catullus at 7.453 with which Josephus concludes not only book 7 but the entire narrative of *War*.

> He, no less than any other, became a proof of God's providence—that God punishes the wicked.

οὐδενὸς ἧττον ἑτέρου τῆς προνοίας τοῦ θεοῦ τεκμήριον γενόμενος ὅτι τοῖς πονηροῖς δίκην ἐπιτίθησιν.

Thus, the contents of *War* 7 are framed by statements about God's justice, and besides accounting for how the Romans progressively reduced the last remaining rebellion in Judea, this episode illustrates that theme with the capture of Judas b. Ari.

After telling of the imposition of the tax on the Jews (216–18), Josephus returns to the fortunes of Antiochus, king of Commagene (219–43). Josephus had first mentioned Antiochus in passing at 5.461 as the father of Antiochus Epiphanes, who led some Macedonians in a reported attack on the walls of Jerusalem. There Josephus stated that Antiochus, the father, at the peak of fortune suffered reverse and showed, paraphrasing Solon in Herodotus *Histories* 1.30f., that no one should be called blessed before death.[3] Josephus does not refer to him again until the passage in question at book 7. Here he tells how Antiochus was falsely accused by Caesennius Paetus, governor of Syria, of being in revolt with Parthia against Rome. Though his sons, Epiphanes and Callinicus, fought against the invasion of Paetus when the latter invaded, Antiochus twice refused. He was arrested at Tarsus, but while on the way to Rome had his fortunes restored by Vespasian. Father and sons were eventually reunited in Rome, where they lived in honor.

The allusion to Herodotus (Solon) is unmistakable (*Histories* 1.32). Pressed by Croesus, Solon stated that one should never call a man happy until one saw the manner of his death. Croesus soon thereafter lost all in defeat to Cyrus. Herodotus told that story in part to illustrate how the sin of Gyges, who spied on Candaules' wife and then usurped the throne after killing him, would be repaid, as foretold by the priestess at Delphi, in the fifth generation: that is, in the person of Croesus (*Histories* 1.13). After his capture, legend has Croesus saved from his pyre and either established as advisor to Cyrus or taken to the land of the Hyperboreans (Bacchylides, 3.57). Antiochus, therefore, is not quite so neat an example of the maxim sounded at 5.461, for the allusion to Croesus is somewhat inexact. Josephus tells us of no long-standing sin within the family line of Antiochus. Yet the story fits in a general way with Josephus's two framing statements about God's justice.

At several points, however, the narrative illustrates Antiochus's refusal to take up arms against Rome (227–28, 231, 234, 242), and perhaps this serves as a clue as to why Josephus places the story here. Aside from the opportunity of a (somewhat inexact) rhetorical trick, Antiochus's family serves as a contrast to

---

3. "For of all the kings under the Romans, the king of Commagene happened to be particularly blessed before he experienced a reversal of fortune. So he also showed in his old age how no one should be called happy before death" (εὐδαιμονῆσαι γὰρ δὴ μάλιστα τῶν ὑπὸ Ῥωμαίοις βασιλέων τὸν Κομμαγανὸν συνέβη πρὶν γεύσασθαι μεταβολῆς· ἀπέφηνε δὲ κἀκεῖνος ἐπὶ γήρως ὡς οὐδένα χρὴ λέγειν πρὸ θανάτου μακάριον).

Jewish rebels in general and the Sicarii in particular. The latter took up arms not only against Rome but also against their own people and finally killed one another in a desert fortress. Antiochus, on the other hand, refused to take up arms, though his sons did for a time out of honor. The story ends with an accent on Vespasian's gentleness (ἡμέρως) and the family living in honor in Rome. The message, though implicit, is clear enough. Even for those who are falsely accused, who fight to protect their honor, and who have in that fight lost their homeland, there is a place in Rome to live with honor. We reasonably conjecture that this message would not be lost on Josephus's Jewish readers.

Finally, Josephus tells of the invasion of Media by the Alani (244–51). Pacorus, the king of that country, fled before them, and the Alani raided his country unopposed. After wreaking havoc also in Armenia, they returned to their own land. Though Josephus states that he has mentioned them "somewhere before" (πρότερόν που δεδηλώκαμεν 7:244), this is, in fact, the first and only time Josephus refers to them in *War*.[4] Either Josephus made this comment intentionally or unintentionally. If the latter, explanation is provided by appeal to some (unrecoverable) source thoughtlessly copied by Josephus, though such thoughtlessness is difficult to reconcile with the care Josephus generally exercises in the management of source material elsewhere, as evidenced for example in the *Antiquities*.[5] If the former, this would be an example of an unresolved reference and a loose end that easily surfaces in a work of sufficient magnitude. We would conclude that Josephus intended to introduce them at some earlier point of *War* but neglected to do so. This supposition is strengthened somewhat by the fact that the Alani were contentious neighbors of the Parthians, and these latter, appearing as they do only in books 1 and 7, are indeed structural components in the overall chiastic arrangement of *War*.[6] We might reasonably conclude that Josephus had intended to introduce the Alani in book 1 as well. Whatever narrative and structural intent Josephus might have had in mind for the Alani, we may note at least how the narrative in question contrasts generally with the Antiochus narrative.

Such are the episodes that precede and build to the Masada narrative. They showcase how the Romans are steadily advancing to suppress all rebellion, with Masada being the last. And in contrast with the behavior of the Sicarii, they also present the possibility of an honorable life apart from one's homeland in Flavian Rome. Implicit also in the background is the working of divine justice, which will take center stage at Masada. Having said all this, in view of the transitional statement at 252 and the long summary of rebel crimes that follows, we see that the Masada narrative nevertheless stands somewhat apart from these preceding

---

4. Curiously, the only other time Josephus mentions them is in *Ant.* 18.97, and there only in passing.

5. See L. H. Feldman, *Flavius Josephus: Judean Antiquities 1–4. Translation and Commentary*, by Louis Feldman; ed. Steve Mason (Leiden: Brill, 2001).

6. See Mason, *Josephus and the New Testament*, 67.

stories. That is, it receives the greater emphasis, obviously by the amount of space Josephus gives it, but also by how he sets the stage.

Following his summary of the Sicarii's transgressions, Josephus parades also other prominent criminals of the revolt. These are the tyrants John of Gischala and Simon b. Giora, the Idumeans, and the Zealots (263–74). Following this Hall of Infamy, Josephus continues the Masada narrative with Flavius Silva's preparations for the siege (275–79). The Hall of Infamy thus serves to introduce the subjugation of the last Jewish rebels. The context might thus be outlined:

    I.   Machaerus, Jardean forest, imposition of Jewish tax (163–218)
    II. Antiochus of Commagene and the Alani (219–51)
   III. Masada
       a. The Hall of Infamy (252–74)
       b. The Strength of the Fortress (275–303)
       c. The Siege (304–19)
       d. The Speeches of Eleazar (320–88)
       e. The Voluntary Deaths (389–406)

Description of Sicarii Activity

Josephus uses Eleazar, the chief of the Sicarii at Masada, as the point of introduction to his summary of the Sicarii's criminal attitudes and behavior. The summary is introduced by τότε γάρ, which follows a statement about Eleazar's ancestor Judas. As noted above, this phrase could conceivably refer to the time of Judas and therefore would summarize the Sicarii's activity at that time. Such a translation, however, produces severe inherent difficulties in what Josephus tells us elsewhere about the rise of the Sicarii and the origins of their name. Moreover, the description of the Sicarii's activities here fits much better with what is said about them in books 2 and 4 than with anything said about the events contemporary with Judas in 6 c.e. It is preferable to coordinate τότε γάρ with ἐγένετο γάρ πῶς ὁ χρόνος ἐκεῖνος at 259, which introduces the rebel characters in the war against Rome. This makes the comment about Eleazar's ancestry parenthetical. Such a translation avoids the inherent difficulties.[7] The point made is that the Sicarii had a leader with a rebel ancestry.

And so Josephus summarizes the activity of the Sicarii in their revolt against Rome. The Sicarii banded together against all who wanted to obey Rome and treated them as enemies—stealing their possessions, rounding up their livestock, and burning their homes. We note that these are the activities of bandits. Josephus nowhere in the summary describes the Sicarii as using daggers or committing assassinations, a point worth noting, inasmuch as this *modus operandi*, according to Josephus, explained the origin of their name. Once again we have evidence of Josephus using the term more broadly.

---

7. See chapter 3 above, "Rise and Activity of Judas in 6 c.e."

The pretext (πρόφασις) given by the Sicarii was that such Jews were just like Gentiles in giving away their freedom, which Jews always fight for, and in having decided to choose slavery to the Romans (255). The real reason according to Josephus was their violence and greed (τῆς ὠμότητος καὶ τῆς πλεονεξίας 256). They made this plain through their activities (256), for when some joined with them in revolt, they suffered worse acts of insolence from the Sicarii (τολμήματα 257) than they experienced previously. And when the pretext was again shown as a lie and they were convicted, the Sicarii mistreated all the more those who, in self-defense, denounced their wickedness (258).

Josephus presents the Sicarii as the first examples of the wickedness of the time, a time when "no wicked deed was left untried, and neither could they have invented a worse crime even if they applied themselves to devise one." Stock phrases follow (259–62).[8] Note the contrasting elements of each statement (public vs. private, impiety toward God vs. injustice toward neighbors, nobles vs. the masses). It was a time "when everyone was infected both in public and in private, when people tried to surpass one another in impious acts toward God and crimes against their neighbor, when the nobles maltreated the masses and masses were eager to destroy the nobles, and when the nobles desired to be tyrants, and the masses to act violently and plunder property." Josephus concludes by saying that the Sicarii first committed crimes and acts of violence against their own people, leaving no word unspoken for insult or deed untried for destruction of those against whom they were plotting.

WORD STUDIES

Josephus employs a veritable cacophony of terms to describe the Sicarii directly or indirectly throughout the context: robbery, plunder, violence, greed, crime,

---

8. "For somehow that time was filled to abundance with every sort of evil among the Judeans so that no wicked deed was left untried, and neither could they have invented a worse crime even if they applied themselves to devise one. Thus everyone was infected both in public and in private, and they tried to surpass one another in impious acts toward God and in crimes against their neighbor, when the nobles maltreated the masses and the masses were eager to destroy the nobles. For the former desired to be tyrants, and the rest desired to act violently and plunder property. Now the Sicarii began the lawlessness and violence against their kinsmen, leaving not a word unspoken for insult nor a deed untried for the destruction of those against whom they plotted" (²⁵⁹ ἐγένετο γάρ πως ὁ χρόνος ἐκεῖνος παντοδαπῆς ἐν τοῖς Ἰουδαίοις πονηρίας πολύφορος, ὡς μηδὲν κακίας ἔργον ἄπρακτον καταλιπεῖν, μηδ᾽ εἴ τι ἐπίνοια διαπλάττειν ἐθελήσειεν, ἔχειν ἄν τι καινότερον ἐξευρεῖν. ²⁶⁰ οὕτως ἰδίᾳ τε καὶ κοινῇ πάντες ἐνόσησαν, καὶ προσυπερβάλλειν ἀλλήλους ἔν τε ταῖς πρὸς θεὸν ἀσεβείαις καὶ ταῖς εἰς τοὺς πλησίον ἀδικίαις ἐφιλονείκησαν, οἱ μὲν δυνατοὶ τὰ πλήθη κακοῦντες, οἱ πολλοὶ δὲ τοὺς δυνατοὺς ἀπολλύναι σπεύδοντες· ²⁶¹ ἦν γὰρ ἐκείνοις μὲν ἐπιθυμία τοῦ τυραννεῖν, τοῖς δὲ τοῦ βιάζεσθαι καὶ τὰ τῶν εὐπόρων διαρπάζειν. ²⁶² πρῶτον οὖν οἱ σικάριοι τῆς παρανομίας καὶ τῆς πρὸς τοὺς συγγενεῖς ἦρξαντο ὠμότητος, μήτε λόγον ἄρρητον εἰς ὕβριν μήτ᾽ ἔργον ἀπείρατον εἰς ὄλεθρον τῶν ἐπιβουλευθέντων παραλιπόντες. 7.259–62).

wickedness, illness, impiety, tyranny, hubris, and the like (ἁρπάζω, περιελαύνω, ὠμότης, πλεονεξία, τόλμημα, κακέω, πονηρία, κακία, νοσέω, ἀσέβια, ἀδικία, τυρρανέω, βιάζομαι, διαρπάζω, παρανομία, ὕβρις). But the summary statements at 255–56 stand out. There Josephus reports that the Sicarii stated that they committed acts of violence against those who ignobly cast away their freedom and preferred slavery, but Josephus interprets these words as a pretext for violence and avarice (τῆς ὠμότητος καὶ τῆς πλεονεξίας).

The first part of the statement, the ignobility of tossing away freedom and preferring slavery (οὕτως ἀγεννῶς τὴν περιμάχητον Ἰουδαίοις ἐλευθερίαν προεμένους καὶ δουλείαν αἱρεῖσθαι τὴν ὑπὸ Ῥωμαίοις ἀνωμολογηκότας), echoes themes sounded by Polybius. Arthur Eckstein has demonstrated that Polybius criticizes characters such as Prusias II of Bithynia (*Histories* 30.18), and countries such as Macedonia (36.17), who adopt without compulsion an unworthy, servile attitude toward Rome.[9] However, Polybius also addresses the irrational and emotional opposition to a greater power, which signals that leaders have become "derelict in their solemn duty to provide guidance to their polities during seasons of difficulties."[10] Polybius thus condemns those who go to war for irrational reasons.

Close attention to the way in which Josephus develops the concept of "freedom" (ἐλευθερία) in *War* is instructive. The principal characters fight to own the term, and all the while Polybius lurks in the background. This is apparent straight away at 2.259, where the word first occurs. Josephus there tells how madmen abused the term. He states, "Deceivers and tricksters, working for revolutionary changes under the pretense of divine revelation, persuaded the people to act as if possessed and led them into the wilderness on the grounds that there God would show them signs of freedom."[11] Similar ideas are found in the second appearance of the word at 2.264, where imposters and bandits (γόητες καὶ λῃστρικοί) incite the people to revolt, applauding them to press on for freedom, and threaten to kill all who submit to Roman hegemony. These two passages thus set the stage for an ongoing struggle in *War* over the use of the term: what is ἐλευθερία, how is it achieved, and by whom is it rightly claimed?

The next eleven occurrences of the noun are in the speech of Agrippa. In good Polybian fashion, Josephus has Agrippa state that as a motive for war against Rome, the hopes for freedom are irrational (ἀλόγιστος 2.346), for the time to fight for freedom was when Pompey first arrived (355). The best course now, according to Agrippa, is to submit. To drive the point home, Agrippa parades many, more

---

9. Arthur M. Eckstein, *Moral Vision in the Histories of Polybius* (Berkeley and Los Angeles: University of California Press, 1995), 221f.

10. Ibid, 210. This latter Polybian theme Eckstein explores at length on 210f.

11. πλάνοι γὰρ ἄνθρωποι καὶ ἀπατεῶνες προσχήματι θειασμοῦ νεωτερισμοὺς καὶ μεταβολὰς πραγματευόμενοι δαιμονᾶν τὸ πλῆθος ἔπειθον καὶ προῆγον εἰς τὴν ἐρημίαν ὡς ἐκεῖ τοῦ θεοῦ δείξοντος αὐτοῖς σημεῖα ἐλευθερίας.

powerful nations, each of which claimed and valued freedom (358, 361, 365, 368, 370, 373, 374) and each of which submitted to the Romans.

Josephus highlights the intensity of the struggle to own the term within the narrative of *War* in a statement made by Jesus against the Idumeans. Jesus observed that because love of freedom was an inborn quality of the Jews, the charge of betraying liberty was infuriating (4.246).[12] For this precise reason Eleazar and his followers murdered Menahem. They were unwilling to surrender their liberty to this tyrant (2.443). The Zealots, when confined in the temple, held out the term in calling for Idumean aid (228), and indeed the Idumeans marched in defense of these "freedom fighters" (τῶν προμάχων τῆς ἐλευθερίας 4.272) and for the freedom of Jerusalem (4.234, 273). Ananus, on the other side, stated that these domestic tyrants (τοὺς τῆς οἰκουμένης δεσπότας 4.178) were in truth those who conspired against liberty (οἱ ἐπίβουλοι τῆς ἐλευθερίας 4.185) as was evidenced by their behavior. Ananus attempted thus to reawaken within the masses a true love of liberty, "that innate and most honorable of the passions" (τὸ τιμιώτατον τῶν παθῶν καὶ φυσικώτατον ἐλευθερίας 4.175), and turn it against the rebels.

Josephus, after he was taken prisoner, spoke to the people of Jerusalem in terms similar to Ananus in attempting to show the folly of revolt (5.365f.). He said the time to fight for freedom was past. Those who were unworthy of freedom lost it to Pompey (5.396). God himself would have granted them liberty if that were his desire (5.408), but in fact God was on the side of the Romans to punish Jewish crimes (5.403, 412). To take up the fight now was characteristic of those who die badly (5.365). Finally, Eleazar, slightly more often than Ananus (eleven times), uses the group of words most frequently in *War* (twelve times). More on this below.

The point to be recognized here is the irony in having the Sicarii brandish such noble-sounding words as the "ignobility of tossing away freedom." In view of how Josephus develops this Polybian concept in the words and events of *War*, the Sicarii sound rather like madmen, and thus are these noble-sounding words subtly undermined.

The second part of the statement, that the noble-sounding slogan of the Sicarii was used for violence and avarice, introduces another loaded concept— "greed" (πλεονεξία). The word occurs in various ethical discussions in Greek philosophy. Greed stands opposite the virtues of equality, partnership, moderation, and decorum (ἰσότης, κοινωνία, σωφροσύνη, κοσμιότης). Greed disrupts not only society but also "disrupts the cosmos, the harmony of the universe and

---

12. "For men who by nature love liberty and are prepared for this reason especially to fight against foreign enemies can be aroused in their savagery against us by no other means than by fabrication of the charge that liberty is absent" (ἄνδρας γὰρ φύσει φιλελευθέρους καὶ διὰ τοῦτο μάλιστα τοῖς ἔξωθεν πολεμίοις μάχεσθαι παρεσκευασμένους οὐκ ἐνῆν ἄλλως ἐξαγριῶσαι καθ᾽ ἡμῶν ἢ λογοποιήσαντας προδοσίαν τῆς ποθουμένης ἐλευθερίας).

of the world of gods and men."[13] So Plato in the *Gorgias* 508a. Similarly, Dio Chrysostom in *Or.* 67.7 states that it is "the greatest evil" for man and that which God punishes.

Here again Josephus probably echoes Polybius, for Eckstein shows how the latter connects turbulence in the social and political realms with greed.[14] Polybius, for example, makes a connection between greed and a bad political constitution in his comments on the Cretan constitution and society. He states,

> As, then, when we see good customs and good laws prevailing among certain people, we confidently assume that, in consequence of them, the men and their civil constitution will be good also, so when we see private life full of covetousness, and public policy of injustice, plainly we have reason for asserting their laws, particular customs, and general constitution to be bad. (*Histories* 6.47)
>
> ὥσπερ οὖν, ὅταν τοὺς ἐθισμοὺς καὶ νόμους κατίδωμεν παρά τισι σπουδαίους ὑπάρχοντας, θαρροῦντες ἀποφαινόμεθα καὶ τοὺς ἄνδρας ἐκ τούτων ἔσεσθαι καὶ τὴν τούτων πολιτείαν σπουδαίαν, οὕτως, ὅταν τούς τε κατ' ἰδίαν βίους τινῶν πλεονεκτικοὺς τάς τε κοινὰς πράξεις ἀδίκους θεωρήσωμεν, δῆλον ὡς εἰκὸς λέγειν καὶ τοὺς νόμους καὶ τὰ κατὰ μέρος ἤθη καὶ τὴν ὅλην πολιτείαν αὐτῶν εἶναι φαύλην.

In turning to Josephus, we note that πλεονέκτημα (four occurrences) and πλεονεκτέω (thirteen occurrences) always mean "advantage" in *War*, such as the advantage in battle (6.77, 79) or the advantage the Greeks have in writing (1.13). πλεονεξία (twelve occurrences), though it does not receive great emphasis, corresponds to established usage. Greed impels the normally mild-mannered citizens at Syria to murder (2.464). It does this because greed is headstrong, innate to all men, and impervious to punishment (5.558), and so, despite Titus's dire warnings, certain individuals persist in cutting open refugees from Jerusalem in search of swallowed wealth. Josephus links the greed of leaders to social disorders in two individuals: Sabinus, whose intent on searching out the temple treasury led to a Jewish uprising (2.41), and Florus, who not only desired to capture the temple (2.331) but also devastated whole cities (2.279).

BOOK CONTEXT

How this passage fits into the context of *War* 7 and its connections elsewhere have been explored above.

---

13. Gerhard Delling, "πλεονέκτης, πλεονεκτέω, πλεονεξία," in *TDNT* XX:267.
14. Eckstein, *Moral Vision*, 70f.

CONCLUSIONS

With this passage Josephus now clearly specifies, although in Polybian terms, the ideology of the Sicarii. They fought against their own countrymen who desired to submit to Rome inasmuch as they considered them enemies and no different from foreigners in so ignobly throwing away their freedom. However, in a manner that also echoes Polybius, Josephus calls the slogan a pretext and in stock terms draws attention to their devastating personal traits, their greed and violence, which lead to social upheaval among those they intended to lead.

Josephus, moreover, states that the Sicarii were the first examples of general lawlessness among the Jews, described by a series of balanced statements. And indeed, in the narrative of *War* they are the first identifiable group to emerge from the nameless hordes of bandits.

The historical question to be asked at this point is what in the mind of Josephus identifies these people as Sicarii. As with prior sections, it cannot be their use of the dagger or assassinations. On the contrary, Josephus again describes them rather like bandits in their behavior. Possibly Josephus identified these particular bandits at Masada as Sicarii in view of the known connection between Eleazar b. Yair and the prior assassinations at Jerusalem, but this again amounts to evidence of a broadening use of the term.

THE MASADA NARRATIVE (7.275, 297, 311)

Josephus now presents one of the more debated narratives of *War*, the voluntary deaths of 960 men, women, and children who would not surrender to the Romans.

LITERARY CONTEXT

Much of what needs to be said about the context can be found above. Here we repeat some of these elements in slightly more detail, and trace the context to the end of *War*. Josephus tells how Flavius Silva established his camps (275–78) and then proceeds to highlight the fortress's strength (279). This is accomplished via a tour both of its physical characteristics to accent the difficulty of approach to the plateau (280–84), and of Herod's fortress, its supplies, and armory to accent its strength and resources (285–303).

Following the speeches of Eleazar and the account of the voluntary deaths of the Sicarii, Josephus concludes the narrative with a summary statement that all of Judea was subdued (407–8) and then proceeds to describe the stasis of the Sicarii in Alexandria (409–36) and the madness of the Sicarii in Cyrene (437–53). He then brings *War* to a conclusion (454–55).

Strictly speaking, Masada is merely the last of the fortresses to be reduced following the destruction of Jerusalem. It would have presented little more than what Jonathan Roth calls a "logistical and engineering challenge for the Romans," one that was well within the capabilities of a single legion and a few auxiliary units to overcome within the span of four to nine weeks.[15] Yet Josephus devotes considerable space (34 percent of book 7) to this single episode, almost as much space as he devotes to Titus's gradual return to Rome, culminating in the triumph (37 percent of book 7). On the one hand, Masada presents unique opportunities for Josephus to show off his rhetorical skill and to present a narrative designed to thrill the reader with its tragic elements. It will be shown, however, that Josephus uses the narrative to weave together several key themes that have been at work throughout *War*, some of which come at a subtle but real "cost to the current Roman image."[16] The context might be outlined in the following manner:

  I.   The Masada narrative
       a. The Hall of Infamy (252–74)
       b. Silva establishes his camp (275–79)
       c. The strength of the fortress (280–303)
       d. The siege (304–19)
       e. The speeches of Eleazar (320–88)
       f. The voluntary deaths (389–406)
 II.   The remnants of Jewish stasis
       a. The Sicarii in Alexandria (407–36)
       b. The madness of the Sicarii in Cyrene and the Catullus affair (437–53)
III.   Epilogue (454–55)

DESCRIPTION OF SICARII ACTIVITY

Within the description of Herod's fortress and its supplies, Josephus states that Eleazar had previously become master of Masada through deceit (δόλῳ 297). This is a new, though not contradictory, bit of information. At 2.408 Josephus only specifies that "those most inclined for war" captured Masada. Josephus does not introduce Eleazar until the death of Menahem at 2.447, where he merely states that Eleazar returned to Masada and later became tyrant there.

After highlighting the strength of Masada, Josephus tells how the Romans raised an embankment to bring their siege engines to bear, which created a breach. The Sicarii answered by erecting a second, earthen and wooden wall (304–14). This the Romans set aflame with arrows, but a north wind at first threatened to

---

15. Jonathan Roth, "The Length of the Siege of Masada," *Scripta Classica Israelica* 14 (1995), 87, 109.

16. Steve Mason, "Essenes and Lurking Spartans in Josephus' *Judean War*: From Story to History," in *Making History: Josephus and Historical Method*, ed. Zuleika Rodgers (Leiden: Brill, 2007), 230.

blow the flames back on the Roman engines (315–17). Just when the Romans were at the point of despair (ἀπέγνωσαν), Josephus reports:

> Then, suddenly changing direction just as by divine providence, a south wind blew full force in the opposite direction against the wall, and now it was burning through and through. (318)
>
> ἔπειτα δ᾽ αἰφνίδιον νότος μεταβαλὼν καθάπερ ἐκ δαιμονίου προνοίας καὶ πολὺς ἐναντίον πνεύσας τῷ τείχει φέρων αὐτὴν προσέβαλε καὶ πᾶν ἤδη διὰ βάθους ἐφλέγετο.

At this point, Josephus tells how the Romans retired for the night rejoicing "to have God as an ally" (τῇ παρὰ τοῦ θεοῦ συμμαχίᾳ 319).

In view of this turn of events, Eleazar deliberated and decided that the death of all was the best option under the present circumstances. Josephus reports that he came to this decision for several reasons. The wind had turned back the flames on the Sicarii wall, and he could contrive no means of deliverance or defense. Moreover, he vividly imagined (ὑπ᾽ ὀφθαλμοὺς αὐτῷ τιθέμενος) what the Romans would do to them, their children, and their wives if they took them captive.

Eleazar then delivered a speech to his "bravest companions" to convince them of the wisdom of this option. This speech is presented here in outline form so as to draw attention to the main points (323–36). Consult the appendix for the original text of both Eleazar's speeches with translations.

I.   The time has come which directs us to put deeds to our words. (323–24).
    a.   We decided long ago not to serve the Romans or any other but God, for God alone is the true and righteous master of people.
    b.   Let us not shame ourselves, we who formerly would not submit to a slavery that had no danger, by now taking along with the slavery incurable punishments if we will go on living under the Romans.
    c.   For we were the first of all to rebel, and we are the last of all to fight.

II. God has granted us this favor—the free choice to die nobly with those who are dearest (ἐλευθέρα δ᾽ ἡ τοῦ γενναίου θανάτου μετὰ τῶν φιλτάτων αἵρεσις), the precise thing that did not come to others who went down in unexpected defeat. (325–26)
    a.   It is obvious that we will be captured tomorrow.
    b.   But we have the free choice of a noble death with our loved ones.
    c.   And neither can our enemy prevent this although they fervently pray to take us alive.
    d.   And neither can we, if we were to fight, still beat them.

III. Perhaps we should have at the beginning guessed at God's plan and recognized that long ago he had passed sentence on the Jewish people, who were once dear to him. (327–28)
    a.   For when we desired to strike out for freedom, everything turned bad among ourselves and even more so from our enemies.
    b.   For if God had remained gracious or a least moderately angry, he would

not have overlooked the destruction of so many people nor advanced against his very holy city with fire and the destructions of enemies.

IV. Did we alone of all the Jewish race expect to go on guarding our freedom as if we had no sin before God and had shared in no crime, we who even taught others (in crime)? (329)

V. Indeed, look! See how God shows that we were hoping in vain for better things by bringing upon us this fate (ἀνάγκην) in these awful events. (330–32)

   a. For not even this fortress, impregnable as it was, was useful for safety.

   b. On the contrary, even though we had ample food and a pile of weapons and all other supplies in abundance, we were denied the hope of safety by God himself, obviously (ὑπ' αὐτοῦ περιφανῶς τοῦ θεοῦ).

   c. For that fire bearing down on our enemies did not turn of its own accord against our prepared wall. Rather these things are (God's) wrath against (our) many crimes that we in our madness arrogantly brought against our own people (ἃ μανέντες εἰς τοὺς ὁμοφύλους ἐτολμήσαμεν).

VI. Let us pay the penalty for these things, not to those hated Romans, but through our own (hands) to God. (333–34)

   a. The latter will be more moderate (μετριώτεραι) than the former.

   b. Indeed, let our wives die suffering no outrage, our children with no experience of slavery, and after them let us offer one another a noble gift by preserving our freedom as a beautiful shroud (εὐγενῆ χάριν ἀλλήλοις παράσχωμεν καλὸν ἐντάφιον τὴν ἐλευθερίαν φυλάξαντες).

VII. But first let us destroy our possessions and the fortress with fire, for I know quite well that the Romans will be distressed if, not even seizing our persons, they also come short of profit. Let us leave the provisions only, for they will testify that we have died, not because we were overcome by need (of food), but just as we determined from the beginning—by choosing death before slavery. (335–36)

Eleazar's first speech had mixed results. Josephus states that some were practically filled with delight in their thinking that this death would be noble (καλόν), but the more tender minded (μαλακωτέρους) hesitated both out of pity for loved ones and at the prospect of their own death. To prevent the latter from weakening (συνεκθηλύνω) the former, Eleazar launched into a speech on the immortality of the soul. Eleazar's second speech, again presented here in outline, may also be found in the appendix.

I. You should not fear death because life, not death, brings misfortune. Death brings liberty to the soul—freeing it from suffering, granting it full use of its own power, and filling it with immortality. (341–48)

   a. Analogy of sleep, which brings release. (349–50)

   b. Indian self immolation—an example of confidence in the release of death. (351–57)

II. God has determined our death. (θεοῦ γνώμη καὶ κατ' ἀνάγκας 358–59)

   a. The Romans can claim no credit or victory. (360)

   b. It mattered not where we Jews lived or with whom we allied ourselves. Consider Caesarea, Scythopolis, Damascus, Egypt. (361–69)

c. It mattered not what preparations we made or resources we had before war. (369–71)

III. Those who died in battle are blessed because they died defending freedom. Those left alive are to be pitied because of the tortures and outrages they endure. (372–77)

IV. Which of us can endure to live and to look upon such things? (378–79)

V. Let us die well. (καλῶς 380)

a. Let us thus take pity on our loved ones, who need not suffer (οὐκ ἔστιν ἀνθρώποις κακόν ἐκ φύσεως ἀνακαῖον) and yet who surely will suffer at the hands of the Romans. (380–86)

b. Our laws enjoin this, our women and children beg for this, and God has sent this fate (ταῦθ᾽ ἡμᾶς οἱ νόμοι κελεύουσι, ταῦθ᾽ ἡμᾶς γυναῖκες καὶ παῖδες ἱκετεύουσι, τούτων τὴν ἀνάγκην θεὸς ἀπέσταλκε 387).

c. Thus, let us be quick to leave them astonishment/shock at our death and wonder/admiration at our bravery (ἔκπληξιν τοῦ θανάτου καὶ θαῦμα τῆς τόλμης καταλιπεῖν 388).

This speech achieved its intent. Josephus reports that the Sicarii rushed to the deed filled with an unstoppable impulse and under divine possession (ἀνεπισχέτου τινὸς ὁρμῆς πεπληρωμένοι καὶ δαιμονῶντες 389). Yet the manner by which Josephus describes the deaths does not allow us to dismiss them as acts of mere blind passion.

[390] And neither when they came to the deed did they lose the edge of their intent, exactly as one might suppose would happen. Rather, they kept their purpose fixed just as they did when they heard the speech. Though intimate and tender compassion came upon all, the consideration that this was the best plan for loved ones won out. [391] Together they embraced their wives and held their children in their arms and clung to them with their last kisses. [392] And together, helped by alien hands as it were, they carried out the plan, holding on to the thought of those evils they were persuaded would happen under their enemies as a consolation against the necessity of killing. (390–92)

[390] καὶ μὴν οὐδ᾽ ὅπερ ἄν τις ᾠήθη τῇ πράξει προσιόντες ἠμβλύνθησαν, ἀλλ᾽ ἀτενῆ τὴν γνώμην διεφύλαξαν οἵαν ἔσχον τῶν λόγων ἀκροώμενοι, τοῦ μὲν οἰκείου καὶ φιλοστόργου πάθους ἅπασι παραμένοντος, τοῦ λογισμοῦ δὲ ὡς τὰ κράτιστα βεβουλευκότος τοῖς φιλτάτοις ἐπικρατοῦντος. [391] ὁμοῦ γὰρ ἠσπάζοντο γυναῖκας περιπτυσσόμενοι καὶ τέκνα προσηγκαλίζοντο τοῖς ὑστάτοις φιλήμασιν ἐμφυόμενοι καὶ δακρύοντες, [392] ὁμοῦ δὲ καθάπερ ἀλλοτρίαις χερσὶν ὑπουργούμενοι συνετέλουν τὸ βούλευμα τὴν ἐπίνοιαν ὧν πείσονται κακῶν ὑπὸ τοῖς πολεμίοις γενόμενοι παραμύθιον τῆς ἐν τῷ κτείνειν ἀνάγκης ἔχοντες.

In the midst of the pathos, Josephus reports that they remained focused on their decision, that reason won out, that this decision was the best possible for those they held most dear, and that indeed avoidance of sufferings necessitated their deaths. Josephus at this point adds an editorial comment.

These were wretched victims of necessity, for whom the lightest of evils seemed to be the killing with their own hands of their wives and children. (393)

ἄθλιοι τῆς ἀνάγκης οἷς αὐτοχειρὶ γυναῖκας τὰς αὐτῶν καὶ τέκνα κτεῖναι κακῶν ἔδοξεν εἶναι τὸ κουφότατον.

The lots are cast, and the killings take place. Seven, two women and five children, are overlooked because they hid in a cistern. The total dead are 960. The date is Xanthicus 15; Passover (394–401). Josephus states that when the Romans entered the fortress the following morning, it was difficult for them to accept the women's report due to the size of the crime/daring act (τῷ μεγέθει τοῦ τολμήματος). Upon seeing the slain, they did not rejoice as over an enemy, but were amazed at the nobility of the plan (τὴν δὲ γενναιότητα τοῦ βουλεύματος) and the unwavering contempt of death shown by such people in carrying it out (402–6).

WORD STUDIES

Josephus employs a variety of positive and negative words throughout the narrative to describe the activities of the Sicarii, and at several points these words even appear to clash by virtue of their close proximity. Three places stand out in particular. First, Josephus has the conversation about voluntary death occur between Eleazar and the "bravest" (ἀνδρωδεστάτους) of his men (322). Interestingly, this is a *hapax legomenon* in the Josephan corpus. Yet at 338, after the Eleazar's first speech, some of the "softer" of the men (τοὺς δ᾽ αὐτῶν μαλακωτέρους) show by the tears in their eyes that they are unwilling to perform the deed. This adjective (μαλακός) is not a standard virtue among the Romans, martial or otherwise, and Josephus himself indicts them of cowardice (πάντως δὲ καὶ τῆς ἑαυτῶν προδήλου τελευτῆς). But he immediately softens the indictment by stating they had compassion also for their wives and children.

More discordant words are used to describe the Sicarii after Eleazar's second speech (389f.). Josephus states that the Sicarii acted like men who were possessed (δαιμονῶντες). In the entire Josephan corpus, this particular verb occurs only here and at *War* 2.259, another clearly negative context. The term appears to be roughly equivalent to "madness" (μαίνομαι), which Josephus uses only slightly more often (eleven times). Here the possession is linked to an uncontrollable impulse (ἀνεπισχέτο τινὸς ὁρμῆς). However, juxtaposed to "madness" and "impulse" are words such as "fixed purpose," "best possible decision," and "holding on to the thought of avoiding suffering as solace for the need to kill" (ἀτενῆ τὴν γνώμην, λογισμοῦ δὲ ὡς τὰ κράτιστα βεβουλευκότες, τὴν ἐπίνοιαν ... παραμύθιον τῆς ἐν τῷ κτείνειν ἀνάγκης ἔχοντες). These words are not appropriate for describing "madness" and "impulse" but rather speak of reason and deliberation.

One final example of how Josephus juxtaposes positive and negative words in seemingly discordant fashion comes by way of the Roman soldiers' reaction to the voluntary deaths (405–6). When they entered the fortress the next day and learned what had happened from the surviving women, Josephus states that the soldiers could hardly believe the "magnitude of the crime" (τῷ μεγέθει τοῦ τολμήματος).[17] Unlike τόλμα, which can have a neutral or a positive meaning (see above), a survey of τόλμημα (ten times in *War* supplemented by its thirteen occurrences in *Antiquities*) shows that in every instance the term is negative. In the majority of contexts it describes (criminal) activity against one's own relations or people such as Joseph's brothers against Joseph (*Ant.* 2.21, 23), children against parents (*Ant.* 4.264), or Aristobulus against his family (*Ant.* 13.316). By extension, it describes acts of violence against one's rulers (*Ant.* 14.310, 17.157), or even intended acts of violence against one's own person—suicide (14.358). This element, the outrage of killing one's own, stands behind all of its prior occurrences in *War*, also. There, Josephus uses the word to describe the acts of violence that the Jewish rebels commit against their own people (4.146, 171, 221, 245, 257), the raid of the Sicarii against their own people at Passover (4.401), a Scythian rebellion against Rome (7.89), and the crimes of the Sicarii against their own people (7.257).

Thus, the evidence would seem to dictate an equivalent translation for the noun's two appearances in the Masada narrative. At 7.393, we should understand Josephus as saying, "No one came short of such a great crime" (οὐδεὶς τηλικούτου τολμήματος ἥττων εὑρέθη) and not "so daring a deed" (so Thackeray). Similarly, the Romans should be understood as showing disbelief at the "magnitude of the crime" on seeing the slain at Masada (τῷ μεγέθει τοῦ τολμήματος ἀπιστοῦντες 405) and not disbelief of such "amazing fortitude" (so Thackeray).

However, such a translation of the term for this last passage (405) leads to an inherent contradiction in light of how the Roman soldiers reacted. Josephus states:

> When they came upon the mass of those who had been murdered, they did not rejoice over them as enemies but were amazed at the nobility of the plan and that their contempt of death in carrying it out remained unwavering in such circumstances. (406)
>
> καὶ τῷ πλήθει τῶν πεφονευμένων ἐπιτυχόντες οὐχ ὡς ἐπὶ πολεμίοις ἥσθησαν τὴν δὲ γενναιότητα τοῦ βουλεύματος καὶ τὴν ἐν τοσούτοις ἄτρεπτον ἐπὶ τῶν ἔργων ἐθαύμασαν τοῦ θανάτου καταφρόνησιν.

Not only is it difficult to understand how the Romans would call such a vast "crime" a "noble" plan, but also "contempt of death" is hardly an appropriate term for murder. Mason shows that Josephus parades the manly characteristics of the Jews in part by this concept.[18] In *Apion* 2.294, Josephus holds out contempt

---

17. On the word group, see above on p. 71f.
18. Mason, "Essenes and Lurking Spartans," 21–23.

of death as one of the admirable traits of the Jews.[19] Similarly, in *Apion* 2.146 contempt of death (θανάτου περιφρόνησιν) takes its place as one of the cardinal virtues produced by the Jewish constitution.[20]

The juxtaposition of such clashing words, apparent especially in the three examples above, can hardly be attributed either to Josephus's ignorance of the language or to his thoughtless and careless employment of source material as an author. The only satisfactory solution is to see this as an intentional manipulation of the text on his part for the purposes of irony, which matter we will address shortly.

At present, we note not only such clashing terminology but also direct our attention to two concepts in particular that stand out in the narrative. The first of these is "necessity/necessary" (ἀνάγκη/ἀναγκαῖος). These words occur seventy-one times in *War*, predominantly in various non-philosophical and non-technical contexts to describe pressing needs or circumstances. Notable here, however, is that Josephus uses the words eight times within the Masada narrative (ἀνάγκη—330, 358, 380, 387, 392, 393; ἀναγκαῖος—352, 382), six times through the course of Eleazar's two speeches and twice in close proximity in describing (392) and editorializing on (393) the voluntary deaths.

The standard text to which the ancients continually referred in the discussion about voluntary death was the *Phaedo*, and central to this discussion was the concept of ἀνάγκη.[21] The starting point of the *Phaedo* is Socrates' statement that one should not take one's life until God sends "some necessity" (ἀνάγκη τινά) upon the person.[22] But when such a time came, as Socrates acknowledged was now upon him, death was not to be feared. Determining when in fact ἀνάγκη was present remained the "center of discussion of voluntary death throughout

---

19. "What is more beneficial than to agree with one another and neither to be divided in bad times nor fall insolently into stasis in good times but instead to show contempt of death in battle" (τί συμφορώτερον τοῦ πρὸς ἀλλήλους ὁμονοεῖν καὶ μήτ' ἐν συμφοραῖς διίστασθαι μήτ' ἐν εὐτυχίας στασιάζειν ἐξυβρίζοντας ἀλλ' ἐν πολέμῳ μὲν θανάτου καταφρονεῖν). Note also that Josephus states it is admirable how Jews are not afflicted by stasis in good times.

20. "For I think that it would be plain that (our laws) are established as the best possible for piety, for communion with one another, for philanthropy toward the whole world, and still more for justice, and endurance in toils, and contempt of death." (οἶμαι γὰρ ἔσεσθαι φανερόν ὅτι καὶ πρὸς εὐσέβειαν καὶ πρὸς κοινωνίαν τὴν μετ' ἀλλήλων καὶ πρὸς τὴν καθόλου φιλανθρωπίαν ἔτι δὲ πρὸς δικαιοσύνην καὶ τὴν ἐν τοῖς πόνοις καρτερίαν καὶ θανάτου περιφρόνησιν ἄριστα κειμένους ἔχομεν τοὺς νόμους). Josephus has Titus admit this quality of the Jews, also (see 6.42).

21. Arthur J. Droge and James D. Tabor, *A Noble Death: Suicide and Martyrdom among Christians and Jews in Antiquity* (San Francisco: HarperSanFrancisco, 1992), 20–21.

22. "Then perhaps from this point of view it is not unreasonable that one should not kill oneself before god sends some necessity, such as is the one now present for me" (ἴσως τοίνυν ταύτη οὐκ ἄλογον μὴ πρότερον αὐτὸν ἀποκτεινύναι δεῖν, πρὶν ἀνάγκην τινὰ θεὸς ἐπιπέμψῃ, ὥσπερ καὶ τὴν νῦν ἡμῖν παροῦσαν [62c]).

antiquity."[23] Thus, Plato in the *Laws*, as presented in the discussion by Tabor and Droge, recognized "at least three" circumstances in which voluntary death was permissible: "(1) if one has been ordered to do so by the polis; (2) if one has encountered devastating misfortune; and (3) if one is faced with intolerable shame."[24] Cicero (*Tusc. Disp.* 1.71–75) compared Cato to Socrates and likewise affirmed that one could depart from life voluntarily only when a signal had been given by the deity.[25] Seneca, however, widened the circumstances in which a person might take his or her life. "Seneca emphasizes the right to die in general. He repeatedly refers to voluntary death as the path to liberty, as proof that an individual cannot be held against his will."[26] Thus, Seneca "represents a considerable shift in Stoic thinking about voluntary death"—from the need for ἀνάγκη to suicide as being a worthy expression of an individual's freedom.[27]

Turning to Josephus, it becomes apparent that he is consciously attempting to place the voluntary deaths of the Sicarii firmly within this philosophical discussion. Josephus has Eleazar interpret the shifting wind and fire as a signal of divine necessity concerning their deaths. Josephus himself has already led the reader to this conclusion at 318 and 319, where he describes the event. There he states the wind suddenly shifted "just as by divine providence" (καθάπερ ἐκ δαιμονίου προνοίας) and that the Romans rejoiced in thus being favored by God's alliance (τῇ παρὰ τοῦ θεοῦ συμμαχίαι κεχρημένοι χαίροντες). Now the point is made repeatedly by Eleazar. He recognized in this shifting wind that God himself brought

---

23. Droge and Tabor, *Noble Death*, 21, 43.

24. Ibid., 22. "But I am speaking about the one who kills himself, turning away by violence his allotted portion of life, when the city has not justly ordered it, and when he is not compelled by some inescapable and terribly painful fate which befalls him, and when he does not have a share of some difficult and intolerable shame" (λέγω δὲ ὅς ἂν ἑαυτὸν κτείνῃ, τὴν τῆς εἱμαρμένης βίᾳ ἀποστερῶν μοῖραν, μήτε πόλεως ταξάσης δίκῃ, μήτε περιωδύνῳ ἀφύκτῳ προσπεσούσῃ τύχῃ ἀναγκασθείς, μηδὲ αἰσχύνης τινὸς ἀπόρου καὶ ἀβίου μεταλαχών [873c]).

25. Particularly in 1.74 he says: "Cato departed from life in such a way that he rejoiced to have found a reason for death. For God, who is master within us, forbids us to leave this place without his command; but when God himself has given just cause, as in the past to Socrates, and at present to Cato, often to many, then truly the wise man will depart joyfully from these shadows to that light, but he will not break the chains of prison—for the laws forbid it—, but just as by a magistrate or some lawful authority, thus he will leave summoned and sent away by God. For the entire life of the philosophers, as I said before, is a careful preparation for death" (Cato autem sic abiit e vita, ut causam moriendi nactum se esse gauderet. vetat enim dominans ille in nobis deus iniussu hinc nos suo demigrare; cum vero causam iustam deus ipse dederit, ut tunc Socrati, nunc Catoni, saepe multis, ne ille medius fidius, vir sapiens laetus ex his tenebris in lucem illam excesserit, nec tamen ille vincla carceris ruperit—leges enim vetant—, sed tamquam a magistratu aut ab aliqua potestate legitima, sic a deo evocatus atque emissus exierit. Tota enim philosophorum vita, ut ait idem, commentatio mortis est).

26. Droge and Tabor, *Noble Death*, 34. The passages the authors cite are *On Anger* 3.15.3–4 and *Epistles* 12.10; 26.10; 66.13; 70.5, 12, 16, 23–24; 77.15.

27. Ibid., 35.

the ἀνάγκη amidst the terrible circumstances (τὴν ἐν τοῖς δεινοῖς ἀνάγκην 330). Eleazar acknowledged this at several points in his speeches. "We die here at God's intent and according to necessity" (θεοῦ γνώμῃ καὶ κατ' ἀνάγκας τελευτήσαντες 358). "Our hope of avenging the city was not ignoble, but it has vanished and left us under necessity (ἐπὶ τῆς ἀνάγκης 380). Let us die well (καλῶς)." And note especially the crescendo of philosophical ideas about voluntary death–freedom, necessity, mandate of law, avoidance of intolerable shame (here brought upon family)—all brought together in the summary of Eleazar's second speech (386–88).

> [386] But as free men let us depart life with our women and children. [387] Our laws order this. Our wives and children beg for this. God has sent the necessity. The Romans desire the opposite, and they are afraid that any of us will die before capture. [388] So let us be quick to leave them, instead of the enjoyment they expect with capture, amazement at our death and wonder at our bravery.

> [386] ἐλεύθεροι δὲ μετὰ τέκνων καὶ γυναικῶν τοῦ ζῆν συνεξέλθωμεν. [387] ταῦθ' ἡμᾶς οἱ νόμοι κελεύουσι, ταῦθ' ἡμᾶς γυναῖκες καὶ παῖδες ἱκετεύουσι· τούτων τὴν ἀνάγκην θεὸς ἀπέσταλκε, τούτων Ῥωμαῖοι τἀναντία θέλουσι, καὶ μή τις ἡμῶν πρὸ τῆς ἁλώσεως ἀποθάνῃ δεδοίκασι. [388] σπεύσωμεν οὖν ἀντὶ τῆς ἐλπιζομένης αὐτοῖς καθ' ἡμῶν ἀπολαύσεως ἔκπληξιν τοῦ θανάτου καὶ θαῦμα τῆς τόλμης καταλιπεῖν.

Finally, we note that Josephus himself essentially endorses Eleazar's assessment, calling the Sicarii "wretched victims of necessity" (ἄθλιοι τῆς ἀνάγκης) in a following statement (392–93).

The second word emphasized heavily in the Masada narrative is "freedom" (ἐλευθερία). The word group is clustered more thickly in the speeches of Eleazar than anywhere else in *War*. We also note that prior to book 7, the term was used exclusively in a political sense.[28] However, in book 7, where the noun appears eight times and the adjective, ἐλευθερός, appears four times, Josephus has Eleazar use the term to denote not only political freedom but also ethical freedom.[29] The two are juxtaposed most clearly at 7.350, where Eleazar states,

> How is it not foolish that we, who pursued (political) freedom in life, should refuse ourselves everlasting freedom (in death)?

> πῶς δ' οὐκ ἀνόητόν ἐστιν τὴν ἐν τῷ ζῆν ἐλευθερίαν διώκοντας τῆς ἀϊδίου φθονεῖν αὑτοῖς;

---

28. On the word group in *War* prior to book 7, see above.

29. So also David Ladouceur, who notes the different use of the term, "a more philosophical or spiritual sense," than that of Josephus at Jotapata. "Josephus and Masada," *Josephus, Judaism, and Christianity*, ed. Louis H. Feldman and Gohei Hata (Detroit: Wayne State University Press, 1987), 98.

As with ἀνάγκη above, connections are made with philosophical discussion about the connection between death and freedom. In good Platonic fashion, Eleazar states that death brings freedom to the soul (344). Like Seneca, he stresses that the choice of a noble death with loved ones is free (ἐλευθέρα δέ ἡ τοῦ γενναίου θανάτου μετὰ τῶν φιλτάτων αἵρεσις 326). He thus urges his compatriots to preserve in death "our freedom as a noble shroud" (καλὸν ἐντάφιον τὴν ἐλευθερίαν 334).

BOOK CONTEXT

Turning now to how the narrative serves the overall structure and outline of *War*, we first note how several themes central to *War* are highlighted within the Masada narrative.[30] Notable in the first place is emphasis on God's authority and desire to punish the rebels. The point is made in rather dramatic fashion when the Romans, seeing the fire suddenly shift against the Sicarii's wall, rejoice in having God as an ally and retire for the evening. The narrative continually comes back to this point. Eleazar admits that the Sicarii should have recognized that God had passed his sentence on the Jewish people (327–28). Eleazar interprets the fire as the signal that God himself was denying the Sicarii hopes. The fire was an indicator of God's wrath against their crimes, which they madly committed against their own people (330–32). God had thus made their death a necessity (338, 387). The Romans, indeed, could only claim the appearance of victory, one that came about after all not because of their might but because of this "necessity" sent by God (358–60). With all these statements Josephus has Eleazar deny the Romans any credit for the death of the Sicarii.

This theme has already been well developed at several key places of *War*. Agrippa had earlier insisted that the Jews should not count on God for an ally (τὴν τοῦ θεοῦ συμμαχίαν) because he has gone over to the side of the Romans (2.390). Vespasian (4.366) and Titus (6.41) point to this divine ally when encouraging their troops. Josephus himself insisted on this point throughout his speech before Jerusalem (5.367–68, 378ff., 412). So also, Josephus relates several divine portents against Jerusalem (6.288–315).

A second theme central to *War* also sounded at Masada is the valor of the Jews. In the proem, Josephus faults previous histories of the Jewish War for distorting facts either out of "flattery toward the Romans or hatred toward the Jews (1.2)."[31] He adds that those who desire to magnify Roman achievements in the war by disparaging those of the Jews miss the mark. "I fail to see how those who have conquered insignificant people can think that they are great (1.8)."[32] Thus

---

30. For scholarly treatment of the following themes, see above under chapter 2.

31. ἡ κολακείᾳ τῇ πρὸς Ῥωμαίους ἢ μίσει τῷ πρὸς Ἰουδαίους καταψεύδονται τῶν πραγμάτων.

32. οὐχ ὁρῶ δέ πῶς ἂν εἶναι μεγάλοι δοκοῖεν οἱ μικροὺς νενικηκότες.

Josephus sounds his intention to highlight those character traits among the Jews that were also valued among the Romans.

The valorous elements of Josephus's presentation of the Sicarii at Masada should in this respect occasion no surprise. It seems undoubtedly present in how Josephus describes the voluntary deaths to his Roman audience. Besides the reaction of the soldiers in the narrative and the legitimacy of the deaths in light of contemporary philosophical discussion, we note also parallels in Polybius as presented by Eckstein. The latter works from Polybius's editorial comment at 30.7.8, where he says, "For to end one's life when one is not conscious of having done anything unworthy is no less a sign of ignobility than to cling to life beyond the point of honor."[33] It was precisely to preserve honor that king Cleomenes III of Sparta took his own life, therefore winning Polybius's approval (18.53.3) for preferring a glorious and noble (καλῶς) death to a life of disgrace (αἰσχρῶς).[34] Eckstein highlights Polybius's approval of the intended mass suicide at Abydus in book 16, which narrative is introduced by a "massing of compliments" and contains bitter comments concerning how the citizens were prevented from carrying out their plan.[35] Eckstein summarizes:

> Heroic suicide, suicide to avoid shame, to avoid adding the burden of shame to an already-existing defeat or disaster, or to make a last defiant gesture of stubborn autonomy in the face of overwhelming power: such action Polybius always found praiseworthy and moving. And insofar as he saw such action as a means of preserving and even enhancing personal reputation in the eyes of posterity, and saw part of the historian's duty to be the preservation and presentation of wholesome *exempla*, Polybius turns out to be the heir of a Homeric attitude toward life.[36]

We should, of course, note this difference—that Josephus is not preserving the memory of the Sicarii as "wholesome *exempla*." He is rather emphasizing how these rebels voluntarily and nobly submitted to appropriate punishment in a manner that also prevented the adding of further shame to themselves, to their wives, and to their children in defeat. Such an emphasis stands in full accord with Josephus's stated themes in *War*.

A recent study by Timothy Hill leads us to similar conclusions, although in a slightly different manner. Throughout his work Hill maintains that Roman con-

---

33. οὐ γὰρ ἔλαττόν ἐστιν ἀγεννίας σημεῖον τὸ μηδὲν αὐτῷ συνειδότα μοχθηρὸν προεξάγειν ἐκ τοῦ ζῆν αὐτόν, ποτὲ μὲν τὰς τῶν ἀντιπολιτευομένων ἀνατάσεις καταπλαγέντα, ποτὲ δὲ τὴν τῶν κρατούτων ἐξουσίαν, τοῦ παρὰ τὸ καθῆκον φιλοζωεῖν.

34. Eckstein, *Moral Vision*, 46.

35. Ibid., 51–52. Eckstein here departs from Walbank and Ladouceur, who conclude that Polybius's presentation is "dry, detached, objective" or ruthlessly pragmatic. See F. W. Walbank, *Polybius* (Berkeley: University of California Press, 1972), 178; and Ladouceur, "Josephus and Masada," 108 n. 42.

36. Eckstein, *Moral Vision*, 55.

siderations about suicide did not center on the rights and wrongs of taking one's life. Thus, while still recognizing *anagke* as a component in assessing suicide, Hill states that it fails to unify Roman ideas about voluntary death.[37] Rather, what runs throughout Roman discussion in various contexts are matters of honor and how an individual expresses himself through suicide. Hill states:

> Good deaths are deaths that serve either to confirm an individual's social stand-
> ing or elevate this. Bad deaths are deaths inappropriate to an individual's social
> status, and therefore act to denigrate it.[38]

If done particularly well, suicide established one as a moral witness in a commu-nity and signaled the attainment of "supreme virtue."[39] Where Roman historians speculate on the motives, they emphasize the implications of avoiding shame and loving honor as reasons for suicide.[40] Hill stresses that this should properly be understood not as individual honor, but the honor of a person in a "social matrix." That is, there is no paradox of a person preserving honor by taking life. Rather, a person establishes identity in society in just such a manner. It consti-tutes the assertion of "one's membership in a group."[41]

> Speaking broadly, then, one can say that suicide in Roman historiography is
> governed by two related principles. First, suicide is the best course to take when
> one's honor is endangered. Second, suicide under such circumstances in most
> cases preserves this honor. So powerful is the force of these principles, further-
> more, that they are taken by Roman historiographers to have the status of trans-
> historical and cross-cultural norms.[42]

Again, Josephus does not intend his readers to understand the Sicarii as those who have attained supreme virtue but rather as those who are under juridical (divine) sentence and who therefore would be expected by a Roman readership to take their own lives. Yet Josephus's accent on avoidance of shame is unmistak-able, and in light of Hill's study we should understand that Josephus intends his Roman readership to see this noble attitude—devotion to ethical standards tak-ing priority over life—as indicative of Jewish character.

There are, moreover, good reasons to suspect that Josephus intends his Jew-ish readers to see valor in the deaths for precisely the same reasons. The qualities of the Jewish people that Josephus extols in *Apion* 2.232–33 correspond to those

---

37. Timothy Hill, *Ambitiosa Mors: Suicide and Self in Roman Thought and Literature* (New York and London: Routledge, 2004), 34–35.

38. Ibid., 11.

39. Ibid., 178.

40. Ibid., 197f.

41. Ibid., 205.

42. Ibid., 198.

reasons given by Eleazar in support of death. Among these is a preference for death rather than doing or saying anything contrary to Jewish law. He writes:

> [232] Does anyone at all know, not a lot of people, but just two or three among us who were betrayers of our laws or fearful of death? I'm not, mind you, speaking about that very easy death that comes to those in war, but that which comes with bodily torture such that it is thought to be the most difficult of all. [233] It seems to me that some of those who conquered us applied (torture) to those under their control not out of hatred but because they wanted to see this amazing sight; whether there exist men who believe that their only crime would be if they were compelled to do or say anything contrary to their laws.

> [232] ἆρ' οὖν καὶ παρ' ἡμῖν, οὐ λέγω τοσούτους, ἀλλὰ δύο ἢ τρεῖς ἔγνω τις προδότας γενομένους τῶν νόμων ἢ θάνατον φοβηθέντας, οὐχὶ τὸν ῥᾷστον ἐκεῖνον λέγω τὸν συμβαίνοντα τοῖς μαχομένοις, ἀλλὰ τὸν μετὰ λύμης τῶν σωμάτων, ὁποῖος εἶναι δοκεῖ πάντων χαλεπώτατος; [233] ὃν ἔγωγε νομίζω τινὰς κρατήσαντας ἡμῶν οὐχ ὑπὸ μίσους προσφέρειν τοῖς ὑποχειρίοις, ἀλλὰ [ὡς] θαυμαστόν τι θέαμα βουλομένους ἰδεῖν, εἴ τινές εἰσιν ἄνθρωποι μόνον εἶναι κακὸν αὐτοῖς πεπιστευκότες, εἰ πρᾶξαί τι παρὰ τοὺς ἑαυτῶν νόμους εἰ λόγον εἰπεῖν παρ' ἐκείνοις παραβιασθεῖεν.

Such a theme is central to Jewish "martyr texts." When presented with a situation that made it impossible for Jews to remain faithful to their God, his law, and their way of life, the noble martyrs chose death rather than compliance. Jan Willem Van Henten notes a redemptive quality to these noble deaths that results in deliverance.[43]

Josephus highlights these very themes at several points in the narrative. Eleazar intended their deaths both to be an atonement for their crimes and to forestall acts of outrage committed against their wives (333–34, 378–86). This is what it meant to die well (καλῶς 380). This thought comforted the Sicarii when the time came to kill their loved ones (390–92). Again, we add that Josephus, by surrounding the voluntary deaths of the Sicarii with noble comments and terminology, is not attempting to turn the Sicarii into heroes. He is rather presenting the motivation for their deaths in a manner that resonates with the Jewish tradition about noble death, as evidenced in 2 Maccabees.

Turning now from themes to structure, we see indications that the Masada narrative brings to a resolution issues raised in connection with the arrival of Pompey, told by Josephus in 1.131f. For by having Eleazar expatiate on "freedom" in its political sense (327, 341, 350, 372), Josephus is reminding his readers of those earlier points in *War* where both Agrippa and Josephus pin the loss of Jewish freedom to the arrival of Pompey (2.355; 5.396). Particularly in the latter

---

43. Van Henten, *The Maccabean Martyrs as Saviors of the Jewish People* (Leiden: Brill, 1997), 8, 140, 155.

passage, Josephus has his own character insist the following in the speech to the rebels in Jerusalem:

> Indeed, was it not from the stasis of our ancestors (that we became enslaved), when the madness of Aristobulus and Hyrcanus and their strife against each other brought Pompey against our city, and God subjected to the Romans those who were unworthy of freedom? (5.396)

> ἆρ᾽ οὐχὶ ἐκ στάσεως τῶν προγόνων, ὅτε ἡ Ἀριστοβούλου καὶ Ὑρκανοῦ μανία καὶ πρὸς ἀλλήλους ἔρις Πομπήιον ἐπήγαγεν τῇ πόλει καὶ Ῥωμαίοις ὑπέταξεν ὁ θεὸς τοὺς οὐκ ἀξίους ἐλευθερίας;

Thus, Josephus firmly links the loss of freedom to the stasis that grew between Aristobulus and Hyrcanus, and it was this stasis that resulted in Roman intervention in Jewish affairs.

The Masada episode brings these issues to a resolution. Stasis broke out among the Jewish civil leaders, Aristobulus and Hyrcanus, in book 1. This stasis among the Jews in Judea, exemplified by the Sicarii, is finally suppressed at Masada. Note how Josephus, after the reduction of the country, summarizes that Judea was finally entirely reduced and not an enemy remained (7.407–8). Moreover, the Romans become involved in connection with Jewish stasis (book 1, especially 1.142) and the Romans leave, having suppressed the stasis. Masada thus takes its place in the chiastic arrangement of *War*.

Turning now to those intra-textual elements that might be brought to bear in the interpretation of Josephus's narrative intent at Masada, we have noted how many scholars present Josephus's speech against suicide at Jotapata (3.362–82) as a clear antithesis to Eleazar's two speeches in favor of suicide. To this we now turn. Before delivering that speech, Josephus had hidden in a cave with forty fellow well-known Jews to escape the Romans. When Josephus was discovered, Vespasian repeatedly encouraged him to surrender, assuring him of safety. However, Josephus decided to surrender only after recalling dreams God had sent him about Vespasian's future. He called God to witness that he would surrender, not as a betrayer but as God's servant (μαρτύρομαι δὲ ὡς οὐ προδότης ἀλλὰ σὸς εἶμι διάκονος 3.354). His compatriots, however, were intent on killing themselves and would not allow Josephus to leave, and so Josephus embarked upon the speech because, as he states, he was bound to obey God's commands and deliver God's message to the Romans. He therefore attempted "to philosophize with them about the necessity (ἐπὶ τῆς ἀνάγης 3.361). His argument is presented here, again in outline form to highlight its emphases. The original text of this speech with a translation may be found in the appendix.

    I. The reasons for killing ourselves are specious. (362–68)

        a. "It is honorable to die in war"—as long as it is at the hands of the enemy. But our enemies intend to spare our lives.

    b. "It is honorable to die for liberty"—as long as one dies fighting those who would take it away.

    c. "We fear slavery, not death"—such freedom we now have!

    d. "Taking one's life is noble"—rather, it is an ignoble and cowardly act.

II. Killing oneself is foreign to nature and an act of impiety (ἀσέβεια) toward God. (369)

    a. Life is a gift from God, who alone has the authority to decide when to take it back. (370–71)

    b. Those who lay mad hands on themselves endure God's punishment. (372–78)

III. Our lives are offered us. Let us live! (379–82)

Now it would certainly be within bounds of rhetorical tradition to argue opposite sides of a particular subject. At the very least, Josephus is demonstrating his rhetorical skill by presenting two seemingly contradictory views on suicide—Josephus's speech at Jotapata and Eleazar's two speeches at Masada. What has not been well observed is how the speech at Jotapata, like those at Masada, also affirms and builds on the idea expressed in the *Phaedo*, that people belong to the gods and therefore are not at liberty to kill themselves. Socrates stated that, just as an owner of animals would be angry with them if they took their own lives against the owner's will, so also must a person not take his life unless god so indicates. Only when god sends some necessity would it then be permissible to take one's life. And so at Jotapata Josephus stated that life is a gift from God, and his alone is the decision when to take it back. The concept of a signal from God that one's life is forfeit—the presence of divine ἀνάγκη—is clearly pronounced in the narrative and speeches of Eleazar. Alternatively, all the arguments of the speech at Jotapata support the point that ἀνάγκη was absent. Not only are "our enemies showing us mercy," but Josephus insisted in that narrative that it was God's will for him to surrender so that he could perform God's service. To take one's life under such circumstances would clearly be an act against nature and God.

In light of Josephus's repeated emphasis on the presence of ἀνάγκη at Masada and the obvious rhetorical antithesis of the speeches of Eleazar for and Josephus against voluntary death, perhaps we should translate ἀνάγκη at 3.361 in like fashion.

> Fearing an assault and thinking that it would be a betrayal of God's commands if he were to die before the delivery of the message, Josephus came to them to speak philosophically about the necessity.
>
> δείσας δὲ τὴν ἔφοδον ὁ Ἰώσηπος καὶ προδοσίαν ἡγούμενος εἶναι τῶν τοῦ θεοῦ προσταγμάτων, εἰ προαποθάνοι τῆς διαγγελίας, ἤρχετο πρὸς αὐτοὺς φιλοσοφεῖν ἐπὶ τῆς ἀνάγκης.

Thackeray translates the phrase ἐπὶ τῆς ἀνάγκης as "in this emergency." This latter idea, however, is expressed more often, not only in *War* but throughout the works of Josephus, as ἐξ ἀνάγκης, κατ' ἀνάγκην, δι' ἀνάγκην, or ὑπ' ἀνάγκης. In the entire Josephan corpus the phrase ἐπὶ τῆς ἀνάγκης is found only three times; here at Jotapata (3.361, 385) and at Masada (7.380). At 3.385 Josephus states that he was torn by various emotions at the need (ποικίλοις διαιρούμενος πάθειν ἐπὶ τῆς ἀνάγκης) as he warded off his compatriots' intention to kill him in the cave at Jotapata. And, as we have seen, at 7.380 Josephus has Eleazar acknowledge that he and the other Sicarii are under necessity.

But we still wonder, in light of the rhetorical antithesis and the emphasis on ἀνάγκη at Masada, why there is no corresponding emphasis in the speech at Jotapata. Nicole Kelly explored these issues in a recent article devoted to how Josephus presents his dual identity as a "prophetic" spokesman in a Roman and Jewish environment. She, too, notes how it would have been natural for Josephus at Jotapata to state that "it is by God's will and of necessity (ἀνάγκη) that we are to *live*."[44] Kelly suggests, however, that Josephus could not do so.

> Josephus cannot make this statement, however, because the ἀνάγκη in this situation applies only to *him*, not to his comrades. In other words, it is God's will and an ἀνάγκη that *Josephus*, but not those in the cave with him, should survive this brush with death. Since his companions, like the Sicarii, prefer death by their own hand to surrender, Josephus cannot hitch the wagon of his fate to theirs. He understands his prophetic calling as a kind of ἀνάγκη which *compels* him to survive by hook or by crook.[45]

In light of how Josephus's speech at Jotapata recalls issues raised in the *Phaedo* that correspond to the absence of "necessity," and in view of Josephus's insistence in the narrative that it was God's will for him to surrender so that he might pronounce God's decree to Vespasian, we conclude that Josephus's speech at Jotapata does not seem to present arguments against self-killing per se. It is rather that taking his own life under those conditions was inappropriate. Indeed, the differences between Josephus's speech at Jotapata and Eleazar's two speeches at Masada seem to have to do more with circumstance and less with a philosophical/religious point of view. Aside from the ambiguous reference to a Jewish law about the burial of a suicide (377), there appears to be little in the speech of Jotapata that one can identify as uniquely Jewish or especially convincing to a Jew. This speech would also seem reasonable to any Greek conversant with the *Phaedo* and later philosophical discussion. Its central point is not that voluntary death is abhorrent to Jewish laws but rather that life belongs to God and one was

---

44. Nicole Kelly, "The Cosmopolitan Expression of Josephus' Prophetic Perspective in the *Jewish War*," *HTR* 97 (2004): 272. Emphasis hers.

45. Ibid., 272. Emphasis hers.

not at liberty to takes one's life arbitrarily. Such is the starting point of the *Phaedo*.[46] The first speech of Eleazar, too, does not sound exclusively Greek. We have seen that in light of Van Henten's work there is good reason to conclude that the arguments therein would sound equally convincing to Jews. True, Eleazar's *second* speech has more points of contact with classical and Hellenistic discussion on the topic. But it seems likely that here Josephus is showing off (to the point of utter historical implausibility) his hard-won cultivation of the Greek language and concepts.[47]

Thus, the crucial difference between Josephus's speech and Eleazar's *first* speech appears to be circumstance. Not only the speeches but the entire narrative emphasizes how ἀνάγκη was present for Eleazar and therefore voluntary death was a divinely sanctioned necessity. The opposite held true for Josephus. He rather had a commission to fulfill before Vespasian, and therefore self-killing, which was always an act of impiety if done arbitrarily, would in this case be a particular act of disobedience.[48]

The story Josephus tells about one Simon of Scythopolis (2.466–76) turns out to be a much more appropriate parallel to the Masada narrative. As the revolt gained strength, Josephus states that Jews at Scythopolis placed their own safety before loyalty to kinsmen and therefore fought against those Jews who were in revolt. The Gentile element of the city, however, did not trust these Jewish allies and killed them by deceit. Simon, one of these Scythopolitan Jews, also fought against his own countrymen, but recognized his error upon seeing the deception and the slaughter of his own people by the Gentile element. At this point he killed his family, who did not resist, and then himself in conspicuous manner. In his final words he stated that his death was to be the punishment for the murder of his kinsmen. Indeed, he stated that he intended to die at his own hands because it was not fitting (πρέπον) that he die at the hands of his enemies. His death would at the same time be a penalty paid in accordance with his defilement and an object of praise for his bravery (τὸ αὐτὸ δ᾽ ἂν εἴη μοι καὶ ποινὴ τοῦ μιάσματος

---

46. So also Ladouceur, who states about Josephus's speech that "Greek philosophy more than Jewish teaching informs its argument against suicide." He notes also the "nearly verbatim citation" of the *Phaedo* in 3.372. See Ladouceur, "Josephus and Masada," 97.

47. For Josephus's own statements about his abilities, see *Apion* 1.50 and *Ant.* 20.263. See also above in chapter two.

48. Kelly makes similar conclusions. "These discourses on collective suicide seem to be included in the *Jewish War* not because Josephus wishes to weigh in on the debate about self-killing, but because they give voice to his conviction that God rewards the righteous and punishes the wicked. Indeed, Josephus seems to be using the idea of ἀνάγκη to express this prophetic principle in the case of the Sicarii. Nowhere do we sense that Eleazar has misinterpreted the fire as a sign from God, and nowhere are we told that the suicides were motivated by anything but necessity. These deaths are not frivolous, not cowardly, not unwarranted. Josephus wants his readers to know that Eleazar correctly interprets the fire as an ἀνάγκη sent by God" (Kelly, "Cosmopolitan Expression," 267).

ἀξία καὶ πρὸς ἀνδρείαν ἔπαινος 2.473). It was done in order that his enemy might not boast or gloat over him. Josephus's editorial comment:

> The youth was deserving of pity because of his bodily strength and courageous spirit, but because of his alliance with foreigners (rather than his own people), he encountered sufferings which were appropriate. (476)
>
> ἄξιος μὲν ἐλέους νεανίας δι᾽ ἀλκὴν σώματος καὶ ψυχῆς παράστημα, τῆς δὲ πρὸς ἀλλοφύλους πίστεως ἕνεκεν ἀκολούθοις πάθεσι χρησάμενος.

Points of contact between this episode and Masada, besides the obvious narrative elements (point of recognition, speech of repentance, killing of family, killing of self, all in public view) are that killing one's own people is an act deserving divine punishment. The punishment that befits (πρέπον) killing one's own people is to kill one's self. At the same time, voluntary death robs the enemy of victory and is praiseworthy for its bravery. Finally, in both narratives voluntary death was intended as the penalty to be paid to God.

CONCLUSIONS

The Masada narrative is extraordinarily rich for its rhetorical devices and inter-play of themes. Focusing first on how the narrative serves the overall structure of *War*, we have seen how Masada answers to the loss of freedom when Romans came because of the stasis in Judea. Josephus already indicated in the proem (1.10) that stasis destroyed the Jewish people. It was left to the Romans to control the stasis. Now Josephus uses the Sicarii to bring this element of *War* to a resolution. In their first public act they murdered the high priest, Jonathan. They supported the first tyrant and leader of the stasis, Menahem. Even though they withdrew after his death and took no further part in the events in Jerusalem, they still were instrumental in the stasis that infected the Judean countryside as a sickness. Their raid on Engaddi is emblematic. Now, in his tale about the final reduction of stasis in Judea by the Romans, Josephus illustrates in the Sicarii its devastating consequences. Those who made war against their own people self-destructed. Ironically, one could say that the Sicarii thus died, inevitably, in accordance with their ideology and activities. Compare here the death of Simon of Scythopolis, whose voluntary death was also befitting of his crime.

Another theme of *War* that is given full prominence at Masada is that God gives the Romans their power and is on their side against the Jewish rebels. But this theme is handled delicately by Josephus in a manner that, while acknowl-edging Roman power, deftly undermines it at the same time. True, Josephus showcases the skill and indefatigability of the Romans in their siege at Masada. The fulsome description of the inapproachable nature of the rock along with the impenetrable fortress and its complete supply serve to highlight the need for

Roman ingenuity (7.279).[49] But when there is a final breach in the walls, there is no culminating display of martial skill. There is no battle, no display of valor, and no sacrifice for honor. Josephus rather has the Romans retire in joy to their camp because of God's "alliance" (συμμάχια). When the Romans return to take up the battle after a good night's rest, God has already seen to their work. In such a manner, Roman power is upstaged by God's.

The voluntary deaths emphasize the point further. That the voluntary deaths are, in the mind of Eleazar, necessitated by God is clear in the speeches. He intends them as the punishment that they are to pay to God (333–34). Nowhere does Josephus have Eleazar confess that their punishment is paid to the Romans. Indeed, nowhere does he have Eleazar refer to Roman military power at all. In the speeches, the Roman military is shunted so far to the sidelines so as to appear almost irrelevant. Even the impregnable and well-supplied fortress, those very things that Josephus had set up to highlight Roman skill, he has Eleazar deftly turn to highlight divine ἀνάγκη (330–32). "Even though our fortress was impregnable and we had an abundance of supplies, *God himself* deprived us of all hope."[50] Finally, in words that sound similar to Simon's at Scythopolis, Eleazar says, "The Romans can claim no credit for the victory" (360). Josephus thus in a rather polite yet insistent manner shifts the focus of Masada away from Roman power to the authority and power of God.

Concerning the valor of the Sicarii, we should emphasize again that Josephus does not turn the Sicarii into heroes. He has already excoriated them in the Hall of Infamy (see above) and presents them as people under God's punishment for their crimes. Yet he clearly highlights also some noble qualities of these criminals. Both the speeches and the nature of voluntary death under these circumstances bear some noble qualities from both Jewish and Roman perspectives. By attaching noble qualities to these enemies of the Romans and of God, Josephus

---

49. "Silva turned his attention to the siege because it required much skill and work in view of the strength of the fortress, which had the following nature" (ὁ Σίλβας ἐπὶ τὴν πολιορκίαν ἐτράπετο πολλῆς ἐπιτεχνήσεως καὶ ταλαιπωρίας δεομένην διὰ τὴν ὀχυρότητα τοῦ φρουρίου τοιοῦδε τὴν φύσιν ὑπάρχοντος).

50. In his social and psychological study of how Rome processed violence and disorder via gladiatorial contests and political suicide, Paul Plass notes how the ancients remarked on the "irrational" element inherent in attempting to assert one's power through suicide, and that the freedom gained in suicide was "at once vacuous and real." Still, preemptive suicide in the political sphere was generally looked upon as a win for the victim; that is, a way of diminishing the emperor's power. See Paul Plass, *The Game of Death in Ancient Rome: Arena Sport and Political Suicide* (Madison: University of Wisconsin Press, 1995), 89–90, 123–24. It would thus be tempting to try to score the voluntary deaths of the Sicarii as a win against Roman power, but in view of how Josephus marginalizes the Roman soldiers, this would be off center to the narrative. The deaths are not primarily acts of defiance directed toward the Romans to make them, albeit in a paradoxical fashion, come away the losers. Rather they take place as obedience to God's punishment, to preserve religious scruples, and to preserve personal dignity.

is developing one of his themes of *War* and, we might add, conforming to the normal standards of character-driven history. Observing that one of the "leading functions of Roman history-writing" was to examine character (ἦθος, *ingenium, mores*), Mason observes the same at work in Josephus.

> Noteworthy in this context is Josephus' effort to achieve balance in his moral assessment and to render his characters plausible human beings with conflicting drives toward good and evil. Such rounded psychological analysis, with its resulting ambiguities, was a hallmark of Roman historiography. Even when describing unrepentant villains, Josephus looks for intelligible motives. They are neither static nor two-dimensional representatives of particular virtues or vices.[51]

Thus there is no need–indeed it is too simplistic–for any blanket assessment on how Josephus presents the Sicarii at Masada as "heroes" or "villains." The narrative is far too complex and finely nuanced. True, Josephus makes the Sicarii emblematic of that stasis which destroyed the Jewish people, but Josephus's Roman readers in particular would not have been troubled by the noble voluntary deaths, particularly in the context of civil war, of those who otherwise have been indicted by the author for their criminal activity.[52]

This observation serves as a point of entrée to how Josephus makes use of irony in the narrative. We note in the first place that Josephus positively invites his readers to explore the narrative more deeply if in no other way than by his employment of intentionally ambiguous, and sometimes seemingly contradictory, words in the narrative above. Eleazar's final encouragement to his compatriots is a good example. At 388 he says, "So let us be quick to leave for them, instead of the enjoyment they expect with our capture, amazement at our death and wonder at our bravery (τόλμης)." Even today scholars are divided as to whether Eleazar leaves amazement at his "arrogance" or his "bravery." Even more striking, as we noted above, is the manner by which Josephus at 405–6 juxtaposes seemingly contradictory words in the Roman assessment of the deaths. This ambiguity of words can only be attributed the "playful distance" of Josephus with his text.[53]

Generally speaking, Josephus employs irony to tease out a number of the themes stated above. He demonstrates a "playful distance" at several points in his free, even seemingly contradictory, manner by which he takes away that which he

---

51. Mason, "Flavius Josephus in Flavian Rome: Reading on and between the Lines," in *Flavian Rome: Culture, Image, Text*, ed. A. J. Boyle and W. J. Dominik (Leiden: Brill, 1991), 559–89, 571.

52. See Catherine Edwards, *Death in Ancient Rome* (New Haven and London: Yale University Press, 2007), 28f.

53. On this aspect of irony, see Mason, "Figured Speech and Irony in T. Flavius Josephus," in *Flavius Josephus and Flavian Rome*, ed. Jonathan Edmondson, Steve Mason, James Rives (New York: Oxford University Press, 2005), 245–49.

simultaneously gives. This is apparent in regard to the Roman victory at Masada. He sets up the narrative in such a manner as to showcase Roman skill and ingenuity. This is especially clear in how he highlights the impregnable nature of the site and the fortress. But then he deftly takes away any claim the Romans might make to victory. Even the nature of the fortress in the end is used to highlight not Roman power but God's providence. He rounds out his assessment of the Roman victory by a telling phrase at 407, "After this capture, *such as it was* (τοιαύτης δὲ τῆς ἀλώσεως γενομένης), the general left a garrison at the fortress." Thus, the irony here is that what on the surface appears to be a magnificent victory for the Romans is indeed not their victory at all.

The same technique is apparent in Josephus's description of the killings at 389–92, where he especially teases the reader. He has already described the "madness" of the Sicarii in prior sections, but when it comes to their voluntary death, he allows a more noble assessment. In the first place, Josephus has Eleazar convince his "bravest" colleagues to submit to death by means of two speeches of the first order. The speeches are well thought out and, especially in regard to the second, filled with philosophical precedent. Yet at the conclusion of the second speech, as we have noted above, Josephus describes the Sicarii as acting out of madness and under irrational impulse—and then juxtaposes rational words denoting a considered plan. He thus permits more honorable traits to attach to these enemies of God and the Jewish people. Finally, his playful distance is certainly evident in the presentation of two equally convincing arguments about voluntary death, one at Jotapata and the other at Masada. The manipulation becomes all the more apparent when Josephus overlays Eleazar's second speech with Greek rhetorical allusions, as if Josephus takes delight in the implausible presentation of a Jewish tyrant in Greek philosophical dress. In such ways Josephus signals to his readers that things are not exactly as they appear on the surface and so invites his readers to examine the Sicarii at Masada more closely. Ironic indeed that these enemies of God and of their own people die so nobly!

At a more fundamental level, however, we see "text-dependent" irony within the narrative in the self-destruction of the Sicarii. The irony present here comes largely through Josephus's attachment of the Sicarii to stasis. These Jews who fought against their own people ironically destroyed themselves. The irony is sharpened, as with the raid on Engaddi, by the fact that the Sicarii killed themselves on 15 Xanthicus, Passover, and even more so by having Eleazar expatiate on freedom. The culminating act of freedom carried out by the Sicarii on Passover was their own death.

We turn now to the irony detected by Ladouceur and followed by Chapman. Recall that Ladouceur has Josephus present Eleazar as one of the Stoic opposition in the Flavian period. Eleazar represents the inappropriate response of a madman to the Flavian regime. Josephus presents the proper response to the Flavians via Josephus's speech at Jotapata. Now, it is indeed true that Vespasian took some measures against Stoic and Cynic philosophers.[54] However, for this irony to work, the deaths of the Sicarii and the speeches of Eleazar would have to emphasize the fact of Roman (read Flavian) power, against which the speeches and deaths would then be directed as acts of defiance. And, indeed, we have seen a note of defiance directed against the Romans in the speeches of Eleazar. Eleazar and the Sicarii, for example, refused to submit to the torture and the slavery they believed they would suffer if they surrendered to the Romans. However, we have seen also that the narrative throughout undermines Roman power, and that the main points of both Eleazar's speeches answer less to Roman power and more to submission to divine ἀνάγκη. In the final analysis, Masada does not highlight Roman power at all. Rather the emphasis is on the final and appropriate end under divine direction of those who committed acts of violence against their own people. Therefore, Josephus does not intend his readers to understand the voluntary deaths primarily as acts of violence against Roman power, and therefore the irony that Ladouceur proposes loses its foundation.

This is not to say that some of Josephus's Roman readers would never have made such connections between the so-called Stoic opposition and the person of Eleazar. Rather, it is to say that, even if such connections were made, these were not central to Josephus's intent. We might point out that the structural arrangement of *War* supports this conclusion. As we have seen above, the Masada narrative responds not so much to issues raised at Jotapata but to those raised in book 1.

The same data speak against any theory that would present Eleazar as a cipher for the wrong choice before Roman power and Josephus at Jotapata as the correct choice.[55] Josephus indeed presents the Sicarii's fight for liberty as ill-timed and characteristic of those who die badly (5.365). And indeed the Sicarii made the wrong choice. Moreover, Josephus did indeed find mercy at the hands of the Romans. However, Masada is not to be understood as a story about the horrendous deaths of those who reject Roman power. Such deaths have already been amply illustrated during the siege and fall of Jerusalem. Rather, Masada is a story about the final recognition of and submission to divine retribution. Neither is the central thrust of Josephus's speech at Jotapata so much about finding mercy by submitting to Roman power as it is about the impiety of taking one's own life for no good reason. Josephus surrendered, according to his explicit statement, not to have Roman mercy but to obey God's commission (3.354). Moreover, all such theories about Masada being an example of an inappropriate response to Roman power are ill-equipped to incorporate the clear textual evidence that,

---

54. For a recent presentation, see Barbara Levick, *Vespasian* (London and New York: Routledge, 1999), 89–90.

55. See above in chapter one, besides Ladouceur and Chapman, also Helgo Lindner, *Die Geschichtsauffassung des Flavius Josephus im Bellum Judaicum* (Leiden: Brill, 1972); and Pierre Vidal-Naquet, "Flavius Josèph et Masada," *Revue Historique* 260 (1978).

besides dying in a fitting manner in accordance with their self-destructive activities, from a Roman perspective Eleazar and his compatriots died well.

Present also here is audience-dependent irony from a Jewish perspective, whereby noble qualities are attached to these criminals. For the manner in which Josephus describes the words and deeds of the Sicarii would remind his Jewish readers of how the author of 2 Maccabees 14:37–46 presents the death of Razis. There we read that Nicanor, sent by Demetrius as governor of Judea, intended to make an example of Razis and show by the latter's death what he intended to bring to the entire Jewish people. But Razis forestalled his intent by taking his own life in the presence of the more than five hundred soldiers sent to arrest him. Van Henten places this suicide as one of the key turning points in the structure of 2 Maccabees in the author's presentation of Nicanor's defeat. "Razis' death turns out to be a demonstration of the nobility, independence and vitality of the Jewish people."[56] Turning his attention to Josephus, Van Henten proposes the following as motifs that are connected to Jewish martyr texts: contempt of death, perseverance during suffering or even contempt of suffering, preference of violent death above a dishonorable continuation of life, total faithfulness to the Lord, obedience to the Torah, Jewish practice and convictions.[57] We have noted that these same noble qualities are emphasized in a different context by Josephus at *Apion* 2.232–34. Here we also note Josephus's statement that the day of Nicanor's defeat was an annual celebration for the Jews (*Ant.* 12.412). Therefore, we should understand that Josephus, in the Masada narrative, presents a subtext to his Jewish readers. For the manner in which he describes the death of the Sicarii would bring these Jewish martyrs to mind and thus allow those readers to hold the Sicarii in admiration for the manner of their death. It is even possible to interpret Josephus's veiled reference to Passover in this manner, for it was a celebration of redemption from slavery to a pagan life and a recreation as a people belonging to God. In other words, it was not merely a celebration of political but also ethical freedom, and it is precisely this freedom that Eleazar is determined also to have the Sicarii preserve by their deaths.

In the end, in part because of Josephus's masterful use of irony, one suspects that readers will see what they desire to see in the death of the Sicarii—criminals or heroes. This, of course, was the goal of literary authors at Rome who used figured speech and irony to make safe criticism. One had to construct a work so that the criticism therein contained could be subject to an alternate interpretation.[58]

---

56. Jan Willem Van Henten, *The Maccabean Martyrs*, 208.

57. Van Henten, "Martyrion and Martyrdom: Some Remarks about Noble Death in Josephus," in *Internationales Josephus-Kolloquium Brüssel 1998*, ed. Jürgen Kalms and Folker Siegert (Münster: Lit Verlag, 1998) 124–41, here 133. Without elaboration, Van Henten lists the events of Masada as illustrative, not of a martyr's death, but of a "noble" death in that the Sicarii are to a certain extent described in terms that pertain to Jewish martyrology (p. 138).

58. See above under "Literary Background."

Indeed, it is a delicate matter for Josephus not only to fulfill his intent, signaled in the proem, to point out noble qualities in those who rebelled against Rome (1.8), but also to set limits to Roman power by placing it under the authority of the God of their defeated enemy. Therefore, Josephus uses irony to showcase both of these intentions in his narrative about Masada. We should at this point recognize also that, in light of the literary tradition at Rome and the rhetorical aims of Josephus, there is no longer any need for us to delve into the so-called "troubled mind" of our author and explain the Masada narrative as his attempt to ease his "tortured conscience" concerning his behavior at Jotapata. In the final analysis, Josephus's connection of stasis to the Sicarii must receive emphasis. These were bandits, who in their blind rebellion against Rome turned against their own people and died fittingly at their own hand under God's sentence. Yet Josephus now adds character to the Sicarii. No longer mere rebellious figures, Josephus gives them plausible motivation, has them repent, and die nobly.

We might at this point make some historical observations about the Sicarii on the basis of the text. We should first recognize that in general, the archaeological finds at Masada harmonize well with the main details of Josephus's narrative. The remains of several Roman encampments surround the cliff. A casemate wall, which shows evidence of destruction by fire, enclosed the entire plateau on which were built a palace, apartments, baths, storerooms, administrative buildings, and numerous cisterns, all of which testify to Herod's elaborate fortified residence as recounted in Josephus. A great variety of objects have been found at the site: jewelry, cosmetic items, cookware, storage jars, lamps, clothing, papyri of various sorts, and weapons.

Among those which are of more interest to this study are a synagogue, several ritual baths (*mikvoth*), certain coins, copies of sacred texts, and a few interesting pottery shards. The Sicarii had added rows of benches and columns to a structure, converting it to a synagogue, and used it as their place of worship. The two *mikvoth* served as places of ritual washing and conform in all respects to rabbinic specifications. The copies of Jewish sacred and sectarian texts include a small fragment identical to one found at Qumran, and for a time this stirred speculation about Essene involvement in the revolt. Among the coins were discovered shekels and half-shekels of all the years of the Judean revolt. Finally, eleven small ostraca, each bearing a name written in Aramaic and one of these displaying the name "ben Yair," were found together. These were immediately thought to be the very lots cast to determine who would carry out the killings in the final desperate moments, as recounted by Josephus.[59] All these fascinating and important discoveries confirm to a remarkable degree what Josephus tells us in general about Masada in *War* and

---

59. See Yigael Yadin, *Masada: The Yigael Yadin Excavations 1963–1965, Final Reports*, 7 vols. (Jerusalem: Israel Exploration Society, 1989 –). For a more popular presentation, see Yadin, *Masada: Herod's Fortress and the Zealots' Last Stand* (New York: Random House, 1966).

about certain of the events during the final siege. Unfortunately, none of them adds significantly to our knowledge of the Sicarii per se.

We note here also that no mass graves have been discovered at Masada, which leads Atkinson to suggest that the defenders did not, in fact, commit mass suicide but were rather taken captive.[60] However, even though the Romans allowed for embellishment of detail in historical narrative, they nevertheless expected that the main facts be true.[61] We legitimately assume that Josephus availed himself of Roman sources, such as *commentarii*, for the major details of the narrative, about which advantage he boasts generally in *Life* 358 and *Apion* 1.56. It is, indeed, difficult for us to imagine how Josephus could have fabricated the voluntary deaths not only in view of such boasting about the accuracy of his history but also in light of the emperor's own endorsement of the completed work. But in regard to the speeches, a more cautious assessment is warranted. Josephus insists that one of the surviving women, a relative of Eleazar, stood out above most women for her intellect and education, presumably to identify her as the source of information for the events and speeches within the fortress (399). There is no compelling reason to deny the existence of such a source. Furthermore, while recognizing that the exact sequence of events is problematic (Shaye Cohen, for example, thinks it unlikely that the Romans would retire for the night after effecting a breach in the walls[62]), we find no compelling reasons to deny that at some point during the siege, Eleazar delivered a speech to his assembled compatriots. But we should also expect that in good historiographical tradition Josephus would have exercised the freedom to compose what he would have thought it appropriate for Eleazar to say, and a cursory glance at the second speech shows that he not only did this, but also allowed his own rhetorical aims to hold sway. The evidence would thus suggest that even if we were to think it likely that Eleazar delivered such speeches, caution is in order when trying to assess what this Sicarii leader actually said. Only some major points indeed seem safe: that Eleazar at some point convinced his compatriots that death was preferable to surrender.

More generally, what identifies these characters as Sicarii? Here Josephus makes clear the Sicarii's motive for their activities. He has already established how they fought against their fellow Jews who sympathized with and paid taxes to the Romans. Now he adds the slogan, "God alone is the true and righteous

---

60. Kenneth Atkinson, "Noble Deaths at Gamla and Masada? A Critical Assessment of Josephus' Accounts of Jewish Resistance in Light of Archaeological Discoveries," in *Making History: Josephus and Historical Method*, ed. Zuleika Rodgers (Leiden: Brill, 2007), 349–71, here 357.

61. This point is made by A. J. Woodman. "The Romans required the hard core of history to be true and its elaboration to be plausible, and further they saw no contradiction between these two requirements but rather regarded them as complementary" (A. J. Woodman, *Rhetoric in Classical Historiography* [Portland, OR: Areopagitica Press, 1966], 91).

62. Cohen, "Masada: Literary Tradition, Archaeological Remains, and the Credibility of Josephus." *JJS* 33 (1982): 385–405, here 396.

master of men" (μόνος γὰρ οὗτος ἀληθής ἐστι καὶ δίκαιος ἀνθρώπων δεσπότης 323). Yet such an agenda, originating with Judas the Galilean and ancestor of Eleazar (2.118), we may legitimately infer was claimed publicly by any number of revolutionary groups and tyrants (see below). And, of course, these Sicarii at Masada are no longer identified by their tactics (use of daggers). Therefore, in the absence of unique rhetoric, behavior, or other external identifiable traits, the only possible historical reason for calling these last rebels Sicarii is their connection to past activities in Jerusalem. That is, the rebels at Masada were clearly connected to those who originally committed stealthy, politically motivated assassinations in Jerusalem. Once again we see in the narrative of *War* how the title "Sicarii" has acquired a somewhat more general application.

THE SICARII IN EGYPT (7.410, 412, 415)

In this first of two smaller episodes that bring *War* to a conclusion, Josephus tells about unrest in Alexandria caused by the Sicarii.

LITERARY CONTEXT

The context of this narrative has been presented above. The narrative serves to bring to a resolution the theme of stasis. We will see, in fact, that it answers more to *War* 1.33f. than it does to its immediate context. The outline of this passage in its context has been presented above.

DESCRIPTION OF SICARII ACTIVITY

Josephus introduces the passage with a transitional statement at 409–10.

> [409] But even still at Alexandria in Egypt it later happened that many of the Jews died. [410] For it was not enough for those from the stasis of the Sicarii who managed to escape there to be saved, and they were again attempting to revolt and were trying to persuade those who were favorably inclined to assert their independence.

> [409] ἔτι δὲ καὶ περὶ Ἀλεξάνδρειαν τὴν ἐν Αἰγύπτῳ μετὰ ταῦτα συνέβη πολλοὺς Ἰουδαίων ἀποθανεῖν· [410] τοῖς γὰρ ἐκ τῆς στάσεως τῶν σικαρίων ἐκεῖ διαφυγεῖν δυνηθεῖσιν οὐκ ἀπέχρη τὸ σῴζεσθαι, πάλιν δὲ καινοτέροις ἐνεχείρουν πράγμασι καὶ πολλοὺς τῶν ὑποδεξαμένων ἔπειθον τῆς ἐλευθερίας ἀντιποιεῖσθαι.

Josephus tells us nothing about the origins of these Sicarii. They could not have come from Masada, according to Josephus's narrative, though E. Mary Smallwood detects a problem with the chronology of these events. Paulinus replaced Lupus as prefect before August 73. To accommodate the sequence of events here reported by Josephus, including an exchange of letters between Lupus and Vespasian and then the arrival of Paulinus after Lupus's death, Smallwood concludes that these events must have taken place before the fall of Masada, despite Josephus's statement.[63]

It would be important for us to determine whether this is in fact the case not only for the possible origins of these Sicarii in Alexandria but also because it would provide evidence that Josephus had reversed the order of historical events for rhetorical reasons. So to this matter we now briefly turn. Smallwood's statements assume that Masada fell in 73, which date is disputed by Werner Eck. On the basis of an inscription found at Urbs Salvia, he stated that Flavius Silva was not appointed procurator of Judea until March 73 because Vespasian and Titus did not become censors until the second quarter of that same year. Allowing enough time for Silva to take office and gather his forces, Eck concludes that Masada could not have been captured until 74.[64] In a review of Eck's arguments, however, Christopher Jones notes how this results in a "serious conflict" in the chronology of Josephus, who reports that the disturbances in Egypt happened when Julius Lupus was prefect and therefore no later than 73. The resolution, presented by Jones, is that the author of the inscription most likely mentioned Judea first "to juxtapose the two adlections in order not to repeat the names of the rulers."[65] That is, the inscription does not represent a chronological order of Silva's political career, and indeed he was sent to Judea before his second adlection. Also, Hannah Cotton has shown that papyri found at Masada point to 73 as the date of its destruction.[66]

On balance, then, it would seem best to date the fall of Masada to April of 73. This, however, does not address Smallwood's contention that the events at Alexandria must have taken place before this date to allow sufficient time for the reported sequence of events. We might point out, however, that the μετὰ ταῦτα ("later") at 409 places only the resulting deaths of the Sicarii subsequent to Masada and not the entire sequence of events, some of which may have taken place before Masada fell. Thus, there is no necessary conflict in Josephus's narrative.

Returning to the origins in Egypt of these Sicarii, we are left with only two options from the narrative of *War*, and neither one has much strength. It is possible that some Sicarii from Masada had fled to Egypt before Masada fell, yet it seems unlikely. M. Stern denies this possibility because all the Sicarii at Masada

---

63. Smallwood, *The Jews under Roman Rule: From Pompey to Diocletion* (Leiden: Brill, 2001): 366 n. 39.

64. Werner Eck, "Die Eroberung von Masada und eine neue Inschrift des L. Flavius Silva Nonius Bassus," *ZNW* 60 (1969): 282f. The inscription, given by Jones, reads, "[legat. Aug. pro pr]ovinciae Iudaeae, adlectus inter patricios [ab divo Vespasiano et di]vo Tito censoribus, ab isdem adlec(tus) inter pr(aetorios), legat. Leg. XXI Rapac(is).

65. Christopher Jones, "Review of Eck, "Senatorem," *AJP* 95 (1974): 90. So also G. W. Bowersock, "Old and New in the History of Judeaea," *JRS* 65 (1975): 184.

66. Hannah M. Cotton, "The Date of the Fall of Masada: The Evidence of the Masada Papyri," *ZPE* 78 (1989): 157–62.

had committed suicide.[67] Yet even if we were to allow the possiblity that some Sicarii left Masada for Egypt prior to that fate, this would still seem unlikely because Josephus has already portrayed those Sicarii as savage animals who were too afraid to wander far from their lair (4.503–8). The only other alternative is that some Sicarii had fled from Jerusalem to Egypt. The problem here is that Josephus tells us nothing about any Sicarii activity in Jerusalem once Eleazar b. Yair leaves after Menahem's murder. Admittedly, this is an argument from silence, but the silence is deafening. In sum, there is simply insufficient evidence at hand for us to determine their origins in Egypt.

Josephus states that these Sicarii, whatever their origins, had a revolutionary agenda though what sort of changes the Jews in Alexandria may have desired or why such revolutionary talk may have been attractive is not specified. Josephus tells us in *Ant.* 12.21 that Titus and Vespasian reaffirmed citizen rights for the Jews of Alexandria despite the urging of the Gentile citizens to deny them. Such evidence speaks of Jewish-Gentile animosity, which we reasonably suppose would have been exacerbated after the war; but in view of the continued Flavian support, there is little data here to enlighten the revolutionary agenda presented in the text. Smallwood conjectures that perhaps the presence of Jews sold into slavery after the revolt, in combination with the newly enacted Judean tax, fostered resentment among Jewish Alexandrian citizens.[68] Her ideas harmonize well with the two-part slogan used by the Sicarii in their revolutionary agenda—"The Romans are no better than you. Regard God alone as Lord!"[69] We have already seen the second part of this phrase in connection with the Sicarii. However, the manner in which Josephus describes the torture of the Sicarii, employing stock ideas of Jewish martyr language, lends a certain religious flavor to the entire close of the narrative. In that light, the slogan, "God alone is master," begins to remind the Jewish reader also of the first statement of Jewish faith, the *Shema* of Deuteronomy 6:4. More on this below.

The Sicarii murdered certain prominent Jews who opposed them, and this motivated the leaders of the Jewish *gerousia* to expose the madness (ἀπόνοιαν) of the Sicarii in a public Jewish assembly. They stated:

> These people, who have no certain hope of safety (for they would straightaway be killed if they were recognized by the Romans), are infecting with their own misfortune those who have no share in their misdeeds. (413)

---

67. M. Stern, "Sicarii and Zealots" in *Society and Religion in the Second Temple Period*, ed. Michael Avi-Yonah and Zvi Baras (Jerusalem: Masada Publishing, 1977), 277. Stern states that these comprised a group independent of those at Masada or Jerusalem, connected to the latter two only via Judas's ideology.

68. Smallwood, *Jews under Roman Rule*, 367.

69. Ῥωμαίους μὲν μηδὲν κρείττους αὐτῶν ὑπολαμβάνειν θεὸν δὲ μόνον ἡγεῖσθαι δεσπότην (410).

καὶ νῦν ἔφασαν αὐτούς, ἐπείπερ οὐδὲ πεφευγότες τῆς σωτηρίας ἐλπίδα
βεβαίαν ἔχουσιν, γνωσθέντας γὰρ ὑπὸ Ῥωμαίων εὐθὺς ἀπολεῖσθαι, τῆς αὐτοῖς
προσηκούσης συμφορᾶς ἀναπιμπλάναι τοὺς μηδενὸς τῶν ἁμαρτημάτων
μετασχόντας.

The leaders encouraged the assembly to be on guard against their destruction
and defend themselves by handing them over to the Romans.

The assembly seized six hundred of the Sicarii on the spot, and the other
Sicarii who had escaped to Egypt were soon arrested and put under torture. Josephus states:

> [417] Everyone was amazed at their endurance and madness or strength of convic
> tion, however it should be called. [418] For under all forms of torture devised for
> the singular purpose of making them confess that Caesar was lord, not one
> gave in. All kept their conviction triumphant over this compulsion and received
> fire and tortures with bodies that seemed to feel no pain and with a spirit that
> just about rejoiced. [419] The age of the children in particular amazed those who
> looked on. Not one of them was forced to name Caesar as lord. Such was the
> degree to which the strength of their bravery held mastery over the weakness of
> their bodies. (417–19)

> [417] ἐφ' ὧν οὐκ ἔστιν ὃς οὐ τὴν καρτερίαν καὶ τὴν εἴτε ἀπόνοιαν εἴτε τῆς
> γνώμης ἰσχὺν χρὴ λέγειν οὐ κατεπλάγη· [418] πάσης γὰρ ἐπ' αὐτοὺς βασάνου καὶ
> λύμης τῶν σωμάτων ἐπινοηθείσης ἐφ' ἓν τοῦτο μόνον, ὅπως αὐτῶν Καίσαρα
> δεσπότην ὁμολογήσωσιν, οὐδεὶς ἐνέδωκεν οὐδὲ ἐμέλλησεν εἰπεῖν, ἀλλὰ πάντες
> ὑπερτέραν τῆς ἀνάγκης τὴν αὐτῶν γνώμην διεφύλαξαν, ὥσπερ ἀναισθήτοις
> σώμασι χαιρούσῃ μόνον οὐχὶ τῇ ψυχῇ τὰς βασάνους καὶ τὸ πῦρ δεχόμενοι. [419]
> μάλιστα δ' ἡ τῶν παίδων ἡλικία τοὺς θεωμένους ἐξέπληξεν· οὐδὲ γὰρ ἐκείνων
> τις ἐξενικήθη Καίσαρα δεσπότην ἐξονομάσαι. τοσοῦτον ἄρα τῆς τῶν σωμάτων
> ἀσθενείας ἡ τῆς τόλμης ἰσχὺς ἐπεκράτει.

The natural interpretation is that for these Sicarii this slogan, "Caesar is lord"
(Caesar dominus est), was used as a test case for *maiestas*. There is some evidence that in Domitian's later years repudiation of the imperial cult was viewed
as *maiestas*, but even then such was not a general policy for Jews. Domitian was
rather more concerned about proselytism.[70] Other than this text, there is no other
evidence for any such policy under Vespasian, making this then a rather isolated
incident.

Lupus reported the commotion to Caesar, who ordered the Jewish temple
to be destroyed because he was suspicious of the revolutionary tendencies of the
Jews, which were hard to put down, and feared that they would gather together

---

70. See Brian W. Jones, *The Emperor Domitian* (London and New York: Routledge, 1992),
117–19; and Smallwood, *Jews under Roman Rule*, 379.

and drag some others along with them (421). Josephus then recounts the temple's origin (421–32). The narrative concludes with its destruction (433–36).

WORD STUDIES

Several of the important words in this narrative we have seen before. Josephus connects the Sicarii to stasis, he employs the ambiguous τόλμα in describing the strength of the Sicarii under torture, and he has the leaders of the *gerousia* dismiss the Sicarii rhetoric and behavior as "madness." With this last term, however, in an editorial comment Josephus opens the door for a different interpretation, explicitly inviting the reader to conclude whether the Sicarii were possessed of "madness" or "strength of conviction" (417). More on this below.

Josephus employs one significant new term for the Sicarii, καρτερία. He stated that those who looked upon the torture of the young children showed amazement at their "endurance." This quality Josephus showcases in *Apion*, where he says that Jewish laws produce endurance in Jewish life (2.146, 170) such that it even surpasses that of the Lacedaemonians (2.228). Here undoubtedly Josephus refers to the popular reputation enjoyed by the Spartans and how καρτερία was "the whole focus" of their training. Mason thus indicates how the word group is an important component of Josephus's presentation of "manly" Jewish character to a Roman audience.[71]

We also note the importance of the term in the Jewish "martyr" tradition. The author of 4 Maccabees, a contemporary of Josephus, therein expanded on the deaths of Eleazar and the seven sons, originally presented in 2 Maccabees, in his treatise on "devout reason's mastery over passions."[72] There καρτερία becomes a theme used to describe their deaths (6:13; 8:26; 11:12; 15:28, 30; 16:14). Note particularly 16:14, where the author says about the mother, "Woman, because of your endurance you even conquered a tyrant and in word and speech were found more powerful than a man."[73]

BOOK CONTEXT

Like the Masada narrative, there are clear indications that this narrative answers in chiastic fashion to the beginning of *War*. Besides the accent on stasis, by which Josephus introduces this section, we note that the commotion caused by the Sicarii

---

71. Mason, "Essenes and Lurking Spartans," 23.

72. H. Anderson, "4 Maccabees: A New Translation and Introduction," in *The Old Testament Pseudepigrapha*, ed. James H. Charlesworth (New York: Doubleday, 1985), 531. Anderson sees this as the theme of the book. He dates the work to the years 63–70 c.e. (533–34).

73. γύναι διὰ καρτερίαν καὶ τύραννον ἐνίκησας καὶ ἔργοις δυνατωτέρα καὶ λόγοις εὑρέθης ἀνδρός.

prompted Lupus to close the temple at Leontopolis, which Josephus then goes on to describe at some length. Josephus reports that Onias promised Ptolemy that the Jews would be his allies against Antiochus (Epiphanes) if he allowed Onias to build a Jewish temple in Alexandria. Ptolemy agreed. Josephus states that Onias's motive was impure for he had a contentious spirit (φιλονεικία) toward the Jews in Jerusalem, bearing anger against them for his exile (431).

Now Josephus first introduced these issues at 1.31–33, the opening paragraphs of *War*. There he states that stasis arose between Onias and the sons of Tobias. The latter, exiled by Onias, gained the support of Antiochus Epiphanes, who used them as guides to invade Judea. Onias escaped to Ptolemy in Egypt. Antiochus plundered the temple and stopped the daily sacrifices there for three and one-half years. Josephus thereupon states that he will dwell on this matter again at the appropriate place (1.33). Josephus does not address the issue again until the passage in question at book 7. Thus, this section answers issues introduced by Josephus at the beginning of *War*. The opening and closing of the temple at Leontopolis, emblematic of Jewish stasis, begins and should properly conclude the narrative of *War*. In this way Josephus links the Sicarii in Alexandria to the vestiges of an ancient internal Jewish stasis that originated with Onias.

CONCLUSIONS

Josephus connects the Sicarii to the long-standing stasis that comprises the beginning of *War*. The narrative about the Sicarii in Alexandria thus brings the history to a satisfying conclusion. We can see this theme more clearly in light of Josephus's statements about the Judean constitution in his later works. For Josephus, the ideal Judean government was a priestly aristocracy. The laws of the Judean constitution were originally given by God to Moses, who in turn entrusted these to the priests (*Ant.* 3.322; 4.304). In consultation with a council (γερουσία) priests oversaw the preservation and administration of the laws that governed the Jewish people (*Ant.* 4.186).[74] Josephus applies the term "theocracy" (θεοκρατία) to this form of government in *Apion* 2.165 and praises it as the best possible form of governments not only because it was established by God, but also because it focused on the administration of worship and everyday activities such that all of life resembled a "sacred rite" (τελετῆς τινός 2.184–89).

Josephus's starting point in *War* stands in accord with these ideas. When stasis first breaks out between Onias and the sons of Tobias, a result is the opening of a rival temple in Egypt. Of necessity, stasis among the Judean leadership, in accordance with the nature of the Judean constitution, is a rebellion also against

---

74. For an exposition of these ideas with particular emphasis on how Josephus articulates these ideas for a Roman audience, see Mason's comments in "Introduction to the *Judean Antiquities*," in Feldman, *Judean Antiquties 1–4*, ed. Steve Mason (Leiden: Brill, 2000), xxiv–xxix.

divinely appointed authority. This symbol of Judean stasis is closed at the conclusion of *War's* narrative. By bracketing *War* in this manner, with the outbreak and resolution of stasis against priestly aristocracy focused as it is on the temple in Alexandria, Josephus gives stasis a theological component, one that ultimately brings divine punishment. It was this stasis that destroyed the people, not the Romans (1.10). Josephus brings these ideas to clear focus and center stage in the concluding episodes of *War* through the Sicarii. We have seen how he highlights divine punishment at Masada to the point were the Romans can claim no victory. Here Josephus illustrates the suppression of this ancient stasis in Alexandria.

But there is a strong note of irony in the death of these Sicarii. Josephus presents their death in ways that even the Spartans would admire, but Josephus wants his Jewish readers also to look deeper. His ambiguous terms invite a more positive assessment of the Sicarii mindset in suffering (417). Jewish readers in particular will detect the language of Jewish "martyrology," the narrative in 2 Maccabees 6 about the mother and her seven sons in particular, when they read about the torture and death of the Sicarii. Strongly pronounced in this tradition is that suffering is to be understood as a mark of God's discipline, atonement for sin, and even his gracious presence among the Jewish people. Before introducing the gruesome accounts of the torture of Eleazar and the mother with her seven sons, the author of 2 Maccabees writes:

> Now I exhort you who come upon this book not to become discouraged because of the sufferings but to consider that these punishments come not for the destruction of our people but their discipline. For it is a sign of great kindness not to allow much time for the impious but to punish them immediately. For the Almighty does not wait patiently with us as with other nations to punish them when they come to the full measure of their sins. He has decided to come upon us so that he might not condemn us when we have come to the completion of our sins. For this reason he never takes his mercy from us and although he disciplines with suffering, he does not forsake his own people. (2 Maccabees 6:12–16)

> παρακαλῶ οὖν τοὺς ἐντυγχάνοντας τῇδε τῇ βίβλῳ μὴ συστέλλεσθαι διὰ τὰς συμφοράς λογίζεσθαι δὲ τὰς τιμωρίας μὴ πρὸς ὄλεθρον ἀλλὰ πρὸς παιδείαν τοῦ γένους ἡμῶν εἶναι. καὶ γὰρ τὸ μὴ πολὺν χρόνον ἐᾶσθαι τοὺς δυσσεβοῦντας ἀλλ᾽ εὐθέως περιπίπτειν ἐπιτίμοις μεγάλης εὐεργεσίας σημεῖόν ἐστιν. οὐ γὰρ καθάπερ καὶ ἐπὶ τῶν ἄλλων ἐθνῶν ἀναμένει μακροθυμῶν ὁ δεσπότης μέχρι τοῦ καταντήσαντας αὐτοὺς πρὸς ἐκπλήρωσιν ἁμαρτιῶν κολάσαι οὕτως καὶ ἐφ᾽ ἡμῶν ἔκρινεν εἶναι ἵνα μὴ πρὸς τέλος ἀφικομένων ἡμῶν τῶν ἁμαρτιῶν ὕστερον ἡμᾶς ἐκδικᾷ διόπερ οὐδέποτε μὲν τὸν ἔλεον ἀφ᾽ ἡμῶν ἀφίστησιν παιδεύων δὲ μετὰ συμφορᾶς οὐκ ἐγκαταλείπει τὸν ἑαυτοῦ λαόν.

By describing the torture of the Sicarii in a manner that recalls the noble suffering described in the Jewish historical tradition, Josephus invites the reader to interpret the torture of the Sicarii as God's discipline and a sign of God's mercy.

True, God had in righteous judgment destroyed the temple in Jerusalem, but Josephus subtly reminds his readers that God has not abandoned his people. The long-standing stasis had been punished and existed no longer. The crimes arising from this stasis had been atoned. *War* thus comes to a close with a subtle but real message of hope for its Jewish readers. At least that is where we would expect *War* to end. But Josephus has one more small and ill-fitting story to tell.

THE SICARII AROUND CYRENE—THE CATULLUS NARRATIVE (7.437, 444)

In this final narrative segment of *War*, Josephus tells how the Sicarii were instrumental in causing unrest in cities around Cyrene.

IMMEDIATE CONTEXT

The context and outline for this section have been presented above. While, strictly speaking, the narrative amounts to another story about the last remnants of Jewish stasis, upon closer examination one suspects that Josephus had other motives for including it in *War*.

DESCRIPTION OF SICARII ACTIVITY

Josephus introduces the section by saying, "The madness of the Sicarii, just like a sickness, affected also the cities around Cyrene" (437).[75] In light of 410 and 412 above, this would be another way of describing the stasis of the Sicarii. Josephus indeed calls their activity stasis in the parallel account in *Life* 424–25 and has, moreover, already connected the ideas of madness and sickness to stasis at 2.256. There we read about activities that are remarkably similar to the text at hand; deceivers and imposters lead Jews into the wilderness, working at revolutionary changes under the pretense of divine revelations.

Josephus proceeds to tell how Jonathan, a very wicked man (πονηρότατος), deceived many of the "indigent" (ἀπόρων), promising "signs and apparitions." In light of the similarities of this account with 2.258, Josephus intends the reader to understand a revolutionary activity here. Jonathan's followers were killed or scattered, but Jonathan for a time eluded capture. When finally caught and brought before Catullus, he blamed the Jewish leaders (ἀξιώμασι προύχοντες). For Catullus, this became an opportunity for injustice (ἀφορμὴν ἀδικημάτων).

Josephus states that Catullus desired to give the appearance that he too had won a Jewish war (Ἰουδαϊκόν τινα πόλεμον κατωρθωκέναι 443), for which purpose he instructed the Sicarii to lie (διδάσκαλος ἦν τῶν σικαρίων τῆς ψευδολογίας 444), using Jonathan in particular to bring allegations against and to murder

---

75. ἥψατο δὲ καὶ τῶν περὶ Κυρήνην πόλεων ἡ τῶν σικαρίων ἀπόνοια καθάπερ νόσος.

a personal Jewish enemy, Alexander, and his wife; to murder wealthy Jews and confiscate their property; and to further slander Jews in Alexandria and Rome, among whom was Josephus.

Vespasian, at Titus's urging, investigated the affair, acquitted the Jews, and had Jonathan killed (450). Catullus suffered only a reprimand because of the leniency of the emperors (451), but he was later tormented in mind and died from an ulcer. Josephus's interpretation of his death: "Thus he died, offering proof no less than any other of God's providence—that he punishes the wicked" (453).[76]

WORD STUDIES

The one significant word used by Josephus for the Sicarii, νόσος, has been dealt with above.

BOOK CONTEXT

This final incident in *War* corresponds also in some degree to the opening narrative at 1:31. Both Catullus and Antiochus have designs against the Jews and use the Jewish divisions/rivalries as opportunities (1.32 vs. 7.441). Both use the immediate occasion to further oppress the Jews. Antiochus, an unjust king, became embroiled in the outbreak of Jewish stasis; Catullus, an unjust governor, became embroiled in the last incident of Jewish stasis, here called the madness of the Sicarii. Antiochus was repulsed by Jewish arms; Catullus was punished directly by God.

This section, however, lacks the note of completion that is highlighted in the previous section. The narrative about the closing of the temple in Leontopolis, emblematic of Jewish stasis, brings closure to the structure of *War*. The stasis that opens the narrative of *War* had now been suppressed. In regard to the narrative about the Sicarii in Cyrene, even though a correspondence is apparent with the opening sections of *War*, there is no clear resolution. It amounts merely to another story of troubling Jewish stasis. In this regard this final section appears as an appendage.

If we were to conjecture about the reasons for its placement, it would seem unlikely that despite the resolution of stasis sounded in the previous narrative, Josephus desired to highlight its insidious nature one last time. This would seem merely superfluous. It seems more likely that Josephus records this incident because it is one in which he became personally involved. He refers to this same incident in *Life* 424–25, where he states that Jonathan accused him of providing arms to the stasis in Cyrene.

---

76. οὕτως ἀπέθανεν οὐδενὸς ἧττον ἑτέρου τῆς προνοίας τοῦ θεοῦ τεκμήριον γενόμενος ὅτι τοῖς πονηροῖς δίκην ἐπιτίθησιν.

CONCLUSIONS

The "madness" of the Sicarii should probably not be understood as consisting in Jonathan's attempt to become the leader of a band of revolutionaries in the wilderness but rather in how he turned upon his own people (444). Aside from this typical trait of the Sicarii, one wonders why Josephus applies the label to these characters. For here Josephus clearly uses the term quite independent of any murdering activity. Neither Jonathan nor his followers committed any such act. Instead, Josephus mentions the Sicarii by name specifically in connection with their giving false witness against fellow Jews. We also note that there is an absence of any emphasis on the ideology of these Sicarii. Such ideology might be inferred from the similarly described events at 2.258, but it is not emphasized here by Josephus. In this narrative, then, "Sicarii" denotes more generically those Jews who turn on other Jews.

CHAPTER FIVE

CONCLUSIONS

THE LITERARY PRESENTATION OF THE SICARII IN *WAR*

Throughout this study we have made many observations concerning how Josephus connects the Sicarii in the various narratives to the structure and themes of *War*. Here we draw all these together in summary fashion. The Sicarii are most clearly connected to stasis, a major theme of *War*. Now it must be admitted that the Sicarii are not the only characters in *War* associated with stasis. The Zealots, the tyrants, and the various bandit gangs also destroyed Jerusalem by their stasis. If we were to draw a distinction between the Sicarii and these other rebel groups, we might suggest that while the latter fight also against the Romans, the Sicarii are shown to fight exclusively against their own people.

Indeed, this is how they are most clearly identified in *War*. Josephus introduces them by drawing attention to their murder of Jonathan, the high priest (2.254–57). This action itself presages the murders of Ananus and Jesus, after which point there is no longer any opportunity either for honorable direction of the war or for peaceful resolution (4.321). The Sicarii add their pivotal strength to the stasis element in the temple and thus critically weaken Jerusalem (2.425). Their first named leader, Menahem, exemplifies the problems of stasis and tyranny (2.433–48). Once they leave Jerusalem, their raid on Engaddi exemplifies how they continue to prey on their own people (4.398–406). At Masada, we note that Josephus has Eleazar confess not to the sin of rebelling against Rome but of murdering his own people (7.332). Such destruction of one's compatriots appears to be the key to understanding the Sicarii in Alexandria (7.410f.). Rebels there are called Sicarii not because they embarked on revolutionary activities but because they murdered their own who did not share their convictions. Similarly, the "madness" of the Sicarii affects Jonathan in Cyrene, who, though he does not himself kill fellow Jews, becomes a tool of Catullus as an informant against his own people.

Not once in *War's* narrative are the Sicarii explicitly connected to the death of Romans. While it is true that there are several places where we should infer this activity, such as when soldiers were slain at the capture of Masada or when Menahem's followers treacherously killed Roman soldiers in Jerusalem, we note that Josephus does not name the Sicarii at these places. Even at Masada, where the Sicarii finally seem about to come to blows with the Romans, no fight takes place. We read about no death of any Roman soldiers. Neither does Josephus mention the Sicarii by name when they accompany Simon on raids into Idumea. He rather identifies them by the more generic term "bandits." Throughout the narrative Josephus seems to be rather careful to name the Sicarii explicitly only when they kill their own people or when they confess to such crimes, as in the Masada narrative.

The connection between the Sicarii and stasis is all the clearer in light of *War*'s structure. Indeed, the two are inseparable. The narrative of *War* begins with an account of the stasis that grew between Onias and the sons of Tobias. This resulted both in the opening of a rival temple in Egypt and ultimately in the arrival of the Romans to control the stasis. Josephus uses the Sicarii to bring these issues to a resolution. The Romans finally leave after the suppression of the last remnants of stasis in Judea at Masada, and the Sicarii activity in Egypt results in the closing of the rival temple. Moreover, Josephus highlights the self-destructive nature of stasis during the course of his narrative by effective use of irony in connection with the Sicarii. These characters, who fight against Roman oppression, become far worse oppressors of the Jewish people. Emblematic are their support of Menahem and their raid at Engaddi. Ultimately and appropriately, they self-destruct at Masada.

Josephus, however, does not employ the Sicarii for purely negative rhetorical purposes, for they also serve in the narrative to illustrate the limits of Roman power, a second major theme in *War*. It is not that he presents the Sicarii as effective fighters. Indeed, early on they withdraw from Jerusalem and take no part in fighting against Rome. Rather, the entire Masada–Sicarii narrative, which is ostensibly set up to highlight Roman ingenuity, finally undermines any notion of Roman victory. Failure to notice this accent has led many scholars astray in their assessment of what Josephus is doing with the Masada narrative. We have noted how Otto Michel, David Ladouceur, Honora Howell Chapman, and others interpret the episode as a "centerpiece example of the greater Roman power encountering the weaker Jewish opponent." Josephus rather insists through the presentation of events and the speeches he gives to Eleazar that Masada should be understood as the culmination of divine punishment. This punishment and accent on God's authority, in light of *War*'s chiastic arrangement, is played out also in the Alexandrian narrative. We naturally conclude that Josephus wants this accent on divine authority, both at Masada and at Alexandria, as the last word in *War* and why he therefore does not end *War* with the Flavian triumph. What Josephus desires to say in connection with the Sicarii about divine authority upstages what he is obligated to say in connection with the Flavians.

A third theme sounded in the proem of *War* is Josephus's intention not to belittle the Jews who fought against Rome, for after all, how can the conquerors of a puny people be accounted great (1.8)? We have seen how Josephus carries out this intention in his description of the Sicarii. In books 2 and 4 they appear as little more than two-dimensional criminals deserving punishment. But in the

Masada narrative Josephus adds texture and even allows his Roman and Jewish readers to detect some noble qualities in these enemies who voluntarily submit to divine punishment and in their deaths forestall any further sacrifice of personal integrity. Moreover, the endurance of those Sicarii put to the test in Egypt amazes all.

This leads to a final note sounded in a subtle but real way by Josephus. His presentation of the Sicarii's death at Masada in some measure recalls the emphases sounded in the noble death of Razis in the Jewish historical tradition. Such connections are more pronounced in the Alexandrian narrative, where Josephus portrays the endurance of Jewish children tortured at the hands of Gentile oppressors expressly intent on having them confess that Caesar was lord. Thus there is a note of irony here. In the final suppression of the criminal Sicarii and their stasis, Josephus also reminds Jewish readers of divine benevolence. God had not abandoned his people. It was rather a sign of his mercy that he visited them with punishment. At least that is how the noble suffering of the Jewish "martyrs" was understood by Josephus's Jewish contemporaries. Indeed, with the Sicarii we see here how Josephus presses beyond purely apologetic themes, whereby he defends his countrymen before the Romans, to defining for Jews "their own self-respect and steadfastness" in a "difficult and uncertain" environment.[1] Writing at the seat of empire subsequent to the destruction of the temple and defeat of his people, Josephus insistently reminds them that God was still in control. They were to remain faithful in covenant for he had not abandoned them. This also Josephus wants to be a final note sounded in *War*.

Finally, we might restate that the narrative and speeches at Masada do not answer well to the needs of irony in the sense that these represented Roman opposition to the Flavians, as some scholars have argued, for the precise reason that the narrative and speeches at Masada are not primarily about Roman power. Neither are such scholarly opinions helped by placing the speeches of Eleazar and voluntary deaths of the Sicarii in apposition to the speech of Josephus and his refusal to take his own life at Jotapata. Certainly there is a rhetorical show between the two speeches, and yes, there is a note of irony that the Sicarii, who fought for liberty from Rome, died in "freedom" on top of a desert fortress. But a fatal problem for all these theories is that the speeches of Eleazar and Josephus do not correspond at the required fundamental level: neither speech is about how Jews ought to respond to Roman power. They rather seem to correspond to the presence or absence of ἀνάγκη. At Jotapata, Josephus was compelled to surrender, he states explicitly, not to have Roman mercy but to obey a divine mandate. Similarly, at Masada, the Sicarii submit to voluntary death, not in view of Roman power but because they stood under a divine sentence.

In sum, while it is true that Josephus stresses in *War* how the Jews should

---

1. Tessa Rajak, "Josephus in the Diaspora," in *Flavius Josephus and Flavian Rome*, ed. Jonathan Edmondson, Steve Mason, and James Rives (New York: Oxford University Press, 2005), 96–97.

submit to the Romans, the (current) divinely appointed world rulers, Josephus nowhere uses the Sicarii to emphasize this point. They serve rather to highlight submission to divine authority, which displaces that of the Romans at Masada.

A Historical Assessment of the Sicarii from *War*

In light of the above rhetorical elements, we now turn to a historical assessment of the Sicarii. We begin with the observation that it cannot be maintained from *War* that the Sicarii are a branch of the Zealots. This long-standing assumption has been buttressed in part by the idea that both the Sicarii and the Zealots originated under Judas in 6 C.E. We have seen, however, that this proposal about the origins of the Sicarii leads to severe problems within the narrative of *War*. Moreover, there is no evidence at all in the narrative of any joint activity between the two. On the contrary, the Sicarii have retired from Jerusalem to Masada before Josephus begins to speak about the Zealots, and there the Sicarii remained throughout the balance of the revolt, never taking part at all from that point onward in the battles at Jerusalem.

Instead, Josephus clearly connects the Sicarii not to the Zealots but to bandits in general. Indeed, they were a "different type of bandit," which sprang up in Jerusalem (2.254f.). What made the Sicarii stand out from the nameless hordes of bandits were the intention and method of their violent activity. Josephus first identifies them in connection with some high profile and politically motivated assassinations in Jerusalem immediately preceding the outbreak of war in Judea. Here we may well note how Josephus emphasizes the connection between the Sicarii and bandits also in the *Ant.* 20.186, where he clearly states that the Sicarii were bandits. Similarly, a few passages later in the same context Josephus calls those who kidnapped the members of Ananias's house both *sicarii* and "bandits" (20.208–10). The two are closely connected if not quite interchangeable.

To what degree were the Sicarii in the narrative of *War* a historically identifiable group? We begin with their name. Josephus explicit states they were first given this label in connection with their assassinations in Jerusalem. If we were to ask who named them "Sicarii," it seems beyond doubt that they acquired the name from the Romans, for this Latin word has no history in Greek or Jewish literature prior to Josephus. After receiving the label, would the Sicarii have willingly adopted it? This we cannot say from *War*. Only in *Ant.* 20.186 does Josephus indicate that they adopted the name for themselves. How long did the label persist? Certainly it lasted beyond the end of the revolt according to the narrative of *War*. And so we might think that certain Jews were known as Sicarii for at least a decade or two in some areas of the Roman Empire under the Flavians. However, our certainty is diminished somewhat when we bear in mind how Josephus makes the label a key rhetorical device. In a sense similar to the use of "banditry" in the Latin tradition, Josephus may at times be using "Sicarii" as nothing more than a literary weapon designed to marginalize and condemn certain rebel activities.

Our suspicion that this may be the case is strengthened somewhat by Josephus's broadening use of the label. While they are at Jerusalem, he emphasizes their assassinations and use of the daggers as those things that particularly gave rise to their name. However, once they leave Jerusalem, Josephus has these unique identifiers fall away, and the Sicarii are no longer identified by their method of violence. Indeed, in their raids from Masada, Josephus describes their behavior in terms similar to general banditry. We note that at times he even declines to refer to the occupiers at Masada as Sicarii at all but merely calls them bandits as he places them in the general background of this infestation throughout Judea. And so it simply cannot be maintained that the Sicarii at Masada were known as such due to any specific method of violence. In the Alexandrian narrative Josephus uses the term in a much more general way to describe those Jews who for political reasons fight against fellow Jews (the theme of stasis). In the Cyrene narrative, even this political motivation is deemphasized. Jonathan appears to be little more than a criminal used by Catullus to slander fellow Jews. All this leads to the inescapable conclusion that "Sicarii" describes more than a person using a dagger in an urban environment.

If the Sicarii are to be understood as an identifiable, historical group, then we would want to know about their organizational principles. What made them Sicarii? We begin with the commonly held assertion that the Sicarii were a distinct party originating with the sect of Judas, the Fourth Philosophy. Although Josephus never specifically links the Sicarii to the Fourth Philosophy, the connection is made via Judas's descendants. This matter involves two questions. The first is this: To what degree was the sect of Judas a clan phenomenon? In other words, when we read about Judas's descendants, do we find clues that they are animated by Judas's teachings? The second question: How firmly are the identity and activities of the Sicarii linked to the clan of Judas? If it could be shown that Judas's Fourth Philosophy continued as a distinct organization with his descendants and that the Sicarii, as an organization, arose from and were continuously linked to this clan, then, indeed, we could conclude that the Sicarii were a direct outgrowth of the sect of Judas.

Let us investigate question one first. Martin Hengel offers a widely held view that the Fourth Philosophy continued to exist as an organization in Judas's descendants. Founded by Judas in 6 C.E., it "reappeared" with his sons, Simon and Jacob, who were crucified by Tiberius Alexander, was continued by Menahem, and came to an end with Eleazar's suicide. Hengel admits that Josephus has little to say about this sect as the rebellion progresses and suggests this was due both to Josephus's reluctance to make any positive statements about those who were primarily responsible for the rebellion and to his lack of source material inasmuch as the Fourth Philosophy would seem to have been a "secret society."[2]

---

2. Hengel, *The Zealots*, trans. David Smith, 2nd ed. (Edinburgh: T & T Clark, 1989), 82–86, with bibliography in the notes.

A recent study by Alexei Sivertsev would also seem to lend support to the clan structure of the Fourth Philosophy. Sivertsev shows how the first century B.C.E. was a time of transition for religious leadership in Judea. Prior to this time, beginning with the return from exile and the building of the second temple, Judaism was largely a "patriarchal" religion with a "family-based nature" that gave shape to its identity and movements. However, with the increase of Hellenization and urbanization after 63 B.C.E., religious traditions began to lose this family-based setting and found new expression in disciple circles that gathered around famous teachers as the "basic social unit of religious learning and piety." In this way the author marks the transition from the second temple, characterized by household religious leadership, to rabbinic Judaism, characterized by "universal teaching that existed independent of families."[3]

Sivertsev's study about the transition in Judea from family-based to rabbinic religious movements is stimulating and convincing, but the evidence brought forward to illustrate the family-based structure of the Fourth Philosophy in particular appears less so. He presents the following: (1) Josephus hints at the family nature of the Fourth Philosophy with the notation that members of this philosophy think little of vengeance falling upon kinsmen and friends" so long as they are not made to call any man "lord." (2) The execution of James and Simon, Judas's sons, makes the connection clear. "In his first reference to the movement after the death (?) of its founder, Josephus discloses one characteristic that persists throughout its history: the leaders of the Fourth Philosophy come from the family (perhaps the extended family) of Judah the Galilean." (3) When the Fourth Philosophy reemerges with Menahem, some of his followers were relatives, such as Eleazar, or "intimate friends" (γνωρίμους). (4) The family nature of the Fourth Philosophy is clearly indicated by the presence of families at Masada.[4] In assessing this data, it may be true that Josephus hints at the family nature of the Fourth Philosophy in his notice that its members think light of punishment falling on family and friends (*Ant.* 18.23), but when Sivertsev states that Simon and James provide evidence that the leaders of the Fourth Philosophy always come from the family of Judas, this begs the question inasmuch as Josephus makes no mention at all of any philosophy, teachings, or activities of these two characters (*Ant.* 20.102). The same might be stated about Menahem, whose religious and philosophical intentions are equally unclear (further below). Finally, the presence of families at Masada, instead of providing evidence of families gathered around a particular religious tradition, can easily be explained by the fact that this fortress was a secure and ultimately the only place of refuge for Eleazar and his followers in time of war.

The philosophical inclinations of Judas's clan appear rather more dubious if, with Emil Schürer, J. Spencer Kennard, Hengel, and others we identify the Judas

---

3. Alexei M. Sivertsev, *Households, Sects, and the Origins of Rabbinic Judaism* (Leiden and Boston: Brill, 2005), 21.

4. Ibid., 169f.

of 4 B.C.E. with the Judas of 6 C.E.[5] With this identification, the patriarch of this "religious" clan would be Hezekiah, whom Josephus describes as a "bandit chief" (ἀρχιληστήν) who once "ravaged" the area in Galilee and was captured and put to death by King Herod in 47 B.C.E. (*War* 1.204; 2.56). Josephus presents him as an example of disorders throughout the country when many aspired to sovereignty (βασιλειᾶν 2.55). Some forty-three years later, we read how Judas, in 4 B.C.E., like his father, also became an object of fear because of his plundering, born from his desire to have royal honor (ζηλώσει βασιλείου τιμῆς, *Ant.* 17.271–72; *War* 2:56). In *War* the next clan member we encounter, Menahem, like his grandfather and great grandfather before him, is aspiring to royalty (2.444).[6] Throughout the narrative Josephus makes clear connections between the clan of Hezekiah and its royal aspirations. We need look no further than bandit lust for power combined with the loss of so many family members for reasons to explain the clan's long fight against Rome and those who would support Roman rule in Judea.

With this line of evidence, Judas's joint activities ten years later with Saddok could naturally be understood as nothing more than an elaborate pretext, an attempt by Judas to further his royal ambitions by more respectable means. True, no mention is made of such ambitions in 6 C.E., but as Kennard notes, "Religion and politics went hand in hand, and no revolutionary leader who proved successful would have disdained the blessings of God. Nor could the Judas of 6 C.E. have failed to distinguish between the rule of self-appointed 'moral men' and the mediation of God Himself through vice-regents."[7] In Menahem, the descendant of this "uncanny teacher," Josephus exposes the ironies inherent in using such high-minded religious sentiments for personal gain, if indeed Menahem held to the same precept of his grandfather that one should call no mortal master "lord." As for Eleazar, Josephus provides contradictory evidence. In the Hall of Infamy, he allows no such high-minded motivation for Eleazar's rebellious

---

5. Schürer, *A History of the Jewish People in the Time of Jesus Christ*, 3 vols. (Edinburgh: T & T Clark, 1890), I.ii.80; J. Spencer Kennard, "Judas of Galilee and His Clan," *JQR* 36 (1946): 281–84; Hengel, *Zealots*, 331, with bibliography in the notes. For an opposing view, see E. Mary Smallwood, *The Jews under Roman Rule: From Pompey to Diocletian* (Leiden: Brill, 2001), 153 n. 40.

6. Josephus tells us nothing about the death of Judas. According to Luke-Acts, it would seem that the sect of Judas did not survive long beyond the death of Judas himself. At Acts 5:33f. Luke states that the Sanhedrin in Jerusalem was debating how to suppress the proclamation of the apostles concerning the resurrection and exaltation of Jesus. Luke tells how Gamaliel counseled that they should take no action against the apostles in part because their proclamation would fail in the end if it had no divine authority. In support of his assertion Gamaliel stated that all the followers of Judas were scattered after his death (Acts 5:37). Josephus mentions in *Antiquities* that two of his sons, Simon and Jacob, were put to death by Tiberius Alexander but offers no reason nor tells us anything at all about their activities (20.102). There is, at least, a long silence of any clan activity from the time of Judas in 6 C.E. to that of Menahem, his likely grandson (see Kennard).

7. Kennard, "Judas of Galilee," 282. See also Hengel, *Zealots,* 82.

activities. Eleazar and the Sicarii had proclaimed a fight against Jews who ignobly tossed away their freedom to Rome, but Josephus calls this a mere pretext
for their violence and greed (7.256). Josephus's presentation turns 180 degrees in
the final hours at Masada. There, Eleazar steps forth as the leader of a principled
group of men, who, driven by their allegiance to God, had unfortunately turned
on their own countrymen, for which sin Eleazar makes confession. However, we
have seen that this sudden shift in presentation is accounted for in light of Josephus's rhetorical aims.

Thus, the evidence used to support the idea that Judas's Fourth Philosophy
was promulgated in his clan is certainly open to contrary interpretation. Josephus
attaches the label to Judas and his teachings, which aroused the entire nation
(*Ant.* 18.4–6). His sons, Simon and Jacob, attracted no such attention. Menahem's philosophical intentions are altogether ambiguous. We might assume that
he employed the propaganda of his grandfather to inspire his following, but his
behavior was, to say the least, incompatible with the Fourth Philosophy's major
precept. Eleazar's speeches clearly connect to the teachings of Judas, yet it is hazardous to press them for precise historical data. Moreover, if the Judas of 4 B.C.E.
is the same as the Judas of 6 C.E. and his father Hezekiah is part of this clan, the
royal ambitions of the clan receive much more emphasis in *War's* narrative, and
Judas's teachings could easily be interpreted as nothing more than an elaborate
pretext.

As to the second question, whether the identity and activities of the Sicarii
are firmly linked to this clan, we have seen that the Sicarii gather around Menahem and Eleazar, but their activities do not begin or end with these leaders. Most
important, they arose independent of any association with the clan of Judas. They
were already active in strengthening the stasis in Jerusalem before the arrival of
Menahem. In addition, after the death of Eleazar, the last known member of the
clan, we still read of their activity in Egypt and Cyrene, and it is highly doubtful
that the Sicarii there had ever associated with Judas's clan.

In conclusion, a careful reading of the Sicarii's relations with the clan of
Judas does not lead to the clear conclusion that the Sicarii were a direct outgrowth of the Fourth Philosophy. Except for the speeches of Eleazar, which are
themselves historically suspect, there is no evidence that Judas's clan held to his
teachings with any precision, and the Sicarii themselves arise and cease to exist
quite independent of any association with the clan. Following Josephus, we must
look for other identifying characteristics. Initially, the Sicarii were known as such
because of their use of the dagger to commit acts of violence in the city against
their own people (2.254f., 425). But when they leave Jerusalem, we are forced to
look for a broader definition because this mode of violence falls away entirely.
Within the narrative of *War*, two identifying characteristics emerge. First is their
slogan, "No lord but God," which Josephus explicitly attaches to the Sicarii in
book 7. Hengel suggests that this amounted to a narrowing and intensification
of the first commandment, held and recited by all Jews daily together with the

Shema.[8] We certainly cannot suggest from the narrative of *War* that this slogan, which was used by Judas to incite the entire nation to rebel, belonged uniquely to the Sicarii. Second is their intention to commit acts of violence exclusively against their own people who say otherwise. This activity, too, was not unique to the Sicarii. It is, however, what sets them apart within the narrative of *War* from Judas's Fourth Philosophy, for although Judas encouraged a fight against Rome, we never read that he taught his followers to kill their fellow countrymen who spoke otherwise. Thus, in the narrative of *War*, the Sicarii took an already-radicalized interpretation of the first commandment, taught by Judas and distinctive of the Fourth Philosophy, and radicalized it still further by systematically using it as justification for fratricide. Josephus presents the Sicarii as motivated exclusively by these two principles in book 7, and these principles indeed explain their behavior in books 2 and 4: their assassination of Jonathan, their fight against the royalist opposition in Jerusalem, and their raid on Engaddi.

Thus, we might reasonably conclude the following. It would seem precarious to insist that the Sicarii were a historically identifiable, card-carrying, banner-waving group during and after the war. The narrative of *War* cannot support such an image for two reasons. First, there is nothing in the narrative of *War* to suggest that they were always identified by unique behavior. Only at first do they carry out assassinations in an urban environment. At Masada they are hardly distinguished from "bandits." Second, their revolutionary agenda, as we have noted, was shared by any number of rebels during the course of the war. Instead, Josephus seems to have adopted this Roman label, attached to perpetrators of high-profile household assassinations carried out at the war's inception, to demonstrate the blindness and folly of such behavior. That is, Josephus uses the term primarily for rhetorical purposes, calling the raiders from Masada "bandits" when they follow Simon and kill Idumeans, but "Sicarii" when they kill fellow Jews at Engaddi. Such an identifying label was of particular use in developing and bringing to a resolution the theme of stasis.

Therefore, if we were to construct a historical image of the Sicarii on the basis of the narrative of *War*, we might suggest the identity of a modern "terrorist" as an analogy. Both labels are highly charged words which bring vividly to mind acts of violence against innocent people for political ends. Both can be used in a variety of political contexts to describe not only those who actually commit such acts, but also for those who merely express the intention or have the clear potential. Both can thus also be used as labels by which to marginalize political enemies. The label *sicarii* first came into use among the Jews to describe terrorist activities in Jerusalem: swift and stealthy acts of violence directed by Jews against their own countrymen. The method of violence distinguished the Sicarii from other bandit gangs so that Josephus could call them "bandits in different form." This activity eventually solidified against Jews in Jerusalem who supported Rome, and

---

8. Hengel, *Zealots*, 98. See his extended discussion there for the slogan, 91–110.

these nameless Sicarii were identified thus not only by their terrorist activities but also by their targets. However, it was not until the rise of Menahem and especially with Eleazar that the Sicarii became a recognizable group. Perhaps what attracted the terrorists to these leaders was the radical teaching of Judas, their ancestor. No doubt some sincerely held to the radicalized slogan "No lord but God," but Josephus signals that others used it merely as a pretext for violence and greed. But what the Sicarii added to this slogan, and what makes them distinct from the Fourth Philosophy, was violent intent against their own countrymen so that Eleazar became known as the leader of a terrorist group, though Josephus sometimes also calls them bandits. Such evidence leads to the conclusion that the label *sicarii* was used not primarily to describe a group of people but to marginalize and condemn certain types of behavior. He and his band of terrorists finally kill themselves, an end which, for rhetorical purposes, Josephus could not resist ennobling. Whether the label was used in Egypt to describe the political assassinations among the Jews is uncertain, but Josephus uses it to condemn such behavior, though he allows his Jewish readers to see a subtext. Finally, it would seem unlikely that the any Jews at Cyrene were labeled Sicarii. Josephus rather seems to use the label to marginalize and condemn a personal enemy.

APPENDIX

RISE AND FALL OF MENAHEM

WAR 2:433–48

433 Now at this time Menahem, a son of Judas called the Galilean (the uncanny teacher who once reproached the Jews at the time of Quirinius because they made themselves subject to the Romans after God), took his friends and left for Masada, 434 where he broke into king Herod's armory and gave weapons to the townspeople and the other bandits. Using these as bodyguards, he returned to Jerusalem just like a king, became leader of the stasis, and took charge of the siege. 435 They had no engines and were unable to dig under the wall out in the open because of the missiles cast from above; so then digging at a distance to one of the towers, they undermined it. Then setting fire to the supporting wood, they left. 436 When the supports were burnt from below, the wall suddenly collapsed, but another wall built on the inside appeared; for since the defenders had foreseen the plan, and perhaps because the tower was shaking as it was being undermined, they prepared a second bulwark for themselves. 437 Because they were convinced that they were just about at the point of victory, the attackers were filled with consternation at the unexpected sight. But those within were sending word to Menahem and the leaders of the stasis, requesting to come out under truce. Since it was granted only to king's men and to the natives of the country, some came

433 κἀν τούτῳ Μανάημός τις υἱὸς Ἰούδα τοῦ καλουμένου Γαλιλαίου σοφιστὴς δεινότατος ὁ καὶ ἐπὶ Κυρινίου ποτὲ Ἰουδαίους ὀνειδίσας ὅτι Ῥωμαίοις ὑπετάσσοντο μετὰ τὸν θεόν ἀναλαβὼν τοὺς γνωρίμους ἀνεχώρησεν εἰς Μασάδαν 434 ἔνθα τὴν Ἡρώδου τοῦ βασιλέως ὁπλοθήκην ἀναρρήξας καὶ πρὸς τοῖς δημόταις ἑτέρους λῃστὰς καθοπλίσας τούτοις τε χρώμενος δορυφόροις οἷα δὴ βασιλεὺς ἐπάνεισιν εἰς Ἱεροσόλυμα καὶ γενόμενος ἡγεμὼν τῆς στάσεως διέτασσεν τὴν πολιορκίαν. 435 ἀπορία δ' ἦν ὀργάνων καὶ φανερῶς ὑπορύττειν τὸ τεῖχος οὐχ οἷόν τε ἦν ἄνωθεν βαλλομένους· ὑπόνομον δὴ πόρρωθεν ἐφ' ἕνα τῶν πύργων ὑπορύξαντες ἀνεκρήμνισαν αὐτόν, ἔπειτα τὴν ἀνέχουσαν ὕλην ἐμπρήσαντες ἐξῆλθον. 436 ὑποκαέντων δὲ τῶν στηριγμάτων ὁ μὲν πύργος ἐξαίφνης κατασείεται, τεῖχος δ' ἕτερον ἔνδοθεν ἀνῳκοδομημένον διεφάνη· τὴν γὰρ ἐπιβουλὴν αὐτῶν προαισθόμενοι, τάχα καὶ τοῦ πύργου κινηθέντος ὡς ὑπωρύττετο, δεύτερον ἑαυτοῖς ἔρυμα κατεσκεύασαν. 437 πρὸς ὃ τῶν ἀδοκήτως ἰδόντων καὶ κρατεῖν ἤδη πεπεισμένων κατάπληξις ἦν. οἱ δὲ ἔνδοθεν πρός τε τὸν Μανάημον καὶ τοὺς ἐξάρχοντας τῆς στάσεως ἔπεμπον ἀξιοῦντες ἐξελθεῖν ὑπόσπονδοι, καὶ δοθὲν μόνοις τοῖς βασιλικοῖς καὶ τοῖς ἐπιχωρίοις οἱ μὲν ἐξῄεσαν. 438 ἀθυμία δὲ τοὺς Ῥωμαίους καταλειφθέντας μόνους

out. [438] A dejected spirit took hold of the Romans left behind and alone; for they did not think they would be able to force their way through so large a crowd and they thought it a reproach to ask for terms and would not even trust them if they were given. [439] And so abandoning their camp on the grounds that it was easily captured, they left for the royal towers, which were called Hippicus, Phasael, and Mariamme. [440] Menahem's troops rushed in from where the soldiers were fleeing, killed as many of them as they caught before they got away, rifled their baggage, and burned the camp. These things happened on the sixth of Gorpiaeus.

[441] On the next day Ananias the high priest was captured as he was hiding near the canal in the royal courtyard, and he, along with his brother Ezekias, was killed by the bandits. The insurrectionists kept continuous watch on the towers so that none of the soldiers might escape. [442] Now the destruction of the places of strength and the death of Ananias the high priest inflated Menahem to violence, and because he thought he had no rival in managing affairs, he became an insufferable tyrant. [443] Eleazar's people rose up against him, saying to one another how those who rebelled against the Romans for freedom should not toss it away to a native hangman and put up with a despot who, even if he should commit no violence, was from a lower class than they. And even if it should be necessary to have one leader, it was better to have anyone instead of that character. So they made plans to seize him at the temple, [444] for he had gone up in pompous fashion to worship, decked out in royal garb and accompanied by his armed fanatics. [445] When Eleazar's people rushed upon him, the rest of the townspeople grabbed stones and threw them at the teacher, thinking that with him out of the way the whole insurrection would go away. [446] Mena-

ὑπέλαβεν· οὔτε γὰρ βιάσασθαι τοσοῦτον πλῆθος ἐδύναντο καὶ τὸ δεξιὰς αἰτεῖν ὄνειδος ὑπελάμβανον πρὸς τῷ μηδὲ πιστεύειν εἰ διδοῖτο. [439] καταλιπόντες δὴ τὸ στρατόπεδον ὡς εὐάλωτον ἐπὶ τοὺς βασιλικοὺς ἀνέφυγον πύργους τόν τε Ἱππικὸν καλούμενον καὶ Φασάηλον καὶ Μαριάμμην. [440] οἱ δὲ περὶ τὸν Μανάημον εἰσπεσόντες ὅθεν οἱ στρατιῶται διέφυγον ὅσους τε αὐτῶν κατελάμβανον μὴ φθάσαντας ἐκδραμεῖν διέφθειραν, καὶ τὰς ἀποσκευὰς διαρπάσαντες ἐνέπρησαν τὸ στρατόπεδον. ταῦτα μὲν οὖν ἕκτῃ Γορπιαίου μηνὸς ἐπράχθη.

[441] κατὰ δὲ τὴν ἐπιοῦσαν ὅ τε ἀρχιερεὺς Ἀνανίας περὶ τὸν τῆς βασιλικῆς αὐλῆς εὔριπον διαλανθάνων ἁλίσκεται καὶ πρὸς τῶν λῃστῶν ἀναιρεῖται σὺν Ἐζεκίᾳ τῷ ἀδελφῷ, καὶ τοὺς πύργους περισχόντες οἱ στασιασταὶ παρεφύλαττον μή τις τῶν στρατιωτῶν διαφύγοι. [442] τὸν δὲ Μανάημον ἥ τε τῶν ὀχυρῶν καταστροφὴ χωρίων καὶ ὁ τοῦ ἀρχιερέως Ἀνανίου θάνατος ἐτύφωσεν εἰς ὠμότητα καὶ μηδένα νομίζων ἔχειν ἐπὶ τοῖς πράγμασιν ἀντίπαλον ἀφόρητος ἦν τύραννος. [443] ἐπανίστανται δὲ οἱ περὶ τὸν Ἐλεάζαρον αὐτῷ καὶ λόγον ἀλλήλοις δόντες, ὡς οὐ χρὴ Ῥωμαίων ἀποστάντας δι' ἐλευθερίας πόθον καταπροέσθαι ταύτην οἰκείῳ δήμῳ καὶ δεσπότην φέρειν, εἰ καὶ μηδὲν πράττοι βίαιον, ἀλλ' οὖν ἑαυτῶν ταπεινότερον· εἰ γὰρ καὶ δέοι τινὰ τῶν ὅλων ἀφηγεῖσθαι, παντὶ μᾶλλον ἢ ἐκείνῳ προσήκειν, συντίθενται καὶ κατὰ τὸ ἱερὸν ἐπεχείρουν αὐτῷ· [444] σοβαρὸς γὰρ ἀναβεβήκει προσκυνήσων ἐσθῆτί τε βασιλικῇ κεκοσμημένος καὶ τοὺς ζηλωτὰς ἐνόπλους ἐφελκόμενος. [445] ὡς δ᾽ οἱ περὶ τὸν Ἐλεάζαρον ἐπ᾽ αὐτὸν ὥρμησαν, ὅ τε λοιπὸς δῆμος ἐπὶ τὰς ὀργὰς λίθους ἁρπάσαντες τὸν σοφιστὴν ἔβαλλον, οἰόμενοι τούτου καταλυθέντος διατρέψειν ὅλην τὴν στάσιν, [446] πρὸς ὀλίγον οἱ περὶ τὸν Μανάημον

hem's adherents, though they offered brief resistance, scattered when they saw the entire crowd had rushed against them. Murder awaited those who were caught, the hunt for those who hid. [447] A few escaped to safety, running away secretly to Masada, among whom was Eleazar b. Yair, a relative of Menahem, who later became the tyrant at Masada. [448] They captured Menahem himself alive, who had fled to the place called Ophlas, where he was meekly hiding. They dragged him out into the open, tortured him in many ways, and killed him. They did the same to his subcommanders and to Absalom, the most notorious servant of his tyranny.

ἀντισχόντες ὡς εἶδον πᾶν ἐπ᾽ αὐτοὺς τὸ πλῆθος ὁρμῆσαν, ἔφυγον ὅπη τις ἴσχυσεν, καὶ φόνος μὲν ἦν τῶν καταληφθέντων, ἔρευνα δὲ τῶν ἀποκρυπτομένων. [447] καὶ διεσώθησαν ὀλίγοι λάθρα διαδράντες εἰς Μασάδαν, σὺν οἷς Ἐλεάζαρος υἱὸς Ἰαείρου, προσήκων τῷ Μαναήμῳ κατὰ γένος, ὃς ὕστερον ἐτυράννησεν τῆς Μασάδας. [448] αὐτόν τε τὸν Μανάημον εἰς τὸν καλούμενον Ὀφλᾶν συμφυγόντα κἀκεῖ ταπεινῶς ὑπολανθάνοντα ζωγρήσαντες εἰς τὸ φανερὸν ἐξείλκυσαν καὶ πολλαῖς αἰκισάμενοι βασάνοις ἀνεῖλον ὁμοίως δὲ καὶ τοὺς ὑπ᾽ αὐτὸν ἡγεμόνας τόν τε ἐπισημότατον τῆς τυραννίδος ὑπηρέτην Ἀψάλωμον.

ELEAZAR'S FIRST SPEECH AT MASADA

WAR 7:323–36

[323] Good men, long ago we resolved to serve neither the Romans nor any other man but God, for he alone is the true and righteous master of men. The time has now come which commands us to prove our resolution by our deeds. [324] Let us not put ourselves to shame, we who in the past would not endure a slavery that had no danger, by now taking along with slavery incurable punishments for ourselves if we will live under the Romans. For we were the first of all to revolt and are the last of all to fight against them. [325] And I think that we have received this as a gift also from God: to be able to die nobly and free, the very thing which did not come to those who were unexpectedly beaten. [326] It is obvious that we will be captured within a day, but the choice of a noble death with loved ones is still free for the taking. Our enemy cannot prevent this though they certainly pray to take us alive, nor can we still win if we go on fighting.

[327] Now perhaps from the very beginning, when we desired to lay claim to freedom and everything turned out

[323] πάλαι διεγνωκότας ἡμᾶς, ἄνδρες ἀγαθοί, μήτε Ῥωμαίοις μήτ᾽ ἄλλῳ τινὶ δουλεύειν ἢ θεῷ, μόνος γὰρ οὗτος ἀληθής ἐστι καὶ δίκαιος ἀνθρώπων δεσπότης, ἥκει νῦν καιρὸς ἐπαληθεῦσαι κελεύων τὸ φρόνημα τοῖς ἔργοις. [324] πρὸς ὃν αὐτοὺς μὴ καταισχύνωμεν, πρότερον μηδὲ δουλείαν ἀκίνδυνον ὑπομείναντες, νῦν δὲ μετὰ δουλείας ἑλόμενοι τιμωρίας ἀνηκέστους, εἰ ζῶντες ὑπὸ Ῥωμαίοις ἐσόμεθα· πρῶτοί τε γὰρ πάντων ἀπέστημεν καὶ πολεμοῦμεν αὐτοῖς τελευταῖοι. [325] νομίζω δὲ καὶ παρὰ θεοῦ ταύτην δεδόσθαι χάριν τοῦ δύνασθαι καλῶς καὶ ἐλευθέρως ἀποθανεῖν, ὅπερ ἄλλοις οὐκ ἐγένετο παρ᾽ ἐλπίδα κρατηθεῖσιν. [326] ἡμῖν δὲ πρόδηλος μέν ἐστιν ἡ γενησομένη μεθ᾽ ἡμέραν ἅλωσις, ἐλευθέρα δὲ ἡ τοῦ γενναίου θανάτου μετὰ τῶν φιλτάτων αἵρεσις. οὔτε γὰρ τοῦτ᾽ ἀποκωλύειν οἱ πολέμιοι δύνανται πάντως εὐχόμενοι ζῶντας ἡμᾶς παραλαβεῖν, οὔθ᾽ ἡμεῖς ἐκείνους ἔτι νικᾶν μαχόμενοι. [327] ἔδει μὲν γὰρ εὐθὺς ἴσως ἐξ ἀρχῆς, ὅτε τῆς ἐλευθερίας ἡμῖν ἀντιποιεῖσθαι θελήσασι πάντα καὶ παρ᾽ ἀλλήλων

difficult among ourselves and worse from our enemies, we should have made a guess at God's plan and known that he had passed sentence on the Jewish people, who were once dear to him. [328] For if he had remained favorable or at least only moderately angry, he would not have overlooked the destruction of so many people nor would he have given his most holy city over to the fire and the destructions of enemies. [329] Did we indeed hope that we alone of all the Jewish race were to remain alive, guarding our freedom as if we were without sin before God and had taken no part in (crime), we who taught others to do so? [330] Indeed, look how he proves that we were hoping in vain by bringing, beyond our expectations, the necessity with these weird events. [331] For not even the nature of this fortress, unassailable as it was, availed for our safety. On the contrary, even though we had boundless supply and a mass of weapons and all other preparations in abundance, we have been denied hope of safety by God himself, obviously. [332] For the fire bearing down on the enemy did not turn all by itself against our prepared wall. On the contrary, these events constitute (his) wrath against our many crimes which in our madness we dared to commit against our own people.

[333] Let us not pay the penalty for these things to those hated Romans but let us do so at our own hands to God. These hands are more tolerable than they. [334] So let our wives die without any maltreatment, our children never having known slavery, and after them let us offer each other a noble gift by preserving our freedom as a beautiful shroud. But first let us destroy the fortress and its items with fire; for I know quite well that the Romans will be distressed if after failing to seize our bodies, they miss out also on their profit. [336] Let us leave only the food; for it will bear witness to how we died; that we

ἀπέβαινε χαλεπὰ καὶ παρὰ τῶν πολεμίων χείρω, τῆς τοῦ θεοῦ γνώμης στοχάζεσθαι καὶ γινώσκειν ὅτι τὸ πάλαι φίλον αὐτῷ φῦλον Ἰουδαίων κατέγνωστο· [328] μένων γὰρ εὐμενὴς ἢ μετρίως γοῦν ἀπηχθημένος, οὐκ ἂν τοσούτων μὲν ἀνθρώπων περιεῖδεν ὄλεθρον, προήκατο δὲ τὴν ἱερωτάτην αὐτοῦ πόλιν πυρὶ καὶ κατασκαφαῖς πολεμίων. [329] ἡμεῖς δ᾽ ἄρα καὶ μόνοι τοῦ παντὸς Ἰουδαίων γένους ἠλπίσαμεν περιέσεσθαι τὴν ἐλευθερίαν φυλάξαντες, ὥσπερ ἀναμάρτητοι πρὸς τὸν θεὸν γενόμενοι καὶ μηδεμιᾶς μετασχόντες — οἳ καὶ τοὺς ἄλλους ἐδιδάξαμεν; [330] τοιγαροῦν ὁρᾶτε, πῶς ἡμᾶς ἐλέγχει μάταια προσδοκήσαντας κρείττονα τῶν ἐλπίδων τὴν ἐν τοῖς δεινοῖς ἀνάγκην ἐπαγαγών· [331] οὐδὲ γὰρ ἡ τοῦ φρουρίου φύσις ἀνάλωτος οὖσα πρὸς σωτηρίαν ὠφέληκεν, ἀλλὰ καὶ τροφῆς ἀφθονίαν καὶ πλῆθος ὅπλων καὶ τὴν ἄλλην ἔχοντες παρασκευὴν περιττεύουσαν ὑπ᾽ αὐτοῦ περιφανῶς τοῦ θεοῦ τὴν ἐλπίδα τῆς σωτηρίας ἀφῃρήμεθα. [332] τὸ γὰρ πῦρ εἰς τοὺς πολεμίους φερόμενον οὐκ αὐτομάτως ἐπὶ τὸ κατασκευασθὲν τεῖχος ὑφ᾽ ἡμῶν ἀνέστρεψεν, ἀλλ᾽ ἔστι ταῦτα χόλος πολλῶν ἀδικημάτων, ἃ μανέντες εἰς τοὺς ὁμοφύλους ἐτολμήσαμεν.

[333] ὑπὲρ ὧν μὴ τοῖς ἐχθίστοις Ῥωμαίοις δίκας ἀλλὰ τῷ θεῷ δι᾽ ἡμῶν αὐτῶν ὑπόσχωμεν· αὗται δέ εἰσιν ἐκείνων μετριώτεραι [334] θνησκέτωσαν γὰρ γυναῖκες ἀνύβριστοι καὶ παῖδες δουλείας ἀπείρατοι, μετὰ δ᾽ αὐτοὺς ἡμεῖς εὐγενῆ χάριν ἀλλήλοις παράσχωμεν καλὸν ἐντάφιον τὴν ἐλευθερίαν φυλάξαντες. [335] πρότερον δὲ καὶ τὰ χρήματα καὶ τὸ φρούριον πυρὶ διαφθείρωμεν· λυπηθήσονται γὰρ Ῥωμαῖοι, σαφῶς οἶδα, μήτε τῶν ἡμετέρων σωμάτων κρατήσαντες καὶ τοῦ κέρδους ἁμαρτόντες. [336] τὰς τροφὰς μόνας ἐάσωμεν· αὗται γὰρ ἡμῖν τεθνηκόσι

were not overcome by need but, just as we resolved from the beginning, we chose death before slavery.

μαρτυρήσουσιν, ὅτι μὴ κατ᾽ ἔνδειαν ἐκρατήθημεν, ἀλλ᾽ ὥσπερ ἐξ ἀρχῆς διέγνωμεν, θάνατον ἑλόμενοι πρὸ δουλείας.

ELEAZAR'S SECOND SPEECH AT MASADA

WAR 7:341–88

[341] I was greatly deceived, he said, in thinking that I was joining with good men in our struggles for freedom; men who had resolved to live well or die. [342] You yourselves are no different from the common people in virtue and bravery, you who are afraid of a death which releases from the greatest evils and for which you should not have delayed or awaited a counselor. [343] For long ago from our very first awareness our ancestral and divine teachings continually instructed us, and our ancestors have confirmed them by spirit and deed, that life, not death, is a misfortune for men. [344] The latter gives freedom to souls and allows them release to their own pure place so that they are without experience of any misfortune. But as long as they are bound in a mortal body and infected with its ills, it is very true to say that they have died. [345] For fellowship with the divine is ill-suited for the mortal.

Now a soul has the power for great things even when it is bound in a body. For it makes it the organ of its perception, setting it in motion and leading it forward to deeds beyond mortal nature. [346] But in truth, after it is released from this weight, which drags it to earth and clings to it, and recovers its own place, then it has a share of a blessed and completely unhindered strength, remaining unseen to human eyes just as God himself. [347] Neither is it seen while it is in the body. For it is invisibly present and is released again unseen, having itself one incorruptible nature and being itself the cause

[341] ἢ πλεῖστον, εἶπεν, ἐψεύσθην νομίζων ἀνδράσιν ἀγαθοῖς τῶν ὑπὲρ τῆς ἐλευθερίας ἀγώνων συναρεῖσθαι, ζῆν καλῶς ἢ τεθνάναι διεγνωκόσιν. [342] ὑμεῖς δὲ ἦτε τῶν τυχόντων οὐδὲν εἰς ἀρετὴν οὐδ᾽ εὐτολμίαν διαφέροντες, οἵ γε καὶ τὸν ἐπὶ μεγίστων ἀπαλλαγῇ κακῶν φοβεῖσθε θάνατον, δέον ὑπὲρ τούτου μήτε μελλῆσαι μήτε σύμβουλον ἀναμεῖναι. [343] πάλαι γὰρ εὐθὺς ἀπὸ τῆς πρώτης αἰσθήσεως παιδεύοντες ἡμᾶς οἱ πάτριοι καὶ θεῖοι λόγοι διετέλουν, ἔργοις τε καὶ φρονήμασι τῶν ἡμετέρων προγόνων αὐτοὺς βεβαιούντων, ὅτι συμφορὰ τὸ ζῆν ἐστιν ἀνθρώποις οὐχὶ θάνατος. [344] οὗτος μὲν γὰρ ἐλευθερίαν διδοὺς ψυχαῖς εἰς τὸν οἰκεῖον καὶ καθαρὸν ἀφίησι τόπον ἀπαλλάσσεσθαι, πάσης συμφορᾶς ἀπαθεῖς ἐσομένας, ἕως δέ εἰσιν ἐν σώματι θνητῷ δεδεμέναι καὶ τῶν τούτου κακῶν συναναπίμπλανται, τἀληθέστατον εἰπεῖν, τεθνήκασι. [345] κοινωνία γὰρ θείῳ πρὸς θνητὸν ἀπρεπής ἐστι.

μέγα μὲν οὖν δύναται ψυχὴ καὶ σώματι συνδεδεμένη· ποιεῖ γὰρ αὐτῆς ὄργανον αἰσθανόμενον ἀοράτως αὐτὸ κινοῦσα καὶ θνητῆς φύσεως περαιτέρω προάγουσα ταῖς πράξεσιν· [346] οὐ μὴν ἀλλ᾽ ἐπειδὰν ἀπολυθεῖσα τοῦ καθέλκοντος αὐτὴν βάρους ἐπὶ γῆν καὶ προσκρεμαμένου χῶρον ἀπολάβῃ τὸν οἰκεῖον, τότε δὴ μακαρίας ἰσχύος καὶ πανταχόθεν ἀκωλύτου μετέχει δυνάμεως, ἀόρατος μένουσα τοῖς ἀνθρωπίνοις ὄμμασιν ὥσπερ αὐτὸς ὁ θεός· [347] οὐδὲ γὰρ ἕως ἐστὶν ἐν σώματι θεωρεῖται· πρόσεισι γὰρ ἀφανῶς καὶ μὴ βλεπομένη πάλιν ἀπαλλάττεται, μίαν μὲν αὐτὴ φύσιν

of change for the body. [348] So great is the soul's immortality that whatever the soul touches lives and flowers, but whatever it leaves withers and dies.

[349] Now let sleep be for you the clearest proof of these truths. While asleep and because the body does not distract them, the souls have the sweetest rest since they are left alone. They go about conversing with God in every way in accordance with their kinship and foretell many things that will be. [350] Why then should we, who love the rest that comes with sleep, fear death? How is it not foolish that we, who pursue freedom in life, refuse ourselves everlasting freedom?

[351] We, who have been taught at home, should be an example to others of being prepared for death. But if we really need convincing from foreigners, let us consider the Indians, who profess to practice wisdom. [352] Being good men, they endure unwillingly the time of life just as if it were some necessary service to nature [353] and they are eager to release their souls from their bodies. Because of a great desire for the immortal abode, they announce to others that they are about to leave although no evil presses on them or drives them out, and there is no one who will prevent them. Rather all rejoice, and each one of them gives letters to those at home [354] so fundamental and true is their belief that the abode for the souls is with one another. [355] And after they have listened to their orders, they surrender the body to fire so that they might separate the soul from the body in a most pure fashion. They die amidst singing. [356] Their loved ones send them forth to death more easily than all people send forth citizens on a very long trip abroad. Though they cry for themselves, they count happy those who have now received the immortal rank. [357] Therefore, do we not shame our ancestral laws by being more low-

ἔχουσα τὴν ἄφθαρτον, αἰτία δὲ σώματι γινομένη μεταβολῆς. [348] ὅτου γὰρ ἂν ψυχὴ προσψαύσῃ, τοῦτο ζῇ καὶ τέθηλεν, ὅτου δ᾽ ἂν ἀπαλλαγῇ μαρανθὲν ἀποθνήσκει· τοσοῦτον αὐτῇ περίεστιν ἀθανασίας. [349] ὕπνος δὲ τεκμήριον ὑμῖν ἔστω τῶν λόγων ἐναργέστατον, ἐν ᾧ ψυχαὶ τοῦ σώματος αὐτὰς μὴ περισπῶντος ἡδίστην μὲν ἔχουσιν ἀνάπαυσιν ἐφ᾽ αὐτῶν γενόμεναι, θεῷ δ᾽ ὁμιλοῦσαι κατὰ συγγένειαν πάντῃ μὲν ἐπιφοιτῶσι, πολλὰ δὲ τῶν ἐσομένων προθεσπίζουσι. [350] τί δὴ δεῖ δεδιέναι θάνατον τὴν ἐν ὕπνῳ γινομένην ἀνάπαυσιν ἀγαπῶντας; πῶς δ᾽ οὐκ ἀνόητόν ἐστιν τὴν ἐν τῷ ζῆν ἐλευθερίαν διώκοντας τῆς ἀιδίου φθονεῖν αὑτοῖς; [351] ἔδει μὲν οὖν ἡμᾶς οἴκοθεν πεπαιδευμένους ἄλλοις εἶναι παράδειγμα τῆς πρὸς θάνατον ἑτοιμότητος· οὐ μὴν ἀλλ᾽ εἰ καὶ τῆς παρὰ τῶν ἀλλοφύλων δεόμεθα πίστεως, βλέψωμεν εἰς Ἰνδοὺς τοὺς σοφίαν ἀσκεῖν ὑπισχνουμένους. [352] ἐκεῖνοί τε γὰρ ὄντες ἄνδρες ἀγαθοὶ τὸν μὲν τοῦ ζῆν χρόνον ὥσπερ ἀναγκαίαν τινὰ τῇ φύσει λειτουργίαν ἀκουσίως ὑπομένουσι, [353] σπεύδουσι δὲ τὰς ψυχὰς ἀπολῦσαι τῶν σωμάτων, καὶ μηδενὸς αὐτοὺς ἐπείγοντος κακοῦ μηδ᾽ ἐξελαύνοντος πόθῳ τῆς ἀθανάτου διαίτης προλέγουσι μὲν τοῖς ἄλλοις ὅτι μέλλουσιν ἀπιέναι, καὶ ἔστιν ὁ κωλύσων οὐδείς, ἀλλὰ πάντες αὐτοὺς εὐδαιμονίζοντες πρὸς τοὺς οἰκείους ἕκαστοι διδόασιν ἐπιστολάς. [354] οὕτως βεβαίαν καὶ ἀληθεστάτην ταῖς ψυχαῖς τὴν μετ᾽ ἀλλήλων εἶναι δίαιταν πεπιστεύκασιν. [355] οἱ δ᾽ ἐπειδὰν ἐπακούσωσι τῶν ἐντεταλμένων αὑτοῖς, πυρὶ τὸ σῶμα παραδόντες, ὅπως δὴ καὶ καθαρωτάτην ἀποκρίνωσι τοῦ σώματος τὴν ψυχὴν ὑμνούμενοι τελευτῶσιν· [356] ῥᾷον γὰρ ἐκείνους εἰς τὸν θάνατον οἱ φίλτατοι προπέμπουσιν ἢ τῶν ἄλλων ἀνθρώπων ἕκαστοι τοὺς πολίτας εἰς μηκίστην ἀποδημίαν, καὶ σφᾶς μὲν αὐτοὺς δακρύουσιν, ἐκείνους

minded than the Indians and by our own timidity shamefully insult that which is envied by all people?

[358] But even if we were taught from the beginning the opposite ideas, that truly the greatest good for people is to live and death is a misfortune, the circumstance at any rate exhorts us to bear it with a stout heart and die in accordance with necessity. [359] For long ago it seems God passed this sentence against the entire Jewish race in common so that we leave life if we do not intend to use it appropriately. [360] Do not attach blame to yourselves or credit the Romans that our fight against them destroyed us all! These things did not happen because of their might. Rather a cause stronger than they has offered them the appearance of victory. [361] For what Roman weapons were those by which the Judeans who dwelled at Caesarea died? [362] On the contrary, they did not even intend to revolt and were feasting during the seventh day when the multitude of Caesareans rushed against them and slew them with wives and children, though they did not resist. They had no regard for the Romans themselves, who considered us their enemy only after we revolted. [363] But someone will say that there was always a dispute between the Caesareans and those Judeans who lived among them, and they took the opportunity to resolve an ancient hatred. [364] Then what should we say about those Jews in Scythopolis? They dared to fight against us on behalf of the Greeks but did not dare to take up a defense against the Romans with us their kinsmen. [365] The goodwill and trust they showed those Greeks sure benefited them a great deal! They were bitterly slain, house and all, by the Greeks and in this manner received a return for their alliance. [366] For what

δὲ μακαρίζουσιν ἤδη τὴν ἀθάνατον τάξιν ἀπολαμβάνοντας. [357] ἆρ᾽ οὖν οὐκ αἰδούμεθα χεῖρον Ἰνδῶν φρονοῦντες καὶ διὰ τῆς αὐτῶν ἀτολμίας τοὺς πατρίους νόμους, οἳ πᾶσιν ἀνθρώποις εἰς ζῆλον ἥκουσιν, αἰσχρῶς ὑβρίζοντες;

[358] ἀλλ᾽ εἴ γε καὶ τοὺς ἐναντίους ἐξ ἀρχῆς λόγους ἐπαιδεύθημεν, ὡς ἄρα μέγιστον ἀγαθὸν ἀνθρώποις ἐστὶ τὸ ζῆν συμφορὰ δ᾽ ὁ θάνατος, ὁ γοῦν καιρὸς ἡμᾶς παρακαλεῖ φέρειν εὐκαρδίως αὐτὸν, θεοῦ γνώμῃ καὶ κατ᾽ ἀνάγκας τελευτήσαντας· [359] πάλαι γάρ, ὡς ἔοικε, κατὰ τοῦ κοινοῦ παντὸς Ἰουδαίων γένους ταύτην ἔθετο τὴν ψῆφον ὁ θεός, ὥσθ᾽ ἡμᾶς τοῦ ζῆν ἀπηλλάχθαι μὴ μέλλοντας αὐτῷ χρῆσθαι κατὰ τρόπον. [360] μὴ γὰρ αὐτοῖς ὑμῖν ἀνάπτετε τὰς αἰτίας μηδὲ χαρίζεσθε τοῖς Ῥωμαίοις, ὅτι πάντας ἡμᾶς ὁ πρὸς αὐτοὺς πόλεμος διέφθειρεν· οὐ γὰρ ἐκείνων ἰσχύι ταῦτα συμβέβηκεν, ἀλλὰ κρείττων αἰτία γενομένη τὸ δοκεῖν ἐκείνοις νικᾶν παρέσχηκε.

[361] ποίοις γὰρ ὅπλοις Ῥωμαίων τεθνήκασιν οἱ Καισάρειαν Ἰουδαῖοι κατοικοῦντες; [362] ἀλλ᾽ οὐδὲ μελλήσαντας αὐτοὺς ἐκείνων ἀφίστασθαι, μεταξὺ δὲ τὴν ἑβδόμην ἑορτάζοντας τὸ πλῆθος τῶν Καισαρέων ἐπιδραμὸν μηδὲ χεῖρας ἀνταίροντας ἅμα γυναιξὶ καὶ τέκνοις κατέσφαξαν, οὐδ᾽ αὐτοὺς Ῥωμαίους ἐντραπέντες, οἳ μόνους ἡμᾶς ἡγοῦντο πολεμίους τοὺς ἀφεστηκότας. [363] ἀλλὰ φήσει τις ὅτι Καισαρεῦσιν ἦν ἀεὶ διαφορὰ πρὸς τοὺς παρ᾽ αὐτοῖς, καὶ τοῦ καιροῦ λαβόμενοι τὸ παλαιὸν μῖσος ἀπεπλήρωσαν. [364] τί οὖν τοὺς ἐν Σκυθοπόλει φῶμεν; ἡμῖν γὰρ ἐκεῖνοι διὰ τοὺς Ἕλληνας πολεμεῖν ἐτόλμησαν, ἀλλ᾽ οὐ μετὰ τῶν συγγενῶν ἡμῶν Ῥωμαίους ἀμύνεσθαι. [365] πολὺ τοίνυν ὤνησεν αὐτοὺς ἡ πρὸς ἐκείνους εὔνοια καὶ πίστις· ὑπ᾽ αὐτῶν μέντοι πανοικεσίᾳ πικρῶς κατεφονεύθησαν ταύτην τῆς συμμαχίας ἀπολαβόντες ἀμοιβήν· [366] ἃ γὰρ ἐκείνους ὑφ᾽ ἡμῶν ἐκώλυσαν,

they prevented them from suffering at our hands, these things they endured as if they desired to make it happen.

Now it would take a long time to speak about each individually. [367] Know that there is not one city in Syria which did not kill the Judeans who inhabited it, being at war with us more than the Romans. [368] The people of Damascus filled their city with a foul slaughter without even being able to invent a good pretext and slew eighteen thousand Judeans with their wives and families. [369] And we heard that the amount of those tortured and killed in Egypt exceeded sixty thousand. Now perhaps they died because in a foreign land they were found to be no match for their enemies. But for every one of those who took up the war against Rome at home, what was lacking which was able to offer the hope of a certain victory? [370] Weapons, walls, impregnable fortresses, an unwavering spirit before the risks on behalf of freedom; these strengthened all to revolt. [371] But these things, which helped for a short time and lifted us with hopes, turned out to be the beginning of greater calamities. For they were all taken. All fell to the enemy just as if they had been prepared to make their victory more famous and not for the safety of those who had prepared them.

[372] Now it is fitting to call those who have died in battle blessed, for they died defending freedom, not throwing it away. But who should not feel pity for the mass of those who come under the Romans? Who would not be quick to die before he suffered these things at their hands? [373] Some died on the rack, tortured with fire and whips, others, half-eaten by wild animals, were kept alive as a second feast for them, in this way affording laughter and sport for their enemies. [374] But we ought to suppose that more wretched than these people are those still alive, who often pray

ταῦθ᾽ ὑπέμειναν ὡς αὐτοὶ δρᾶσαι θελήσαντες.

μακρὸν ἂν εἴη νῦν ἰδίᾳ περὶ ἑκάστων λέγειν. [367] ἴστε γὰρ ὅτι τῶν ἐν Συρίᾳ πόλεων οὐκ ἔστιν ἥτις τοὺς παρ᾽ αὐτῇ κατοικοῦντας Ἰουδαίους οὐκ ἀνῄρηκεν, ἡμῖν πλέον ἢ Ῥωμαίοις ὄντας πολεμίους· [368] ὅπου γε Δαμασκηνοὶ μηδὲ πρόφασιν εὔλογον πλάσαι δυνηθέντες φόνου μιαρωτάτου τὴν αὑτῶν πόλιν ἐνέπλησαν ὀκτακισχιλίους πρὸς τοῖς μυρίοις Ἰουδαίους ἅμα γυναιξὶ καὶ γενεαῖς ἀποσφάξαντες. [369] τὸ δ᾽ ἐν Αἰγύπτῳ πλῆθος τῶν μετ᾽ αἰκίας ἀνῃρημένων ἓξ που μυριάδας ὑπερβάλλειν ἐπυνθανόμεθα. κἀκεῖνοι μὲν ἴσως ἐπ᾽ ἀλλοτρίας γῆς οὐδὲν ἀντίπαλον εὑράμενοι τοῖς πολεμίοις οὕτως ἀπέθανον, τοῖς δ᾽ ἐπὶ τῆς οἰκείας τὸν πρὸς Ῥωμαίους πόλεμον ἀραμένοις ἅπασί τε τῶν ἐλπίδα νίκης ἐχυρᾶς παρασχεῖν δυναμένων οὐχ ὑπῆρξε; [370] καὶ γὰρ ὅπλα καὶ τείχη καὶ φρουρίων δυσάλωτοι κατασκευαὶ καὶ φρόνημα πρὸς τοὺς ὑπὲρ τῆς ἐλευθερίας κινδύνους ἄτρεπτον πάντας πρὸς τὴν ἀπόστασιν ἐπέρρωσεν. [371] ἀλλὰ ταῦτα πρὸς βραχὺν χρόνον ἀρκέσαντα καὶ ταῖς ἐλπίσιν ἡμᾶς ἐπάραντα μειζόνων ἀρχὴ κακῶν ἐφάνη· πάντα γὰρ ἥλω, καὶ πάντα τοῖς πολεμίοις ὑπέπεσεν, ὥσπερ εἰς τὴν ἐκείνων εὐκλεεστέραν νίκην, οὐκ εἰς τὴν τῶν παρασκευασαμένων σωτηρίαν εὐτρεπισθέντα.

[372] καὶ τοὺς μὲν ἐν ταῖς μάχαις ἀποθνήσκοντας εὐδαιμονίζειν προσῆκον· ἀμυνόμενοι γὰρ καὶ τὴν ἐλευθερίαν οὐ προέμενοι τεθνήκασι· τὸ δὲ πλῆθος τῶν ὑπὸ Ῥωμαίοις γενομένων τίς οὐκ ἂν ἐλεήσειε; τίς οὐκ ἂν ἐπειχθείη πρὸ τοῦ ταὐτὰ παθεῖν ἐκείνοις ἀποθανεῖν; [373] ὧν οἱ μὲν στρεβλούμενοι καὶ πυρὶ καὶ μάστιξιν αἰκιζόμενοι τεθνήκασιν, οἱ δ᾽ ἀπὸ θηρίων ἡμίβρωτοι πρὸς δευτέραν αὐτοῖς τροφὴν ζῶντες ἐφυλάχθησαν, γέλωτα καὶ παίγνιον τοῖς πολεμίοις παρασχόντες. [374] ἐκείνων μὲν οὖν ἀθλιωτάτους ὑποληπτέον τοὺς ἔτι ζῶντας, οἳ πολλάκις εὐχόμενοι

to die but do not. [375] And where is the great city, the mother city of the entire Jewish people, fortified by such encircling walls, which presented her many citadels and massive towers and could hardly contain the preparations for war and held so many thousands of men to fight on her behalf? [376] Where has she gone, who was believed by us to have had God as the founder? She has been uprooted to the foundation and plundered, and her only memorials are the names of those killed, which dwell among the remains. [377] Wretched old men sit beside the ashes of the sacred area, and a few women are kept for shameful outrage by their enemies.

[378] Who of us as we think about these things could stand to see the sun even if it were possible to live without danger? Who is so hateful of his fatherland or so fearful and cowardly that he would not regret still being alive? [379] Oh that we had all died before we had seen that holy city torn down by enemy hands, before we had seen the temple so impiously torn out! [380] Now since hope, one not ignoble, deluded us—a hope that we might somehow be able to ward off the enemy on her behalf—and is completely gone and has left us all alone under this necessity, let us be quick to die nobly. Let us take pity upon ourselves and our children and wives, while it is possible to receive this pity at our own hand. [381] For we were born for death, we and those whom we have begotten, and not even the fortunate can escape it. [382] But violation and slavery and the sight of our wives with children led to shame; these are no necessary evils born to man from nature. Rather those who do not want to die when the possibility exists endure these things because of their fear. [383] But we, thinking highly about our bravery, revolted against the Romans and now at last, when they offered us safety, we refused it. [384] To whom now is their rage not apparent, if they will capture us alive?

τὸν θάνατον λαβεῖν οὐκ ἔχουσιν. [375] ποῦ δ᾽ ἡ μεγάλη πόλις, ἡ τοῦ παντὸς Ἰουδαίων γένους μητρόπολις, ἡ τοσούτοις μὲν ἐρυμνὴ τειχῶν περιβόλοις, τοσαῦτα δ᾽ αὐτῆς φρούρια καὶ μεγέθη πύργων προβεβλημένη, μόλις δὲ χωροῦσα τὰς εἰς τὸν πόλεμον παρασκευάς, τοσαύτας δὲ μυριάδας ἀνδρῶν ἔχουσα τῶν ὑπὲρ αὐτῆς μαχομένων; [376] ποῦ γέγονεν ἡμῖν ἡ τὸν θεὸν ἔχειν οἰκιστὴν πεπιστευμένη; πρόρριζος ἐκ βάθρων ἀνήρπασται, καὶ μόνον αὐτῆς μνημεῖον ἀπολείπεται τὸ τῶν ἀνῃρημένων ἔτι τοῖς λειψάνοις ἐποικοῦν. [377] πρεσβῦται δὲ δύστηνοι τῇ σποδῷ τοῦ τεμένους παρακάθηνται καὶ γυναῖκες ὀλίγαι πρὸς ὕβριν αἰσχίστην ὑπὸ τῶν πολεμίων τετηρημέναι.

[378] ταῦτα τίς ἐν νῷ βαλλόμενος ἡμῶν καρτερήσει τὸν ἥλιον ὁρᾶν, κἂν δύνηται ζῆν ἀκινδύνως; τίς οὕτω τῆς πατρίδος ἐχθρός, ἢ τίς οὕτως ἄνανδρος καὶ φιλόψυχος, ὡς μὴ καὶ περὶ τοῦ μέχρι νῦν ζῆσαι μετανοεῖν; [379] ἀλλ᾽ εἴθε πάντες ἐτεθνήκειμεν πρὶν τὴν ἱερὰν ἐκείνην πόλιν χερσὶν ἰδεῖν κατασκαπτομένην πολεμίων, πρὶν τὸν ναὸν τὸν ἅγιον οὕτως ἀνοσίως ἐξορωρυγμένον. [380] ἐπεὶ δὲ ἡμᾶς οὐκ ἀγεννὴς ἐλπὶς ἐβουκόλησεν, ὡς τάχα που δυνήσεσθαι τοὺς πολεμίους ὑπὲρ αὐτῆς ἀμύνασθαι, φρούδη δὲ γέγονε νῦν καὶ μόνους ἡμᾶς ἐπὶ τῆς ἀνάγκης καταλέλοιπεν, σπεύσωμεν καλῶς ἀποθανεῖν, ἐλεήσωμεν ἡμᾶς αὐτοὺς καὶ τὰ τέκνα καὶ τὰς γυναῖκας, ἕως ἡμῖν ἔξεστιν παρ᾽ ἡμῶν αὐτῶν λαβεῖν τὸν ἔλεον. [381] ἐπὶ μὲν γὰρ θάνατον ἐγεννήθημεν καὶ τοὺς ἐξ αὐτῶν ἐγεννήσαμεν, καὶ τοῦτον οὐδὲ τοῖς εὐδαιμονοῦσίν ἐστι διαφυγεῖν· [382] ὕβρις δὲ καὶ δουλεία καὶ τὸ βλέπειν γυναῖκας εἰς αἰσχύνην ἀγομένας μετὰ τέκνων οὐκ ἔστιν ἀνθρώποις κακὸν ἐκ φύσεως ἀναγκαῖον, ἀλλὰ ταῦτα διὰ τὴν αὐτῶν δειλίαν ὑπομένουσιν οἱ παρὸν πρὸ αὐτῶν ἀποθανεῖν μὴ θελήσαντες. [383] ἡμεῖς δὲ ἐπ᾽ ἀνδρείᾳ μέγα φρονοῦντες Ῥωμαίων ἀπέστημεν καὶ τὰ τελευταῖα νῦν ἐπὶ σωτηρίᾳ προκαλουμένων ἡμᾶς οὐχ ὑπηκούσαμεν. [384] τίνι τοίνυν οὐκ

Wretched will be the young, characterized as they are by strong bodies sufficient for many tortures, and those advanced to an age that is unable to bear the distress. [385] Will someone see a wife taken for violation, or with bound hands listen to the cry of his child crying out, "Father"? [386] No! While our hands are free and have a sword, let them give us a noble service! Let us die un-enslaved to our enemies and as free men let us depart life together with our children and wives. [387] Our laws order this. Our wives and children beg for this. God has sent the necessity. The Romans desire the opposite and are afraid that any of us will die before capture. [388] So let us be quick to leave for them, instead of the enjoyment they expect with our capture, amazement at our death and wonder at our bravery.

ἔστιν ὁ θυμὸς αὐτῶν πρόδηλος εἰ ζώντων ἡμῶν κρατήσουσιν; ἄθλιοι μὲν οἱ νέοι τῆς ῥώμης τῶν σωμάτων εἰς πολλὰς αἰκίας ἀρκέσοντες, ἄθλιοι δὲ οἱ παρηβηκότες φέρειν τῆς ἡλικίας τὰς συμφορὰς οὐ δυναμένης. [385] ὄψεταί τις γυναῖκα πρὸς βίαν ἀγομένην, φωνῆς ἐπακούσεται τέκνου πατέρα βοῶντος χεῖρας δεδεμένος; [386] ἀλλ᾽ ἕως εἰσὶν ἐλεύθεραι καὶ ξίφος ἔχουσιν, καλὴν ὑπουργίαν ὑπουργησάτωσαν· ἀδούλωτοι μὲν ὑπὸ τῶν πολεμίων ἀποθάνωμεν, ἐλεύθεροι δὲ μετὰ τέκνων καὶ γυναικῶν τοῦ ζῆν συνεξέλθωμεν. [387] ταῦθ᾽ ἡμᾶς οἱ νόμοι κελεύουσι ταῦθ᾽ ἡμᾶς γυναῖκες καὶ παῖδες ἱκετεύουσι· τούτων τὴν ἀνάγκην θεὸς ἀπέσταλκε, τούτων Ῥωμαῖοι τἀναντία θέλουσι, καὶ μή τις ἡμῶν πρὸ τῆς ἁλώσεως ἀποθάνη δεδοίκασι. [388] σπεύσωμεν οὖν ἀντὶ τῆς ἐλπιζομένης αὐτοῖς καθ᾽ ἡμῶν ἀπολαύσεως ἔκπληξιν τοῦ θανάτου καὶ θαῦμα τῆς τόλμης καταλιπεῖν.

Josephus's Speech at Jotapata

War 3:362–82

[362] Why, he said, this great desire that we kill ourselves, comrades, or that we separate body and soul, things most dear? Someone says that I have changed. [363] But the Romans know about this at least. "It's noble to die in war"—but by the rule of battle; that is, by those who conquer. [364] Now if I am turning and fleeing from the sword of the Romans, truly I deserve to die by my own sword at my own hand. But if they have a sparing attitude toward an enemy, how much more right is it that we should spare ourselves? For it is foolish that we do to ourselves those things concerning which we are fighting against them. [365] "It is noble to die for freedom"; I agree, but when we are at war and fighting those who would take it away. But they are now neither coming to meet us in battle

[362] τί γὰρ τοσοῦτον, ἔφη, σφῶν αὐτῶν, ἑταῖροι, φονῶμεν; ἢ τί τὰ φίλτατα διαστασιάζομεν, σῶμα καὶ ψυχήν. ἠλλάχθαι τις ἐμέ φησιν. [363] ἀλλ᾽ οἴδασιν Ῥωμαῖοι τοῦτό γε. καλὸν ἐν πολέμῳ θνήσκειν, ἀλλὰ πολέμου νόμῳ, τουτέστιν ὑπὸ τῶν κρατούντων. [364] εἰ μὲν οὖν τὸν Ῥωμαίων ἀποστρέφομαι σίδηρον, ἄξιος ἀληθῶς εἰμι τοὐμοῦ ξίφους καὶ χειρὸς τῆς ἐμῆς· εἰ δ᾽ ἐκείνους εἰσέρχεται φειδὼ πολεμίου, πόσῳ δικαιότερον ἂν ἡμᾶς ἡμῶν αὐτῶν εἰσέλθοι; καὶ γὰρ ἠλίθιον ταῦτα δρᾶν σφᾶς αὐτούς, περὶ ὧν πρὸς ἐκείνους διιστάμεθα. [365] καλὸν γὰρ ὑπὲρ τῆς ἐλευθερίας ἀποθνήσκειν· φημὶ κἀγώ, μαχομένους μέντοι, καὶ ὑπὸ τῶν ἀφαιρουμένων αὐτήν. νῦν δ᾽ οὔτ᾽ εἰς μάχην ἀντιάζουσιν ἡμῖν οὔτ᾽ ἀναιροῦσιν ἡμᾶς· δειλὸς δὲ ὁμοίως ὅ τε

nor killing us. The one who does not want to die when it is necessary is just as cowardly as the one who wants to die when it is unnecessary. [366] What do we fear that causes us not to go out to the Romans? [367] Isn't it death? Then this thing which we fear and suspect from our enemy, should we make it certain for ourselves? "No, it is slavery we fear," someone will say. Well, we're certainly free now! [368] "It is noble to kill oneself," someone will say. Not at all! Rather it is ignoble. I at least think that such a person would be like a terrified pilot who sank his boat intentionally before the rain came because he was afraid of the storm.

[369] To die at one's own hand is both alien to the nature held in common by all living things and an impious act against God, who created us. [370] For of all the animals there is not one that contemplates or causes its own death. For the desire to live is a law of nature, strong in all things. For this reason we consider those who openly take life away from us to be enemies, and those who do so by stealth we punish. [371] Do you not think that God is exasperated when a person despises his gift. For from him we have received our existence and to him we leave its end. [372] The bodies of all things are mortal and crafted from corruptible matter, but the soul is forever immortal and takes its dwelling in the bodies as a portion of God. Now if someone destroys a human deposit or manages it badly, he is thought to be wicked and untrustworthy. So if a person casts God's deposit away from his own body, do you think he will escape the notice of the One who is wronged? [373] It is lawful to punish household slaves who run away, even if they are leaving wicked masters. Won't it appear as if we ourselves are committing sacrilege if we run away from the noblest master, God? [374] Don't you know that everlasting fame belongs to those who depart life in accordance with the law of

μὴ βουλόμενος θνῄσκειν ὅταν δέῃ καὶ ὁ βουλόμενος, ὅταν μὴ δέῃ. [366] τί δὲ καὶ δεδοικότες πρὸς Ῥωμαίους οὐκ ἄνιμεν; [367] ἆρ' οὐχὶ θάνατον; εἶθ' ὃν δεδοίκαμεν ἐκ τῶν ἐχθρῶν ὑποπτευόμενον, ἑαυτοῖς βέβαιον ἐπιστήσομεν; ἀλλὰ δουλείαν, ἐρεῖ τις. πάνυ γοῦν νῦν ἐσμεν ἐλεύθεροι. [368] γενναῖον γὰρ ἀνελεῖν ἑαυτόν, φήσει τις. οὐ μὲν οὖν, ἀλλ' ἀγενέστατον, ὡς ἔγωγε καὶ κυβερνήτην ἡγοῦμαι δειλότατον, ὅστις χειμῶνα δεδοικὼς πρὸ τῆς θυέλλης ἐβάπτισεν ἑκὼν τὸ σκάφος.

[369] ἀλλὰ μὴν ἡ αὐτοχειρία καὶ τῆς κοινῆς ἁπάντων ζῴων φύσεως ἀλλότριον καὶ πρὸς τὸν κτίσαντα θεὸν ἡμᾶς ἐστιν ἀσέβεια. [370] τῶν μέν γε ζῴων οὐδέν ἐστιν ὃ θνῄσκει μετὰ προνοίας ἢ δι' αὐτοῦ· φύσεως γὰρ νόμος ἰσχυρὸς ἐν ἅπασιν τὸ ζῆν ἐθέλειν· διὰ τοῦτο καὶ τοὺς φανερῶς ἀφαιρουμένους ἡμᾶς τούτου πολεμίους ἡγούμεθα καὶ τοὺς ἐξ ἐνέδρας τιμωρούμεθα. [371] τὸν δὲ θεὸν οὐκ οἴεσθε ἀγανακτεῖν, ὅταν ἄνθρωπος αὐτοῦ τὸ δῶρον ὑβρίζῃ; καὶ γὰρ εἰλήφαμεν παρ' ἐκείνου τὸ εἶναι καὶ τὸ μηκέτι εἶναι πάλιν ἐκείνῳ δίδομεν. [372] τὰ μέν γε σώματα θνητὰ πᾶσιν καὶ ἐκ φθαρτῆς ὕλης δεδημιούργηται, ψυχὴ δὲ ἀθάνατος ἀεὶ καὶ θεοῦ μοῖρα τοῖς σώμασιν ἐνοικίζεται· εἶτ' ἐὰν μὲν ἀφανίσῃ τις ἀνθρώπου παρακαταθήκην ἢ διαθῆται κακῶς, πονηρὸς εἶναι δοκεῖ καὶ ἄπιστος, εἰ δέ τις τοῦ σφετέρου σώματος ἐκβάλλει τὴν παρακαταθήκην τοῦ θεοῦ, λεληθέναι δοκεῖ τὸν ἀδικούμενον; [373] καὶ κολάζειν μὲν τοὺς ἀποδράντας οἰκέτας δίκαιον νενόμισται, κἂν πονηροὺς καταλείπωσι δεσπότας, αὐτοὶ δὲ κάλλιστον δεσπότην ἀποδιδράσκοντες τὸν θεὸν οὐ δοκοῦμεν ἀσεβεῖν; [374] ἆρ' οὐκ ἴστε, ὅτι τῶν μὲν ἐξιόντων τοῦ βίου κατὰ τὸν τῆς φύσεως νόμον καὶ τὸ ληφθὲν παρὰ τοῦ θεοῦ χρέος ἐκτινύντων, ὅταν ὁ δοὺς

nature and who repay the debt which was received from God when the one who gave it wants to receive it back again; that their homes and families are secure; that their souls remain pure and obedient; that they inherit a heavenly and very holy place, from where in the turning of the ages they are transferred again into holy bodies? [375] But for as many as lay insane hands upon themselves, the darker realm of the dead receives their souls and God, their Father, punishes their descendants for the insolent deeds of their fathers. [376] Therefore this crime is hateful to God and punished by the most wise lawgiver. [377] At least among us the laws have decreed that those who kill themselves are to be cast out and remain unburied until the sun sets, although they think it proper to bury even enemies of war. [378] Among other peoples also they ordered that the right hands of those who died in this way, and by which they made war against themselves, be cut off, reasoning that just as the body was cut off from the soul in an alien fashion, so also the hand be cut off from the body.

[379] Therefore, comrades, it is good that we consider things aright and not add to our human misfortunes impiety against the one who created us. [380] If it seems good to be saved, let us be saved! For safety among those to whom we have shown our virtues by so many deeds is not without glory. If it seems good to die, it is good to die at the hand of those who have taken us. [381] But I will not go over to the enemies' rank so that I might be a traitor to myself. For I would be much more foolish than those who have deserted to the enemy, if they do this for safety, and I to destruction—my own at that. [382] However, I pray for the Romans' ambush; for if am killed by them after their pledge, I will die in good spirit because I will take away as comfort the faithlessness of those who lied, a thing better than victory.

κομίσασθαι θέλῃ, κλέος μὲν αἰώνιον, οἶκοι δὲ καὶ γενεαὶ βέβαιοι, καθαραὶ δὲ καὶ ἐπήκοοι μένουσιν αἱ ψυχαί, χῶρον οὐράνιον λαχοῦσαι τὸν ἁγιώτατον, ἔνθεν ἐκ περιτροπῆς αἰώνων ἁγνοῖς πάλιν ἀντενοικίζονται σώμασιν· [375] ὅσοις δὲ καθ᾽ ἑαυτῶν ἐμάνησαν αἱ χεῖρες, τούτων ᾅδης μὲν δέχεται τὰς ψυχὰς σκοτεινότερος, ὁ δὲ τούτων πατὴρ θεὸς εἰς ἐγγόνους τιμωρεῖται τοὺς τῶν πατέρων ὑβριστάς. [376] διὰ τοῦτο μεμίσηται παρὰ θεῷ τοῦτο καὶ παρὰ τῷ σοφωτάτῳ κολάζεται νομοθέτῃ· [377] τοὺς γοῦν ἀναιροῦντας ἑαυτοὺς παρὰ μὲν ἡμῖν μέχρις ἡλίου δύσεως ἀτάφους ἐκρίπτειν ἔκριναν, καίτοι καὶ πολεμίους θάπτειν θεμιτὸν ἡγούμενοι, [378] παρ᾽ ἑτέροις δὲ καὶ τὰς δεξιὰς τῶν τοιούτων νεκρῶν ἀποκόπτειν ἐκέλευσαν, αἷς ἐστρατεύσαντο καθ᾽ ἑαυτῶν, ἡγούμενοι, καθάπερ τὸ σῶμα τῆς ψυχῆς ἀλλότριον, οὕτως καὶ τὴν χεῖρα τοῦ σώματος.

[379] καλὸν οὖν, ἑταῖροι, δίκαια φρονεῖν καὶ μὴ ταῖς ἀνθρωπίναις συμφοραῖς προσθεῖναι τὴν εἰς τὸν κτίσαντα ἡμᾶς δυσσέβειαν. [380] εἰ σώζεσθαι δοκεῖ, σωζώμεθα· καὶ γὰρ οὐκ ἄδοξος ἡ σωτηρία παρ᾽ οἷς διὰ τοσούτων ἔργων ἐπεδειξάμεθα τὰς ἀρετάς· εἰ τεθνάναι, καλὸν ὑπὸ τῶν ἑλόντων. [381] οὐ μεταβήσομαι δ᾽ ἐγὼ εἰς τὴν τῶν πολεμίων τάξιν, ἵν᾽ ἐμαυτοῦ προδότης γένωμαι. καὶ γὰρ ἂν εἴην πολὺ τῶν αὐτομολούντων πρὸς τοὺς πολεμίους ἠλιθιώτερος, εἴ γ᾽ ἐκεῖνοι μὲν ἐπὶ σωτηρίᾳ τοῦτο πράττουσιν, ἐγὼ δὲ ἐπὶ ἀπωλείᾳ, καί γε τῇ ἐμαυτοῦ. [382] τὴν μέντοι Ῥωμαίων ἐνέδραν εὔχομαι· μετὰ γὰρ δεξιὰν ἀναιρούμενος ὑπ᾽ αὐτῶν εὔθυμος τεθνήξομαι, τὴν τῶν ψευσαμένων ἀπιστίαν νίκης μείζονα ἀποφέρων παραμυθίαν.

BIBLIOGRAPHY

Ahl, Frederick. "The Art of Safe Criticism." *AJP* 105 (1984): 174–208.

Anderson, H. "4 Maccabees: A New Translation and Introduction." In *The Old Testament Pseudepigrapha*. Edited by James H. Charlesworth. New York: Doubleday, 1985.

Appelbaum, S. "The Zealots: The Case for Revaluation." *JRS* 61 (1971): 155–70.

Atkinson, Kenneth. "Noble Deaths at Gamala and Masada? A Critical Assessment of Josephus' Accounts of Jewish Resistance in Light of Archaeological Discoveries." Pages 349–71 in *Making History: Josephus and Historical Method*. Edited by Zuleika Rodgers. Leiden: Brill, 2007.

Attridge, Harold. "Jewish Historiography." Pages 311–43 in *Early Judaism and Its Modern Interpreters*. Edited by Robert A. Kraft and George W. E. Nickelsburg. Philadelphia: Fortress, 1986.

———. "Josephus and His Works." Pages 185–232 in *Jewish Writings of the Second Temple Period*. Edited by Michael E. Stone. Philadelphia: Fortress, 1986.

Barclay, John M. G. "The Empire Writes Back: Josephan Rhetoric in Flavian Rome." Pages 315–32 in *Flavius Josephus and Flavian Rome*. Edited by Jonathan Edmondson, Steve Mason, and James Rives. New York: Oxford University Press, 2005.

Barish, David A. "The 'Autobiography' of Josephus and the Hypothesis of a Second Edition of His 'Antiquities.'" *HTR* 71 (1978): 61–75.

Barnes, T. D. "The Sack of the Temple in Josephus and Tacitus." Pages 129–44 in *Flavius Josephus and Flavian Rome*. Edited by Jonathan Edmondson, Steve Mason, and James Rives. New York: Oxford University Press, 2005.

Bauernfeind, O., and O. Michel. "Die beiden Eleazarreden in Jos. Bell. 7, 323–336; 7, 341–388." *ZNW* 58 (1965): 267–72.

Baumbach, Gunther. "Zeloten und Sikarier." *TLZ* 90 (1965): 727–40.

Beard, Mary. "The Triumph of Flavius Josephus." Pages 543–58 in *Flavian Rome: Culture, Image, Text*. Edited by A. J. Boyle and W. J. Dominik. Leiden and Boston: Brill, 2003.

Begg, Christopher. *Josephus' Story of the Later Monarchy*. Leuven: Leven Universtiy Press, 2000.

Ben-Yehuda, Nachman. *The Masada Myth: Collective Memory and Mythmaking in Israel*. Madison: University of Wisconsin Press, 1995.

———. *Sacrificing Truth: Archaeology and the Myth of Masada*. Amherst: Humanity Books, 2002.

Bilde, Per. "The Causes of the Jewish War According to Josephus." *JSJ* 10 (1979): 179–202.

————. *Flavius Josephus between Jerusalem and Rome*. JSPSup 2. Worcester: Sheffield Academic Press, 1988.

Bowersock, G. W. "Old and New in the History of Judaea." *JRS* 65 (1975): 180–85.

Brunt, Peter A. "Josephus on Social Conflicts in Roman Judaea." *Klio* 59 (1977): 149–53.

Bünker, Michael. "Die rhetorische Disposition der Eleazarreden." *Kairos* 23 (1981): 101–7.

Chapman, Honora Howell. "Spectacle and Theater in Josephus's *Bellum Judaicum*." Ph.D. diss., Stanford University, 1998.

————. "Spectacle in Josephus' *Jewish War*." Pages 289–313 in *Flavius Josephus and Flavian Rome*. Edited by Jonathan Edmondson, Steve Mason, and James Rives. New York: Oxford University Press, 2005.

Cloud, J. D. "How Did Sulla Style His Law *De Sicariis*?" *The Classical Review* 18 (1968): 140–43.

————. "The Primary Purpose of the Lex Cornelia." *Zeitschrift der Savigny-Stiftung für Rechtsgeschichte* 86 (1969): 258–86.

Cohen, Shaye J. D. *From Maccabees to the Mishnah*. Philadelphia: Westminster, 1987.

————. *Josephus in Galilee and Rome*. Leiden: Brill, 1979.

————. "Josephus, Jeremiah, and Polybius." *History and Theory* 21 (1982): 366–81.

————. "Masada: Literary Tradition, Archaeological Remains, and the Credibility of Josephus." *JJS* 33 (1982): 385–405.

Cotton, Hannah M. "The Date of the Fall of Masada: The Evidence of the Masada Papyri." *ZPE* 78 (1989): 157–62.

Cotton, Hannah M., and Werner Eck. "Josephus' Roman Audience: Josephus and the Roman Elites." Pages 37–52 in *Flavius Josephus and Flavian Rome*. Edited by Jonathan Edmondson, Steve Mason, and James Rives. New York: Oxford University Press, 2005.

D'Huys, Viktor. "How to Describe Violence in Historical Narrative." *Ancient Society* 18 (1987): 209–50.

Drexler, Hans. "Untersuchungen zu Josephus und zur Geschichte des jüdischen Aufstandes." *Klio* 19 (1925): 277–312.

Droge, Arthur J. "Josephus between Greeks and Barbarians." In *Josephus' Contra Apionem*. Edited by Louis H. Feldman and John R. Levison. New York and Leiden: Brill, 1996.

————, and James D. Tabor. *A Noble Death: Suicide and Martyrdom among Christians and Jews in Antiquity*. San Francisco: HarperSanFrancisco, 1992.

Eck, Werner. "Die Eroberung von Masada und eine neue Inschrift des L. Flavius Silva Nonius Bassus." *ZNW* 60 (1969): 282–89.

Eckstein, Arthur M. "Josephus and Polybius: A Reconsideration." *CQ* 9 (1990): 175–298.

————. *Moral Vision in the Histories of Polybius*. Berkeley and Los Angeles: University of California Press, 1995.

Edwards, Catharine. *Death in Ancient Rome*. New Haven and London: Yale University Press, 2007.

Fatham, Elaine. *Roman Literary Culture: From Cicero to Apuleius*. Baltimore: Johns Hopkins University Press, 1996.

Farmer, William Reuben. *Maccabees, Zealots, and Josephus*. New York: Columbia University Press, 1956.

Feldman, L. H. *Flavius Josephus: Judean Antiquities 1–4*. Translation and Commentary. Edited by Steve Mason. Leiden: Brill, 2000.

————. "Flavius Josephus Revisited: The Man, His Writings, and His Significance." In *ANRW* II.21.2 (1984).

————. "Introduction." In *Josephus, the Bible, and History*. Edited by Louis H. Feldman and Gohei Hata. Leiden: Brill, 1989.

————. *Jew and Gentile in the Ancient World*. Princeton: Princeton University Press, 1993.

————. *Josephus and Modern Scholarship (1937–1980)*. New York: Walter de Gruyter, 1984.

————. *Josephus: A Supplementary Bibliography*. New York: Garland, 1986.

————. *Josephus: Jewish Antiquities Book XX*. Translated by Louis H. Feldman. Cambridge, MA: Harvard University Press, 1965.

————. "Masada: A Critique of Recent Scholarship." Pages 218–48 in *Christianity, Judaism and Other Greco-Roman Cults: Studies for Morton Smith*. Edited by J. Neusner. Leiden: Brill, 1975.

————. *Studies in Josephus' Rewritten Bible*. Boston: Brill, 1998.

Ferrary, Jean-Louis. "Lex Cornelia de Sicariis et Veneficis." *Athenaeum* 69 (1991): 417–34.

Foucher, Antoine. "Nature et formes de l'histoire tragique à Rome." *Latomus* 59 (2000): 773–801.

Garnsey, Peter, and Richard Saller. *The Roman Empire: Economy, Society and Culture*. Berkeley and Los Angeles: University of California Press, 1987.

Goodblatt, David. "Priestly Ideologies of the Judean Resistance." *JSQ* 3 (1996): 225–49.

————. "Suicide in the Sanctuary: Traditions on Priestly Martyrdom." *JJS* 46 (1995): 10–29.

Goodman, Martin. "The *Fiscus Iudaicus* and Gentile Attitudes to Judaism in Flavian Rome." Pages 167–77 in *Flavius Josephus and Flavian Rome*. Edited by Jonathan Edmondson, Steve Mason, and James Rives. New York: Oxford University Press, 2005.

————. *The Ruling Class of Judaea*. Cambridge: Cambridge University Press, 1987.

Goold, G. P., ed. *Josephus*, Loeb Classical Library. Cambridge, MA: Harvard University Press, 1927–1965.

Griffin, Miriam. "Philosophy, Cato, and Roman Suicide." *Greece & Rome* 33 (1986): 64–77.

———. "Philosophy, Cato, and Roman Suicide: II." *Greece and Rome* 33 (1986): 192–202.

Grisé, Yolande. *Le suicide dans la Rome antique.* Montreal: Bellarmin, 1982.

Groag, Edmund, Arthur Stein, and Leiva Petersen, eds. *Prosopographia Imperii Romani.* Berlin and Leipzig: Walter de Gruyter, 1933.

Gruen, Erich S. *Diaspora: Jews amidst Greeks and Romans.* Cambridge, MA, and London: Harvard University Press, 2002.

———. "Roman Perspectives on the Jews in the Age of the Great Revolt." Pages 27–42 in *The First Jewish Revolt: Archaeology, History, and Ideology.* Edited by Andrea M. Berlin and J. Andrew Overman. London and New York: Routledge, 2002.

———. *Roman Politics and the Criminal Courts, 149–78 B.C.* Cambridge, MA: Harvard University Press, 1968.

Grünewald, Thomas. *Bandits in the Roman Empire: Myth and Reality.* Translated by John Drinkwater. London and New York: Routledge, 2004.

Habinek, Thomas N. *The Politics of Latin Literature: Writing, Identity, and Empire in Ancient Rome.* Princeton: Princeton University Press, 1998.

Hadas-Lebel, Mireille. *Flavius Josephus: Eyewitness to Rome's First-Century Conquest of Judea.* Translated by Richard Millar. New York: Macmillan, 1993.

Harris, William V. *Ancient Literacy.* Cambridge, MA, and London: Harvard University Press, 1989.

Hengel, Martin. *The Zealots: Investigations into the Jewish Freedom Movement in the Period from Herod I until 70 A.D.* Second edition. Translated by David Smith. Edinburgh: T & T Clark, 1989.

Hill, Timothy. *Ambitiosa Mors: Suicide and Self in Roman Thought and Literature.* Studies in Classics. Edited by Kirk Obbink and Andrew Dyck. New York and London: Routledge, 2004.

Hoenig, Sidney B. "The Sicarii in Masada—Glory or Infamy?" *Tradition* 11 (1970): 5–30.

Horsley, Richard A. *Galilee: History, Politics, People.* Valley Forge, PA: Trinity Press International, 1995.

———. "Josephus and the Bandits." *JSJ* 10 (1979): 35–63.

———. "Menahem in Jerusalem: A Brief Messianic Episode among the Sicarii—Not 'Zealot Messianism.'" *NT* 27 (1985): 334–48.

———. "Popular Prophetic Movements at the Time of Jesus: Their Principle Features and Social Origins." *JSNT* 26 (1986): 3–27.

———. "The Sicarii: Ancient Jewish 'Terrorist.'" *JR* 59 (1979): 435–58.

Horsley, Richard A., and John S. Hanson. *Bandits, Prophets, and Messiahs.* San Francisco: Harper & Row, 1985.

Jacobs, I. "Eleazar Ben Yair's Sanction for Martyrdom." *JSJ* 13 (1982): 183–86.

Jones, Brian W. *The Emperor Domitian*. London and New York: Routledge, 1992.

Jones, Christopher P. Review of Eck, "Senatorem." *AJP* 95 (1974): 89–90.

―――. "Towards a Chronology of Josephus." *Scripta Classica Israelica* 21 (2002): 113–21.

Josephus. Translated by H. St. J. Thackeray et al. 10 vols. LCL. Cambridge, MA: Harvard University Press, 1926–1965.

Kelly, Nicole. "The Cosmopolitan Expression of Josephus's Prophetic Perspective in the *Jewish War*." *HTR* 97, no. 3 (2004): 257–74.

Kennard, J. Spencer. "Judas of Galilee and His Clan." *JQR* 36 (1946): 281–86.

Kennedy, George A. *A New History of Classical Rhetoric*. Princeton: Princeton University Press, 1994.

Klassen, William. "The Archaeological Artifacts of Masada and the Credibility of Josephus." Pages 456–73 in *Text and Artifact in the Religions of Mediterranean Antiquity: Essays in Honour of Peter Richardson*. Edited by Stephen Wilson and Michel Desjardins Wilson. Waterloo, ON: Wilfrid Laurier University Press, 2000.

Kittel, G., and G. Friedrich, eds. *TDNT*. Translated by G. W. Bromiley. 10 vols. Grand Rapids: Eerdmans, 1964–1976.

Kraus, C. S., and A. J. Woodman. *Latin Historians*. Oxford: Oxford University Press, 1997.

Ladouceur, David J. "Josephus and Masada." Pages 95–113 in *Josephus, Judaism, and Christianity*. Edited by Louis H. Feldman and Gohei Hata. Detroit: Wayne State University Press, 1987.

―――. "Masada: A Consideration of the Literary Evidence." *GRBS* 21 (1980): 245–60.

Laqueur, Richard. *Der jüdische Historiker Flavius Josephus*. Darmstadt: Wissenschaftliche Buchgesellschaft, 1920. Reprint, 1970.

Leon, Harry J. *The Jews of Ancient Rome*. Peabody: Hendrickson, 1960. Reprint, 1995.

Levene, D. S. "Pity, Fear and the Historical Audience: Tacitus on the Fall of Vitellius." Pages 128–49 in *The Passions in Roman Thought and Literature*. Edited by Susanna Morton Braund and Christopher Gill. Cambridge: Cambridge University Press, 1997.

Levick, Barbara. *Vespasian*. London and New York: Routledge, 1999.

Levine, Lee. "Synagogue Leadership: The Case of the Archisynagogue." Pages 195–213 in *Jews in a Graeco-Roman World*. Edited by Martin Goodman. Oxford: Clarendon, 1998.

Liddell, Henry George, Robert Scott, and Henry Stuart Jones. *A Greek-English Lexicon*. Oxford: Clarendon, 1969.

Lindner, Helgo. *Die Geschichtsauffassung des Flavius Josephus im Bellum Judaicum*. Leiden: Brill, 1972.

Lintott, Andrew. *Violence, Civil Strife and Revolution in the Classical City 750–330 BC*. London and Canberra: Croom Helm, 1982.

————. *Violence in Republican Rome*. Second edition. Oxford: Oxford University Press, 1999.

Luttwak, Edward N. *The Grand Strategy of the Rome Empire from the First Century A.D. to the Third*. Baltimore: Johns Hopkins University Press, 1976.

Luz, Menahem. "Eleazar's Second Speech on Masada and Its Literary Precedents." *Rheinisches Museum für Philologie* 126 (1983): 25–43.

Macleod, Colin. "Thucydides and Tragedy." In *Collected Essays*, 140–58. Oxford: Clarendon, 1983.

MacMullen, Ramsay. *Enemies of the Roman Order*. Cambridge, MA: Harvard University Press, 1966.

Mader, Gottfried. *Josephus and the Politics of Historiography: Apologetic and Impression Management in the* Bellum Judaicum. Leiden: Brill, 2000.

Marincola, John. *Authority and Tradition in Ancient Historiography*. Cambridge: Cambridge University Press, 1997.

Mason, Steve. "Of Audience and Meaning: Reading Josephus' *Bellum Judaicum* in the Context of a Flavian Audience." Pages 71–100 in *Josephus and Jewish History in Flavian Rome and Beyond*. Edited by Joseph Sievers and Gaia Lembi. Leiden: Brill, 2005.

————. "Contradiction or Counterpoint? Josephus and Historical Method." *Review of Rabbinic Judaism* 6 (2003): 145–88.

————. "Essenes and Lurking Spartans in Josephus' *Judean War*: From Story to History." Pages 219–61 in *Making History: Josephus and Historical Method*. Edited by Zuleika Rodgers. Leiden: Brill, 2007.

————. "Figured Speech and Irony in T. Flavius Josephus." Pages 243–88 in *Flavius Josephus and Flavian Rome*. Edited by Jonathan Edmondson, Steve Mason, and James Rives. New York: Oxford University Press, 2005.

————. "Flavius Josephus in Flavian Rome: Reading on and between the Lines." Pages 559–89 in *Flavian Rome: Culture, Image, Text*. Edited by A. J. Boyle and W. J. Dominik. Leiden and Boston: Brill, 2003.

————. *Flavius Josephus on the Pharisees*. Boston and Leiden: Brill, 1991.

————. "Introduction to the *Judean Antiquities*." In *Flavius Josephus: Judean Antiquities 1–4*. Translation and Commentary. Edited by Steve Mason. Leiden: Brill, 2000.

————. *Josephus and the New Testament*. Second edition. Peabody: Hendrickson, 2003.

————. "Josephus, Daniel, and the Flavian House." Pages 161–91 in *Josephus and the History of the Greco-Roman Period: Essays in Memory of Morton Smith*. Edited by Fausto Parente and Joseph Sievers. Leiden: Brill, 1994.

————. *Life of Josephus*. Flavius Josephus. Translation and Commentary. Edited by Steve Mason. Boston and Leiden: Brill, 2003.

————. "'Should Any Wish to Enquire Further' (*Ant.* 1.25): The Aim and Audience of Josephus's *Judean Antiquities/Life.*" Pages 64–103 in *Understanding Josephus: Seven Perspectives.* Edited by Steve Mason. Sheffield: Sheffield Academic Press, 1998.

Mattern, Susan P. *Rome and the Enemy: Imperial Strategy in the Principate.* Berkeley and Los Angeles: University of California Press, 1999.

McGuire, Donald T. "Textual Strategies and Political Suicide in Flavian Epic." In *Ramus: Critical Studies in Greek and Roman Literature,* 18. Edited by A. J. Boyle. Victoria, Australia: Aureal Publications, 1989.

McLaren, James. *Turbulent Times? Josephus and Scholarship on Judaea in the First Century.* Sheffield: Scheffield Academic Press, 1998.

Metzger, Bruce M. *An Introduction to the Apocrypha.* New York: Oxford University Press, 1957.

Michel, Otto. "Die Rettung Israels und die Rolle Roms nach den Reden im 'Bellum Iudaicum.'" *ANRW* 21.2:945–76. Edited by Wolfgang Hasse, II. New York and Berlin: Walter de Gruyter, 1984.

Millar, Fergus. "Last Year in Jerusalem: Monuments of the Jewish War in Rome." Pages 101–28 in *Flavius Josephus and Flavian Rome.* Edited by Jonathan Edmondson, Steve Mason, and James Rives. New York: Oxford University Press, 2005.

Moehring, Horst R. "Joseph Ben Matthia and Flavius Josephus: The Jewish Prophet and Roman Historian." *ANRW* 21.2:865–944. Edited by Wolfgang Hasse, II. Berlin and New York: Walter de Gruyter, 1984.

Morel, W. "Eine Rede bei Josephus." *Rheinisches Museum für Philologie* 75 (1926): 106–14.

Morton, Andrew, and Sidney Michaelson. "Elision as an Indicator of Authorship." Pages 33–56 in *Revue—Organisation Internationale pour l'etude des langues anciennes par ordinateur.* 1973.

Muecke, D. C. *The Compass of Irony.* London: Metheun, 1969.

Newell, Raymond R. "The Forms and Historical Value of Josephus' Suicide Accounts." Pages 278–94 in *Josephus, the Bible, and History.* Edited by Louis H. Feldman and Gohei Hata. Leiden: Brill, 1989.

Nickelsburg, George E. W. *Jewish Literature between the Bible and the Mishnah.* Philadelphia: Fortress, 1981.

Niese, B., ed. *Flavii Josephi Opera.* Vols. 1–7. Berlin: Weidmann, 1887–1904.

Nikiprowetzky, Valentin. "Josephus and the Revolutionary Parties." Pages 216–36 in *Josephus, the Bible, and History.* Edited by Louis H. Feldman and Gohei Hata. Leiden: Brill, 1989.

———. "La Mort d'Éléazar fils de Jaïre et les courants apologétiques dans le De Bello Judaico de Flavius Josèphe." Pages 461–90 in *Hommages à André Dupont-Sommer.* Paris: Librairie d'Amerique et d'Orient Adrien-Maisonneuve, 1971.

———. "Sicaires et Zélotes—une Reconsidération." *Semitica* 23 (1973): 51–64.

Noy, David. *Foreigners at Rome: Citizens and Strangers*. London: Duckworth, 2000.

———. *Jewish Inscriptions of Western Europe, 2: The City of Rome*. Cambridge: Cambridge Univeristy Press, 1995.

Ogilvie, R. M. *Roman Literature and Society*. Penguin Books, 1980.

Overman, J. Andrew. "The First Revolt and Flavian Politics." Pages 211–20 in *The First Jewish Revolt: Archaeology, History, and Ideology*. Edited by Andrea M. Berlin and Andrew J. Overman. London and New York: Routledge, 2002.

Pearlman, Moshe. *The Zealots of Masada*. Herzlia: Palphot.

Penwill, John L. "Expelling the Mind: Politics and Philosophy in Flavian Rome." Pages 345–68 in *Flavian Rome: Culture, Image, Text*. Edited by A. J. Boyle and W. J. Dominik. Leiden and Boston: Brill, 2003.

Petersen, Hans. "Real and Alleged Literary Projects of Josephus." *AJP* 79 (1958): 259–74.

Plass, Paul. *The Game of Death in Ancient Rome: Arena Sport and Political Suicide*. Madison: University of Wisconsin Press, 1995.

Price, Jonathan. *Jerusalem under Siege: The Collapse of the Jewish State 66–70 C.E.* Leiden: Brill, 1992.

———. "Josephus' Reading of Thucydides: A Test Case in the BJ." Available at http://pace.mcmaster.ca/media/pdf/sbl/price2003.pdf.

———. "The Provincial Historian in Rome." Pages 101–18 in *Josephus and Jewish History in Flavian Rome and Beyond*. Edited by Joseph Sievers and Gaia Lembi. Leiden: Brill, 2005.

———. *Thucydides and Internal War*. Cambridge: Cambridge University Press, 2001.

Rahlfs, Alfred, ed. *Septuaginta*. Stuttgart: Deutsche Bibelstiftung, 1935.

Rajak, Tessa. "Dying for the Law." Pages 99–133 in *The Jewish Dialogue with Greece and Rome*. Leiden: Brill, 2002.

———. "Josephus in the Diaspora." Pages 79–97 in *Flavius Josephus and Flavian Rome*. Edited by Jonathan Edmondson, Steve Mason, and James Rives. New York: Oxford University Press, 2005.

———. *Josephus, the Historian and His Society*. Second edition. London: Gerald Duckworth, 2002.

Redondo, Jordi. "The Greek Literary Language of the Hebrew Historian Josephus." *Hermes* 128 (2000): 420–34.

———, ed. *A Complete Concordance to Flavius Josephus*. Leiden: Brill, 2002.

Rives, James. "Flavian Religious Policy and the Destruction of the Jerusalem Temple." Pages 145–66 in *Flavius Josephus and Flavian Rome*. Edited by Jonathan Edmondson, Steve Mason, and James Rives. New York: Oxford University Press, 2005.

Roller, Matthew B. *Constructing Autocracy: Aristocrats and Emperors in Julio-Claudian Rome*. Princeton and Oxford: Princeton University Press, 2001.

Roth, Jonathan. "The Length of the Siege of Masada." *Scripta Classica Israelica* 14 (1995): 87–110.

Runnalls, Donna R. "The Rhetoric of Josephus." Pages 737–754 in *Handbook of Classical Rhetoric in the Hellenistic Period*. Edited by Stanley E. Porter. Leiden: Brill, 1997.

Rutgers, Leonard Victor. *The Jews in Late Ancient Rome: Evidence of Cultural Interaction in the Roman Diaspora*. Leiden and New York: Brill, 1995.

Sacchi, Paolo. *The History of the Second Temple Period*. Sheffield: Sheffield Academic Press, 2000.

Schäfer, Peter. *Judeophobia: Attitudes toward the Jews in the Ancient World*. Cambridge, MA: Harvard University Press, 1997.

Schürer, Emil. *A History of the Jewish People in the Time of Jesus Christ*. 3 vols. Edinburgh: T & T Clark, 1890.

Schwartz, Daniel. "Once Again: Who Captured Masada? On Doublets, Reading against the Grain, and What Josephus Actually Wrote." *Scripta Classica Israelica* 24 (2005): 75–83.

Schwartz, Seth. "The Composition and Publication of Josephus's Bellum Iudaicum Book 7." *HTR* 79 (1986): 373–86.

Shargel, Baila R. "The Evolution of the Masada Myth." *Judaism* 28 (1979): 357–71.

Shaw, Brent. "Bandits in the Roman Empire." *Past and Present* 105 (1984): 3–52.

———. "Josephus: Roman Power and Responses to It." *Athenaeum* 73 (1995): 357–90.

———. Review of *Räuber, Rebellen, Rivalen, Rächer: Studien zu Latrones im römischen Reich*. Forschungen zur Antiken Sklaverei, Bd. 31, by Thomas Grünwald. *Bryn Mawr Classical Review* (February 2000) Available at http://ccat.sas.upenn.edu/bmcr/2000/2000-02-12.html..

Shutt, R. J. H. *Studies in Josephus*. London: S.P.C.K., 1961.

Sievers, Joseph. "Reponse to Steve Mason, 'At Play Seriously': Irony and Humour in the *Vita* of Josephus." Online: http://pace.cns.yorku.ca/York/york/conference2001-ext.htm.

Silberman, Neil Asher. "The First Revolt and Its Afterlife." Pages 237–52 in *The First Jewish Revolt: Archaeology, History, and Ideology*. Edited by Andrea M. Berlin and Andrew J. Overman. London and New York: Routledge, 2002.

Sivertsev, Alexei M. *Households, Sects, and the Origins of Rabbinic Judaism*. Leiden and Boston: Brill, 2005.

Smallwood, E. Mary. *The Jews under Roman Rule: From Pompey to Diocletian*. Leiden: Brill, 2001.

Smith, Morton. "Zealots and Sicarii, Their Origins and Relation." *HTR* 64 (1971): 1–19.

Smyth, Herbert Weir. *Greek Grammar*. Cambridge, MA: Harvard University Press, 1956.

Sterling, Gregory E. "Historiography and Self-Definition: Josephus, Luke-Acts and Apologetic Historiography." Leiden: Brill, 1992.

Stern, M. "Sicarii and Zealots." Pages 263–301 in *Society and Religion in the Second Temple Period*. Edited by Michael Avi-Yonah and Zvi Baras. Jerusalem: Masada Publishing, 1977.

———. *Josephus the Man and the Historian*. New York: Jewish Institute of Religion, 1929.

Van Henten, Jan Willem. *The Maccabean Martyrs as Saviours of the Jewish People*. Leiden: Brill, 1997.

———. *Martyrdom and Noble Death: Selected Texts from Graeco-Roman, Jewish and Christian Antiquity*. London and New York: Routledge, 2002.

———. "Martyrion and Martyrdom. Some Remarks about Noble Death in Josephus." Pages 124–41 in *Internationales Josephus-Kolloquium Brüssel 1998*. Edited by Jürgen Kalms and Folker Siegert. Münster: Lit Verlag, 1998.

Van Hoof, Anton J. L. *From Autothanasia to Suicide*. London and New York: Routledge, 1990.

Vidal-Naquet, Pierre. "Flavius Josèphe et Masada." *Revue Historique* 260 (1978): 13–21.

Villalba I Varneda, Pere. *The Historical Method of Flavius Josephus*. Leiden: Brill, 1986.

Walbank, F. W. "History and Tragedy." In *Selected Papers: Studies in Greek and Roman History and Historiography*. Cambridge: Cambridge University Press, 1985.

———. *Polybius*. Berkeley: University of California Press, 1972.

———. "Tragic History: A Reconsideration." *Bulletin of the Institute of Classical Studies* 2 (1955): 4–14.

———. "'Treason' and Roman Domination: Two Case-Studies, Polybius and Josephus." Pages 273–85 in *Rom und der griechische Osten: Festschrift für Hatto H. Schmitt sum 65. Geburtstag*. Edited by Ch. Schubert and K. Brodersen. Stuttgart: Franz Steiner Verlag, 1990.

Walker, Andrew D. "*Enargeia* and the Spectator in Greek Historiography." *TAPA* 123 (1993): 353–77.

Weiss-Rosmarin, Trude. "Masada and Yavneh." *Jewish Spectator* 31 (1966): 4–7.

———. "Masada, Josephus and Yadin." *Jewish Spectator* 32 (1967): 2–8, 30–32.

———. "Masada Revisited." *Jewish Spectator* 34 (1969): 3–5, 29–32.

Welch, John W., ed. *Chiasmus in Antiquity*. Hildesheim: Gerstenberg Verlag, 1981.

Williams, David S. *Stylometric Authorship Studies in Flavius Josephus and Related Literature*. Lewiston: Edwin Mellen, 1992.

———. "Thackeray's Assistant Hypothesis: A Stylometric Evaluation." *JJS* 48 (1992): 262–75.

Williams, Margaret. "The Structure of the Jewish Community in Rome." Pages

215–28 in *Jews in a Graeco-Roman World*. Edited by Martin Goodman. Oxford: Clarendon, 1998.

Willmes, Bernd. *Menschliches Schicksal und ironische Weisheitskritik im Koheletbuch: Kohelets Ironie und die Grenzen der Exegese*. Neukirchen-Vluyn: Neukirchener Verlag, 2000.

Woodman, A. J. *Rhetoric in Classical Historiography*. Portland: Areopagitica, 1988.

Yadin, Yigael. *Masada: The Yigael Yadin Excavations 1963–1965, Final Reports*. Seven vols. Jerusalem: Israel Exploration Society, 1989–.

————. *Masada: Herod's Fortress and the Zealots' Last Stand*. New York: Random House, 1966.

Zeitlin, Solomon. "Masada and the Sicarii. The Occupants of Masada." *JQR* 55 (1965): 299–317.

————. "The Sicarii and Masada." *JQR* 57 (1967): 251–70.

————. "Zealots and Sicarii." *JBL* 81 (1962): 395–98.

Zerubavel, Yael. "The Death of Memory and the Memory of Death: Masada and the Holocaust as Historical Metaphors." *Representations* 45 (1994): 72–100.

INDEX OF MODERN AUTHORS

INDEX OF ANCIENT AUTHORS AND TEXTS

INDEX OF SUBJECTS

CPSIA information can be obtained
at www.ICGtesting.com
Printed in the USA
FSOW01n1128200416
19432FS